African Pasts, Presents, and Futures

After the Empire: The Francophone World and Postcolonial France

Series Editor: Valérie Orlando, University of Maryland

Recent Titles

African Pasts, Presents, and Futures: Generational Shifts in African Women's Literature, Film, and Internet Discourse, by Touria Khannous

Writing the Nomadic Experience in Contemporary Francophone Literature, by Katharine N. Harrington

The Body Besieged: The Embodiment of Historical Memory in Nina Bouraoui and Leïla Sebbar, by Helen Vassallo

Writerly Identities in Beur Fiction and Beyond, by Laura Reeck

France's Lost Empires: Fragmentation, Nostalgia, and la fracture coloniale, edited by Kate Marsh and Nicola Frith

Globalizing the Postcolony: Contesting Discourses of Gender and Development in Francophone Africa, by Claire H. Griffiths

Writing and Filming the Genocide of the Tutsis in Rwanda: Dismembering and Remembering Traumatic History, by Alexandre Dauge-Roth

The Star, the Cross, and the Crescent: Religions and Conflicts in Francophone Literature from the Arab World, by Carine Bourget

African Pasts, Presents, and Futures

Generational Shifts in African Women's Literature, Film, and Internet Discourse

Touria Khannous

LEXINGTON BOOKS
Lanham • Boulder • New York • Toronto • Plymouth, UK

Published by Lexington Books
A wholly owned subsidiary of Rowman & Littlefield
4501 Forbes Boulevard, Suite 200, Lanham, Maryland 20706
www.rowman.com

10 Thornbury Road, Plymouth PL6 7PP, United Kingdom

British Library Cataloguing in Publication Information Available

Library of Congress Cataloging-in-Publication Data
Khannous, Touria, 1968– author.
African pasts, presents, and futures : generational shifts in African women's literature, film, and internet discourse / Touria Khannous.
pages cm.—(After the empire : the Francophone world and postcolonial France)
Includes bibliographical references and index.
ISBN 978-0-7391-7041-0 (cloth : alk. paper)—ISBN 978-0-7391-7042-7 (electronic)
1. African literature—Women authors—History and criticism. 2. Women and literature—Africa—History—20th century. 3. Women and literature—Africa—History—21st century. 4. Motion pictures—Africa. 5. Women motion picture producers and directors—Africa. 6. Internet—Social aspects—Africa. 7. Internet and women—Africa. I. Title. II. Series: After the empire.
PL8010.K47 2013
809.89287096—dc23
2013022296

∞™ The paper used in this publication meets the minimum requirements of American National Standard for Information Sciences Permanence of Paper for Printed Library Materials, ANSI/NISO Z39.48-1992.

Printed in the United States of America

Contents

Acknowledgments

I would like to thank the people who knowingly or unknowingly contributed to the writing of my book. Particular acknowledgement goes to Dr. Neil Lazarus, my original supervisor at Brown University, who motivated me to do research in this field and offered me invaluable help and encouragement. At Brown, I would also like to thank Dr. Philip Rosen, Dr. Madhu Dubey, Dr. William Keach, Dr. Dorothy Denniston, and Dr. Coppelia Kahn. Gratitude is also due to Dr. Valerie Orlando, who read the manuscript with meticulous care, offering me her brilliant advice and making substantive suggestions. I am also indebted to colleagues and friends who kindly read and commented on parts of the book: Dr. Sandra Carter, Dr. Amy Elder, Dr. Mildred Mortimer, Dr. Pallavi Rastogi, Dr. Dorobta Pucherva, Dr. Iyunolu Folayan Osagie, and Dr. Maureen Eke. Acknowledgments must also include my colleagues at Louisiana State University who have supported me directly or indirectly in ways that have affected my research. In particular, I am grateful to Dr. John Pizer, my chair in Foreign Languages, Dr. Leonard Ray, my chair in International Studies, and my former chair Dr. Emily Batinsky. I also would like to thank the Dean's Office in the College of Humanities & Social Sciences for a junior faculty research leave that enabled me to finish writing parts of the manuscript.

Theoretical Introduction

Refocusing Critiques of African Women's Writing

The decade after 1960 in Africa was marked not only by decolonization, but also by the proliferation of works by a number of important women writers. Since then, critics have actively engaged with the sociocultural and political themes of these works. Carole Boyce Davies' and Anne Adams Graves' pioneering book *Ngambika: Studies of Women in African Literature* (1986) is a significant precursor in the development of feminist scholarship on African literature. While the book attempts to construct a literary canon for African women writers, it limits itself solely to the study of representations of women in African literature, and not women's texts per se. The emergence of new women writers marked a distinctive shift in feminist literary studies in the 1990s. For the first time, critics engaged in debates surrounding gender, race, class, female identity, and subjectivity in African women's literary texts. Florence Stratton's book *Contemporary African Literature and the Politics of Gender* (1994) traces the voices of newly emerging women writers such as Grace Ogot, Flora Nwapa, Buchi Emecheta, and Mariama Bâ.[1]

Stratton takes to task scholars of African literature for ignoring the writings of African women. Juliana Nfah-Abbenyi likewise addresses this oversight in her 1997 book, *Gender in African Women's Writing: Identity, Sexuality and Difference*.[2] While Nfah-Abbenyi applies feminist theory to her reading of African women's literature, she also derives theoretical insights about indigenous African feminism from the published works themselves. Most timely in its criticism is Susan Andrade's recent book, *The Nation Writ Small: African Fictions and Feminisms, 1958-1988* (2011), wherein she discusses the work of Africa's first generation of postindependence writers. Andrade challenges the way literary works by men were seen as engaged with politics, whereas the very notion of "women's literature" was associated with personal experience and the realm of the feminine. This criticism leveled at the writings of African women tended to rely on the opposition between the personal and the political, which in turn justified the dismissal of women's literature as irrelevant to politically engaged literature. Andrade explains further that the reason novels authored by African women were considered inferior or unrelated to political and national concerns was because they centered on domestic stories and family. In her view, it would be a mistake to take into account critiques that rest on the idea that the writings of African women were apolitical. On the contrary, these writers were consciously dedicated to "politically engaged" literature, but their writings were largely articulated through allegory: "To invert the cliché, in the narratives of many African female writers, the family becomes the nation writ small." [3] Andrade goes on to analyze novels by the first generation of postindependence African writers, both male and female. These include works by Flora Nwapa, Buchi Emecheta, Ousmane Sembène, Mariama Bâ, Aminata Sow Fall, Tsitsi Dangarembga, Nuruddin Farah, and Assia Djebar.

My book encompasses more recent examples of literature, film, and Internet discourse produced by African women, thus recognizing new developments in feminist consciousness and feminist activism across the continent. The book focuses on works produced by women in the Maghreb (Morocco, Algeria, and Tunisia), as well as Ghana, Nigeria, South Africa, and Zimbabwe. It explores different aspects of women's agency at the political, cultural, social, religious, and aesthetic levels, and highlights their civil society activism and push for legal reform. Authors whose work is analyzed include Assia Djebar, Leila Abouzeid, Ama Ata Aidoo, Bessie Head, Moufida Tlatli, Farida Benlyazid, Tess Onwueme, Yvonne Vera, Malika Oufkir, Leila Merrakshi, and feminist activists who use social media to campaign for equal rights and effect sociopolitical change in their home countries. It tracks not only their opinions on a range of social and political questions but also fundamental shifts in their positions and concerns through the different generations. The book is timely in that it discusses the work of some of the most creative and prolific women writers, filmmakers, and feminist activists from across the continent. It not only sheds new light on their discursive mediations but exposes the breadth of their cultural forms of expression, their feminisms, and their unwavering commitment to social and political change. Equally important, it examines to what extent they produce films, new feminist discourses, and literary texts that aim to challenge the sociopolitical and cultural climates of their respective countries, thereby marking their roles as agents of social transformation and political change. Women authors create narrative strategies of resistance to the pressures their societies exert on them as authors and as women. They position themselves within the contexts of Islam, feminism, nationalism, modernity, and global and postcolonial politics, thus engaging in the construction of sociopolitical platforms for reform in their home countries. Whether fictional or nonfictional, autobiographical or testimonial, their texts dwell on certain key themes. These include the struggle for independence, nationhood, the sociopolitical status of women, Islam, the failure of postcolonial regimes, confrontations between tradition and modernity, linguistic tensions between colonial and local languages, as well as concern with an authentic identity vis-à-vis the global spread of consumerist culture.

The texts included are selected because of the range of issues and questions they represent. I chose these specific texts because of their subversive nature and their authors' preoccupation with change. The authors foreground the issue of gender as the vantage point of their rhetorical critique. Studying gender within the contexts of colonial history, indigenous patriarchy, and contemporary globalization is part of an effort to establish evidence of commonalities across the continent in a shared discourse. I particularly chose Assia Djebar's film *La Nouba* (1978) to begin my book because, although the events take place in a different historical context, the film lends itself to contemporary theoretical analysis and shares similarities with the work of Ama Ata Aidoo and Bessie Head. I chose to discuss Bessie Head largely because of the universality of her work and its enduring relevance. Leila Merrakshi's film *Marock* (2005) is studied largely because of its transgressive nature, in terms of the issues it raises regarding gender and sexuality. Yvonne Vera is an obvious choice because her novel *The Stone Virgins* (2002) is openly subversive. The chapters on Oufkir, Vera, and Onwueme are grouped sequentially because all three authors are openly engaged in critiquing abusive dictatorships, which are prevalent in Africa. I conclude my book with a chapter on women's use of social media to effect change, because it is the new form of writing that will take the causes of African women into the next century.

The book covers the works of women writers and filmmakers in Arabic, French, and English in various regions of Africa. It also meaningfully links the works of North African and Sub-Saharan authors, underscoring their similarities and differences. Given the geographical expansiveness of Africa, and the diversity of experiences among African women, this project defines what we mean by "African" and African women. Therefore, the title of the book is purely descriptive, denoting authors who are women and come from countries geographically located on the African continent. The fact that the women writers, filmmakers, and activists in this study come from Arabophone, Francophone, and Anglophone regions in Africa attests to the linguistic polyvalence of their texts and multiplicity of their cultural locations. Their works transgress borders and engage in transnational and intertextual exchanges. Their grouping under the category "African women" is deliberately inclusive, overlooking artificial boundaries imposed by language, religion, or former colonial powers. The category "African women" itself, as some have suggested, is an artificial and arbitrary designation that is too broad and internally diverse. In terms of historical development, ethnicity, and social structure, Moroccan, Algerian, and Tunisian women might have more in common with Middle Eastern women than they do, for instance, with Ghanaian and Nigerian women. Using "African women," however, as a conceptual category that fuses geographical and historical factors, and takes into account Africa's shared colonial past, provides a more meaningful justification for grouping these women authors together. When Algerian writer Assia Djebar received the Prix Fonlon prize at the African Literature Association in 1997, she used the prize as an occasion to state her affiliation with Africa and insist that she does not ascribe to Europe's colonial or geographical mapping of Africa with its artificial partitioning of North and Sub-Saharan.[4] It is hoped that this work expands the notion of a canon of African women's cultural production, promoting it in a broad, new-world context.

I have given more space to North Africa because of the diversity of its narratives. I have also excluded some well-known writers because their works have already received extensive scholarly attention, preferring instead to focus on lesser known authors like Tess Onwueme. The sections in this book are divided not geographically, but thematically and linguistically, to reflect common concerns and experiences across geographical boundaries. It is also important to note that some of the writers and filmmakers (Djebar, Merrakshi, Oufkir, and Aidoo) have themselves migrated either to Europe or North America, which extends the discussion beyond the African continent. The book engages with an almost fifty-year tradition of writing, film, and feminist activism by African women. It also surveys alternative feminisms women authors propose, considering the contexts from which they emerge, the choice of language used, the impact of new media on their work, and the complexity of their relationships with both artistic forebears and contemporary audiences.

In offering analyses of texts from 1968 to 2011, the book has two main goals. The first is to analyze and place into context women's texts, which redefine the political in terms that appropriate women's experiences and gender politics. The second is to provide an analysis of the social, political, and biographical contexts of the texts in question. Situating women's texts within their sociopolitical contexts will establish the vital role that these texts, taken collectively, play in effecting change within the public sphere. It will also help bring aesthetics into alliance with the historical and the political. In fact, authors such as Assia Djebar and Bessie Head see the purpose of their authorship as political and aesthetic. Their work is immersed in political consciousness, and there is a clear connection between the political and the aesthetic in their artistic expressions, as they experiment with new forms and points of view to express their political convictions. The boundaries between the political and aesthetic are at times breached as rhetorical conventions are subverted to meet their political ends. In her essay "A Postcolonial Aesthetic: Repeating Upon the Present," Elleke Boehmer draws attention to the contention that "postcolonial aesthetic" is an oxymoron in terms as within postcolonial criticism "there is little sense in which postcolonial writing can be both political and implicated in a (purely) aesthetic stance."[5] Boehmer calls on critics of postcolonial literature to investigate its aesthetic dimensions as well as its political implications.[6]

The women authors and activists included in this book reconcile how best to further their political commitment and dedicate themselves to their art. Their ideas are propelled by social and political objectives, even when they seem concerned with their art. Furthermore, they have moved the terms of discourse beyond the private sphere of femininity, thus explicitly expressing their commitment to women's causes and politics in texts that promote reform. Through journalistic and narrative writings, participation in public forums, and political discussions, writers like Leila Abouzeid, Assia Djebar, Bessie Head, and Ama Ata Aidoo have, at one point or another, touched on the issue of gender-related reform. Their focus on women has its roots in their political activism, which manifests itself in political reform, revolution, civil rights, and humanism. Moreover, by virtue of their use of various forms of new media, women authors have increasingly important roles in the public realm, challenging traditional divisions between public and private spheres, and calling for women's engagement in social and political activities. Thus, they invoke woman's experience in private as well as public forms of expression, encompassing the philosophical, spiritual, social, psychological, sexual, political, and aesthetic. Through their writings, authors such as Bessie Head, Malika Oufkir, and Yvonne Vera have also chosen to share their pain with the public. By extending women's experience into the public domain, they have shifted the terms of discourse from woman as victim to woman as agent of change. In transposing the feminine, often associated with the private sphere, into public spaces, they have embraced a new activist feminist poetic that valorizes a way of reimagining nation marked by the presence of women in the public sphere. What unites them is their objective to find a feminine, public voice in nations where female agency has been suppressed.

Even though writers are expected to be committed politically in Africa, there has been little attempt to read African women's texts as political, an attitude that is based on the traditional assumption regarding women and politics, and the idea that women cannot write about what is outside the private sphere. The questions are these: What has empowered these women to speak in countries where they have been excluded from politics? What does politics mean for them? The authors covered in this book are concerned with political issues such as elections and legal issues, but more broadly they are promoting a feminist agenda that allows for a greater participation of women in the public sphere. It is commitment to such a feminist agenda that allows them to contribute to their countries' sociopolitical transformation.

Drawing on examples from works published between the 1960s and 2000s, I examine women's texts as engaged implicitly or explicitly with social and political concerns—the common concerns of the Habermasian public sphere of questioning national politics and challenging prevailing ideologies and laws. Jürgen Habermas defines the public sphere as "the domain of our social life in which such a thing as public opinion can be formed."[7] His concept of public sphere has been criticized by philosophers and social scientists as emphasizing a unitary, bourgeois public sphere that has effaced difference in gender, culture, and identity. Critics have countered the dominant model of the bourgeois public sphere with the concept of a proletarian public sphere. American feminist Nancy Frazer, for instance, points out that it is only through these subaltern, counter-public spheres that inequalities come to light, and groups that are marginalized on the basis of class or gender are able to attain a voice. She adds that an "egalitarian, multicultural society only makes sense if we presuppose a plurality of public arenas in which groups with diverse values and discourses participate. By definition, such a society must contain a multiplicity of publics."[8] The women authors whose work is analyzed in this book have used the public sphere as Nancy Frazer describes it. One needs to only look at the work of Assia Djebar, Bessie Head, and Yvonne Vera, among others, to see how powerful the political interventions of these women are.

While some women authors claim a feminist position, others reject it. Yet, foregrounding their feminism is essential to tracing their political activism. Women writers who reject feminism are reluctant to accept definitions associated with Western feminist models. Nigerian scholar Molara Ogundipe-Leslie laments the fact that many African women writers insist "they are not feminists, as if it were a crime to be a feminist."[9] According to her, African feminism is a political ideology that needs to be seen as part and parcel of the worldwide feminist movement to improve women's conditions and protest constraints on their autonomy: "Feminism . . . must always have a political and activist spine to its form."[10] For some critics, however, the specificity of the African experience makes application of the term "feminist" to women's political activism untenable. Nigerian scholar Obioma Nnaemeka explains that African women do not feel the need to articulate their feminism: "They just do it. . . . It is *what* they do and *how* they do it that provides the 'framework.'"[11] Nnaemeka's definition favors action over words, focusing more on practical details of political activism and one's connection to the community. Such nondefinition of feminism, however, is a bit misleading as any politically motivated action necessarily means articulating one's needs, ideas, demands, and visions.[12]

Being aware of the dangers of trying to reduce feminism to its "essential" trait, and of excluding women writers like Bessie Head, who reject the feminist label, African feminist scholars have tried to fashion new concepts of African feminism. Ogundipe-Leslie coined the word "stiwanism," an "acronym for *Social Transformation Including Women in Africa* [author's emphasis]."[13] Through this concept, she places feminism in an African context and stresses the active role women can play in Africa's sociopolitical transformation. The term stiwanism thus allows her to recognize African women's political activism and the cultural specificity of African women within "the spaces and strategies provided in indigenous cultures for the social being of women."[14] Nigerian feminist Mary Kolawole created an African version of Alice Walker's womanist theory, which recognizes the intersections between race, class, and gender in black women's oppression. The African womanist, according to Kolawole, aims for local-level social transformation of existing structures of power that shape women's subordination while drawing upon her own cultural contexts. She insists that "womanism" is an integrated philosophy that does not adhere to the rigid compartmentalizing that some critics ascribe to it:

> Womanism does not require compartmentalization and one does not need to identify radical, liberal, psycho-analytic and other categories of womanism. Any African woman who has the consciousness to situate the struggle within African cultural realities by working for a total and robust self-retrieval of the African woman is an African . . . womanist.[15]

As a woman-centered philosophy, African womanism is the manifestation of the social and political consciousness of African women who strive to change the oppressive social and patriarchal structures of their societies.

Younger African feminist scholars, some emerging from feminist university programs, are increasingly attracted to the feminist movement and are often critical of their forebears. These younger scholars have now branched into several other topics such as sexuality studies. One such scholar is Ugandan Sylvia Tamale, who contests the view that feminism is irrelevant to African women's experience, as issues like sexuality, reproduction, and domestic violence are as relevant and important to African women as they are to white women. She states: "We must reject the argument that Africa is not ready for radical feminism. . . . Our sexuality has a lot to do with women's oppression. We can see it in ideologies such as 'heteronormativity,' 'marriagenormativity,' and 'mothernormativity.'"[16] In the introduction to her recently published book, titled *African Sexualities*, Sylvia Tamale explores the connection between gender, sexuality, and the power of the state in Africa, especially as it relates to issues of development. For her, there is a link between sustainable development and the sexual and reproductive health services that the state delivers. In many parts of Africa, "the law turns sexualities into a space through which instruments of state control and dominance can be deployed. . . . The offences of prostitution, abortion and adultery clearly curtail both women's and men's sexual autonomy, . . . and the criminalization of homosexuality affects both men and women who do not conform to the dominant ideology of heterosexuality."[17] By making reproductive and sexual rights integral to the political agenda, second-wave feminists insist that personal rights are also political. They defend reproductive choice while they seek to eliminate genital mutilation and domestic violence. Amina Mama is another prolific young feminist scholar who has touched on the topic of sexuality in her writings. In her essay, "Sheroes and Villains: Conceptualizing Colonial and Contemporary Violence against Women in Africa," she describes the violent treatment of women in colonial states. She also points out that sexual and coercive controls over women continue unabated in postcolonial African states. This is exemplified by the "Clean-up Operations" that took place in a number of African countries, including Zimbabwe, Gambia, Zambia, and Tanzania, and were accompanied by "widespread abuse of women." There is a second-wave literature that reflects such feminist theory. Yvonne Vera's novel *The Stone Virgins* documents the abuses of Robert Mugabe's government against civilians and women in particular. Beyond documenting such abuses at the national level, feminists like Amina Mama also petition international human rights organizations such as International Women's Rights Action Watch to include African women and to report abuses. Amina Mama has also written extensively on how to build gender into educational systems in Africa. She has been very interested in the extent to which feminism is absent from institutions (like schools and universities) that are supposed to emancipate women and other marginalized groups.[18]

Feminist activism in North Africa, where Arabic and Islam have a dominant stronghold, is different from feminism in Africa south of the Sahara. In her essay "Bargaining with Patriarchy," Deniz Kandioti argues that the coping mechanisms of Muslim women, with regard to patriarchy, differ from women's resistance strategies in Sub-Saharan Africa, a region where the system of male dominance is also rampant. Here, patriarchy is balanced out by areas of "relative autonomy" that women strive to achieve.[19] In contrast, "accommodations to the system" of "classic patriarchy" made by Muslim women can be attributed to the fact that these women have traditionally lacked economic autonomy, making them more likely to internalize and adhere to patriarchal rules in return for patriarchal protection and security.[20] While patriarchy in North Africa rests on deep cultural foundations, it was also exacerbated by colonialism and the new family laws instituted by emerging African states in the aftermath of independence. There were tensions between those who advocated women's liberation, and were thus associated with discourses of secularism and modernity, and those who adhered to religion and traditionalism. The most coherent rendition of such conflict is manifested in Frantz Fanon's two essays, "Algeria Unveiled" and "The Algerian Family." Fanon became convinced that the Arab woman's entry into public space, due to the revolution, heralded her emancipation once and for all from patriarchy. The modernity he saw embodied in the figure of the woman liberator was, however, misleading. According to Neil Lazarus, the conflation of independence with the liberation of Arab women is the product of "a utopian conceptualization of the national liberation struggle."[21] Thus, Fanon's own claims that women have achieved their goal of liberation need to be weighed against the "demobilization" and "disenfranchisement" of the people soon after independence was achieved in 1962.[22] Following independence, women faced gender-based discrimination in family legal codes of almost all North African countries. According to Algerian feminist Marie Aimée Lucas, the family code, which was instated in 1984, highlights the ambiguous nature of Algeria's dominant ideology and its own brand of nationalist socialism. For Lucas, the code aligns women with tradition, against a masculine sphere of modernity.[23] Apart from leftist activism, what really sparked the feminist movement in North Africa were the personal status codes, dictated by judicial officials and generally viewed as discriminatory against women.[24] Throughout the history of the feminist movement in Morocco,[25] for instance, male and female activists protested the existing *Moudawana* (Family Code), and their efforts bore fruit when King Mohammed VI introduced radical reforms in 2004, thus initiating a new era in women's rights.

According to feminist activists, however, such legal victories did not translate into any notable change in women's living conditions. In Tunisia, where liberalism prevailed in the aftermath of independence, national leaders stressed women's rights and equal education opportunities for both men and women. President Bourguiba, first president of independent Tunisia, instituted the personal status code (*Code du statut personnel*) in 1956, which recognized the juridical equality between men and women. Some feminists have contended, however, that the postcolonial state granted women rights to advance its own liberal agenda in its competition against Islamic conservatives. Therefore, the rights granted to women resulted from the state's decision and not from the activism of the feminist movement.[26] The texts analyzed in this book are reflective of such feminist discourses and their central theoretical concerns. The authors span three distinct generations delineated by both biological age and experiential differences.

FIRST GENERATION OF AUTHORS: NATIONALIST STRUGGLES AND LITERARY MODERNISM (1957–1980s)

First-generation authors like Assia Djebar, Ama Ata Aidoo, and Bessie Head articulated the first wave of thought against racism and colonial occupation. Their writings and films were influenced by anticolonial struggle and early experiences of independence, and thus reflected classic postcolonial paradigms of nation-building, as well as the aspirations of independence and the creation of the postcolonial nation-state. The era of national liberation struggles saw the emergence of prolific writers who associated themselves with liberation and who believed that revolution, and the sociopolitical transformations it caused, could be a valuable topic to promote in their writings.[27] These factors paved the way for a unique form of modernism marked along gender lines, as women joined men in nationalist and socialist movements, participating in political activities to alter the status quo. Literature and film played a critical role in shaping modern nationhood in Africa due to the emergence of a new group of writers who desired to exercise control not only upon their own literary texts but also upon national history as well.[28] Anthony Appiah emphasizes the "post-realist" mode of postcolonial African fiction in its refusal to legitimize nationalism. Appiah cites *Le Devoir de Violence* by Malian writer Yambo Ouologuem as an example of African works that delegitimize a realism that "only legitimates a nationalism that failed,"[29] thus discarding realism as a possible form for political engagement in postcolonial African fiction. However, Appiah's focus is exclusive of African women who engaged equally in a struggle to create their own voices, thereby securing for themselves a visible place on the modern fiction scene. Women's response to the modernist project follows practices that constituted the literature of this period. Taking part in the literary tradition of the day, and conscious of their gendered condition, women writers engaged national issues and experimented with new aesthetic forms and styles. They also had a vital role to play in the direction African feminism took. While they were the product of modernization and the colonial education promoted by nationalists, their modernization was also characterized by struggle against male dominance, with men seeking to defend an exclusive claim to writing. The modernism of early women authors was, at the very least, a result of their struggle for their place in the literary and cinematographic world.

During the colonial period, African women were largely invisible in public versions of history. The history of women's silencing in Africa is intertwined with the history of colonization, as women were denied speech not only by the male patriarchy within their own cultures, but also by the European colonizer. Such politics of exclusion also resulted in the obliteration of their voices in nationalist discourses.[30] That women were denied freedom of speech reveals how language had been used as a patriarchal weapon. It is this historical context of denying the colonized access to language that makes African women writers aware of the implications of writing and filming in the language of the colonizer. Such censorship and silencing might also have facilitated development of their writing. Emerging women writers and filmmakers like Assia Djebar (originally named Fatima-Zohra Imalayan) had to adopt a pen name. Djebar's unease with self-representation is apparent in her choice of the pen name, "Assia Djebar," upon publication of her first autobiographical novel, *La Soif* (1957). She used a pen name because, at the age of twenty-one, by writing about an "emancipated" Algerian woman, she risked embarrassing her family. She still uses, however, the name she was given at birth for her civil identity. One of the notable themes in the texts of first-generation authors like Assia Djebar, Ama Ata Aidoo, and Bessie Head was the need to write. The theme of writing features prominently in novels such as Assia Djebar's *Fantasia* (1985) and Bessie Head's *A Question of Power* (1974), where the female protagonists come to writing in an effort to come to terms with their identity. Bessie Head writes against the censorship and constraints placed on her writing by the apartheid regime.

Women fought side-by-side with men for independence in Ghana, Morocco, and Algeria, and for revolutionary change in South Africa. But they will later realize that issues of primary concern to them, such as economic, social, and legal equality, were considered of secondary concern to the nationalist liberation movements. The gap between women's struggle to be included as equals and their exclusion from patriarchal and racist structures of the liberation movements had its equivalent in the struggle against women's literary exclusion in the same era. Overall, there is an underlying theme that motivates their writings and films. This theme fundamentally echoes their preoccupation with the failed promise of liberation and the demise of ideals professed by the nationalist revolutionaries who fought for independence. Thus, their texts bring to light the hidden mechanisms by which the male nationalist elite have succeeded in reproducing their patriarchal advantages to the exclusion of women.

SECOND GENERATION OF AUTHORS: REINSCRIBING HUMAN RIGHTS ABUSES (1980s–2000s)

The second generation of authors write about the failure of the nation-state in a particularly African context. Even in Latin America there are dictatorships, but the dramatic failure of the nation-state in the twentieth century is a uniquely African problem. In this sense, the second generation seems to be more distinctively African than the first generation of authors, whose writings seem to fall along more conventionally postcolonial lines. The second generation consists of women authors who reached adulthood either during or after the colonial period. The earliest of this generation include Yvonne Vera, who was concerned not only with analyzing the relations between colonizer and colonized, but also with staking out a place in postcolonial Zimbabwe, a nation tainted by despotism and violence. Belonging to this second generation are also authors like Leila Abouzeid, Malika Oufkir, and Tess Onwueme, who turned their social critique to the corruption and human rights abuses characterizing postcolonial regimes rather than the oppression inflicted by the former colonizer. The struggle for human rights provides one of the most impressive examples of human agency in the writings and films of this generation of women authors. Testimonial works, such as Vera's *The Stone Virgins* and Oufkir's *Stolen Lives*, embody a genre of writings by survivors of state terror and oppression.[31] In this context, African women's writings are worth studying as examples of humanitarian intervention through literature. Women authors such as Malika Oufkir, Yvonne Vera, and Tess Onwueme claim the primacy of literary discourse as a powerful tool for remembering, accountability, and social justice in the face of violence, particularly against women, by repressive state regimes. Their human rights discourse depends on international audiences, or as Joseph Slaughter puts it, "a public, international space that empowers all human beings to speak."[32] The collapse of the African nation-state such as Zimbabwe has thus had its impact on women's writing in significant ways.

THIRD GENERATION OF AUTHORS: NEW TRENDS IN LITERATURE, FILM, AND SOCIAL MEDIA (2000–PRESENT)

The third generation, as I construct it, includes emerging writers, feminist activists, and filmmakers who have been influenced by globalization and mass culture. With this third generation, writing is no longer about the post-colonial experience, for authors have moved beyond the old tropes of independence and maligning the colonizer to explore new themes, and new forums, engaging a new discourse in a world context. African women authors writing and filming in the twenty-first century have gone beyond the nationalist discourse to tackle more contemporary issues as they strive to link individual characters with a newly emerging global culture that is driven by commercialization and capitalism. For instance, Leila Merrakshi's film *Marock* (2005) reveals how globalization is changing the lives of youth in contemporary Morocco. The context of the film is the global city of Casablanca, which has been impacted in significant ways by Morocco's market reforms in the 1980s. Globalization has influenced people by transforming identities, something more evident among youth exposed to popular cultural trends and foreign media. The film's incorporation of gender allows exploration and understanding of the contested meanings of globalization that influence women's lives. The controversy surrounding the film also shows how globalization has been used to recover conservative notions of femininity, with many conservative voices denouncing the blurred gender identity lines that accompany global politics.

TODAY'S GENERATION: THE NET, YOUNG ACTIVISTS, AND NEW FORMS OF FEMINISM

Globalization has also shaped women's agency, as it has made public spaces equally accessible for women, and helped feminist activists to come together through global forums and transnational networks in their call for equal rights. Fourth-generation feminist activists have embraced the community and instant connectivity offered by social media, like blogs and Facebook, in an effort to better engage feminist goals with dynamic developments on the ground. As they voice their concerns, they are making feminism relevant to the unique challenges their generation faces. Feminist activists are increasingly resorting to the Internet to cultivate their own feminism and to disseminate their views to a wider public. They are using new forms of feminist discourse, and the technology to fuel such discourse, to promote change from within. The context of African women's Internet activism is global, highly political, and important worldwide, especially in light of the recent uprisings sweeping North Africa. Facebook use and blogging are timely, and the international responses take on more importance than the blogs themselves. Where books and films reach a limited number of people at a given time, blogging and cyberspace offer endless potential and endless audiences. Whether transcribed through film, prose, or social media, African women's voices ring out loud and clear, proclaiming their countries' most neglected ideals of justice, freedom, and liberty, and urging for reform. By incorporating film and Internet discourse, the book attempts to move beyond the purely literary and toward a broader view of African women's cultural production.

The ten chapters in this volume treat seven countries from Africa: Morocco, Algeria, Tunisia, Ghana, Zimbabwe, Nigeria, and South Africa. Three chapters in Part I illustrate political debates over women's participation in anticolonial movements and their position in nationalist discourses. Chapter 1, "Algerian Women in the Public Sphere: Remaking / Her / Story in Assia Djebar's Film *La Nouba des femmes du Mont Chenoua*," traces Assia Djebar's representations of the voices and presence of women in the Algerian revolution. The film explicitly and powerfully engages with the political. Djebar gives this film's audiences her own representation of colonialism and Algerian women's cultural and political agency. Chapter 2, "Ama Ata Aidoo's Modernism and the Politics of Postcolonialism" discusses the ways in which Aidoo engages politically with Kwame Nkrumah's nationalism, the perverse effects of neocolonialism, and the corruption of the elite in Africa. Through her female protagonist's critique of African politics and European hegemony, Aidoo initiates a kind of political mobility and agency for the African woman. Chapter 3, "Rewriting Power: Bessie Head's Revolutionary Politics" introduces a different approach and locus to Bessie Head's writings, from which to consider women's potential and actual political agency in subverting power relationships and effecting change.

In Part II, women's agency against human rights abuses and repressive regimes is underlined in three chapters. Chapter 4, "National Reconciliation through Narrative: Malika Oufkir's *Stolen Lives*," analyzes Malika Oufkir's memoir, which broaches the topic of human rights abuses in postindependence Morocco. The author's journey from wealth to imprisonment, escape, and expatriation beguiles her readers, as does her public persona, which positioned her to be a spokeswoman for political reform. The chapter addresses questions of truth and denial, frames the discussion in the context of pain, and compares reception of the book in three countries: Morocco, the United States, and France. Chapter 5, "National Violence and Male Crisis Discourse in Yvonne Vera's *The Stone Virgins*" focuses on a Zimbabwean writer who writes against official silencing by a government intent on wiping from public memory the history of its violent repression of the civilians of Matabeleland. The novel re-presents events concomitant with colonialism, the war of liberation, and postcolonial violence in terms of a crisis of masculinity. This narrative angle helps undermine male dominance, leaving much room for female agency and liberation. Vera's use of innovative narrative strategies, the layering of narrative voices, and intertexuality resists the established practice of traditional narrative. Thus, the narrative itself becomes an act of resistance against Robert Mugabe's regime. Chapter 6, "Political Satire in Tess Onuweme's Play *No Vacancy*," examines Nigerian writer Tess Onuweme's play *No Vacancy* (2005), an allegorical satire of Nigerian politics as well as of post-9/11 America. The author frames the issues of unemployment and poverty at the global level in order to avoid persecution and censorship by Nigerian authorities. Through satire, she aims to raise political consciousness and to issue a call for reform of Nigeria's politics. The play's characters are assembled in a staged forum, waging a revolution against the system.

Part III includes three chapters. Chapter 7, "Islam, Gender, and Identity in Leila Abouzeid's *The Last Chapter*: A Postcolonial Critique," examines Leila Abouzeid's *The Last Chapter* (2004), in which she questions women's subjugation within the context of both secularism and Islam in postindependent Morocco. The novel establishes a hierarchy of narrative voices that challenge a residual patriarchal ideology, touted as national and religious authenticity. It also emphasizes the female protagonist's social emancipation and agency through access to education, while problematizing different individual and political male identities. Chapter 8, "Strategies of Representation and Postcolonial Identity in Farida Benlyazid's *Door to the Sky* (1988) and Moufida Tlatli's *Silences of the Palace* (1994)," analyzes these two well-known iconic films. Tlatli's film offers an early critique of Arab-Muslim decadence, through its depiction of female slaves, and a general attitude toward women in Muslim society, while hinting at the urgency for reform. Tlatli experiments with modern filmic techniques to highlight women's agency and strategies of resistance. Benlyazid, on the other hand, explores a liberating and empowering space for women, while inscribing traditional Islam with a feminist consciousness that questions not only Islamic fundamentalist representations of women but also European imperialism. In both films, Benlyazid and Tlatli construct a world of political possibility, one where female agency and gender solidarity undermine homogeneous religious and national identification. Chapter 9, "Islam, Youth, and the Global: Leila Merrakshi's Controversial Film *Marock*" examines Merrakshi's film *Marock*, (2005) which foregrounds female sexual agency to a public that had previously repressed it. The filmmaker's construction of the protagonist's agency relies on notions borrowed from a global consumer culture that positions the woman as spectacle.

Part IV underlines feminist activism in the field of civil society and legal reform. Chapter 10, "Debating Islam, Gender, and the Arab Spring: Moroccan and Tunisian Women's Cyberspace," analyzes the role played by social media in recent years as a tool for networking with other feminists to effect reforms. The section on Morocco includes the debate on the *Moudawana* (Family Law) and its impact on women's agency. The section on Tunisia analyzes the role played by women's Internet activism in the 2011 Jasmine revolution as well as women's civic and public participation. Overall, the primary objective of this book is to shed light on women's agency and their political interventions in male-dominated spaces. The book bears witness to the transformative powers of representation and seeks to engage women as authors and critics in a timely study that marks a new beginning for African women authors who will write, produce films, and use social media in the twenty-first century.

NOTES

1. Florence Stratton, *Contemporary African Literature and the Politics of Gender* (New York: Routledge, 1994).
2. Juliana Nfah-Abbenyi, *Gender in African Women's Writing: Identity, Sexuality and Difference* (Bloomington, IN: Indiana University Press, 1997).
3. Susan Andrade, *The Nation Writ Small: African Fictions and Feminisms, 1958-1988* (Durham, NC: Duke University Press, 2011), 21.

4. For the full text of Assia Djebar's speech, refer to Assia Djebar, "Untitled Speech for 1997 Prix Fonlon-Nichols," *The African Literature Association Bulletin* 23, no. 2 (September 1997): 21–22.

5. Elleke Boehmer, "A Postcolonial Aesthetic: Repeating Upon the Present," in *Rerouting the Postcolonial: New Directions for the New Millennium*, eds. Janet Wilson (et al) (Abingdon: Routledge, 2010), 170.

6. Ibid., 170.

7. Jürgen Habermas, "The Public Sphere," in *Media Studies: A Reader*, eds. Paul Marris and Sue Thornham (Edinburgh, UK: Edinburgh University Press, 1996), 55.

8. Nancy Frazer, "Rethinking the Public Sphere: A Contribution to the Critique of Actually Existing Democracy," in *Habermas and the Public Sphere*, ed. Craig Calhoun (Cambridge, MA: MIT Press, 1992), 126.

9. Morala Ogundipe-Leslie, "The Female Writer and Her Commitment," *African Literature Today* 15 (1987): 5–13.

10. Molara Ogundipe-Leslie, "Stiwanism: Feminism in an African Context," in *African Literature: An Anthology of Criticism and Theory*, eds. Tejumola Olaniyan and Ato Quayson (Oxford: Blackwell Publishing Ltd., 2007), 547.

11. Obioma Nnaemeka, "Introduction: Reading the Rainbow," in *Sisterhood, Feminism, and Power: From Africa to the Diaspora* (Trenton, NJ: Africa World Press, 1998), 5.

12. An article by Indian activist Madhu Kishwar touches upon these issues. Refer to Madhu Kishwar, "Why I Do Not Call Myself A Feminist," *Manushi: A Journal of Women and Society* 61 (1990): 3.

13. Ibid., 550.

14. Ibid.

15. Mary Modupe Kolawole, *Womanism and African Consciousness* (Trenton, NJ: Africa World Press, 1997), 34.

16. Syvlia Tamale, "African Feminism: How Should We Change?" *Development* 49, no. 1 (2006): 40.

17. Sylvia Tamale, ed., *African Sexualities: A Reader* (Oxford: Pambazuka Press, 2011), 3.

18. Amina Mama, "Sheroes and Villains: Conceptualizing Colonial and Contemporary Violence Against Women in Africa," in *Feminist Genealogies, Colonial Legacies and Democratic Futures*, eds. M. Jacqui Alexander and Chandra Mohanty (New York: Routledge, 1997), 57.

19. Deniz Kandioti, "Bargaining with Patriarchy," in *Gender and Society* 2, no. 3 (September 1988), 276.

20. Ibid., 280.

21. Neil Lazarus, *Resistance in Postcolonial African Fiction* (New Haven, CT: Yale University Press, 1993), 5.

22. Neil Lazarus, "Disavowing Decolonization: Fanon, Nationalism, and the Problematic of Representation in Current Theories of Colonial Discourse," in *Nationalism and Cultural Practice in the Postcolonial World* (Cambridge: Cambridge University Press, 1999), 92.

23. Marie Aimée Hélie-Lucas, "Women, Nationalism and Religion in the Algerian Liberation Struggle," in *Opening the Gates: A Century of Arab Feminist Writing*, eds. Margot Badran and Miriam Cooke (London: Virago Press, 1990), 105.

24. In her book *The Eloquence of Silence*, Marnia Lazreg succinctly summarizes the origins of the Algerian feminist movement, which emerged in response to the controversy surrounding the draft of the family code in 1984. The preface to the code stipulates many discriminatory laws against women regarding marriage, divorce, and guardianship. Refer to the source for a detailed account of the code. Marnia Lazreg, *The Eloquence of Silence: Algerian Women in Question* (New York: Routledge, 1994), 151–155.

25. In Morocco, early feminists were leftist activists who vehemently questioned patriarchy. Within Moroccan feminist discourses, the idea of gendered space has been very influential. Moroccan scholar Fatima Sadiqi refers to public space as men's space where social norms are dictated. For Moroccan feminist scholar Fatima Mernissi, this dichotomy is in accordance with the Arab-Muslim tradition, which explains the entrenchment of patriarchal power and social institutions through segregation and legal subordination in the family, which limit women's autonomy and impede their efforts to achieve power. Refer to Fatima Sadiqi, "Feminization of

Public Space: Women's Activism, the Family Law and Social Change in Morocco" *Journal of Middle East Women's Studies* 2, no. 2 (2006): 25; and Fatima Mernissi, *The Veil and the Male Elite: A Feminist Interpretation of Women's Rights in Islam*, first published in 1975, trans. Mary Jo Lakeland (Bloomington: Indiana University Press, 1987), 19.

26. Refer to Faegheh Shirazi, ed., *Muslim Women in War and Crisis: Representation and Reality* (Austin: University of Texas Press, 2010), 200.

27. Evan Mwangi sees literary modernism in Africa manifested in the proliferation of metafictions and self-reflexive novels he attributes to social and political developments happening in the second half of the century. Evan Mwangi, *Africa Writes Back to the Self: Metafiction, Gender, Sexuality* (Albany, NY: State University of New York Press, 2009), 27–28.

28. Postcolonial scholars have contested the common view that modernism is an exclusively European movement, which ignores the complex relationship that Africa has had with the modernist project. African philosopher Valentin Y. Mudimbe argues that colonial European writers often viewed Africa as a primitive continent that served only as a source of raw material for development of European modernism. Edward Said argues that European writers had revolutionized art and writing based on ideas borrowed from outside the West—from urban centers in Africa, Asia, and Latin America. Neil Lazarus raises the question of European modernism's relation to colonialism and concludes that while modernism as an aesthetic movement is "intrinsic to the socio-historical project of modernity," it does not have, "for all its dissidence, an anti-colonial dimension." African scholar Simon Gikandi takes this argument one step further, arguing that modernism has sustained nationalist anticolonial struggle, thus subverting the common perspective of modernism as the handmaid of colonialism. According to him, modernism is not a cultural imposition by the colonizer, but rather the collective resistance of the colonized. Refer to Valentin Mudimbe, *The Invention of Africa: Gnosis, Philosophy, and the Order of Knowledge* (Bloomington: Indiana University Press, 1988), 107; Edward Said, *Culture and Imperialism* (New York: Vintage Books, 1993), 227; Neil Lazarus, *The Postcolonial Unconscious* (Cambridge: Cambridge University Press, 2011), 28; and Simon Gikandi, "The Short Century: On Modernism and Nationalism," *New Formations*, 51 (2004), 19.

29. Kwame Anthony Appiah, *In My Father's House*: *Africa in the Philosophy of Culture* (New York: Oxford University Press, 1992), 150.

30. In his book *The Rhetoric of Empire*, David Spurr argues that the colonized are denied language in a double sense. On the one hand, they are not allowed to speak; on the other hand, they are considered incapable of speech.

31. Recent scholarship has focused on the intersection of human rights and literature. In his groundbreaking book *The Human Rights, Inc.: The World Novel, Narrative Form and International Law*, Joseph Slaughter stresses the interdependence between the social work of literature and the cultural work of law. His goal, he states, is to reveal particular ways human rights law and literature make human rights legible.

32. Joseph Slaughter, "Narration in International Human Rights Law," in *Comparative Literature and Culture* 9, no. 1 (March 2007), http://docs.lib.purdue.edu/clcweb/vol9/iss1/19.

I

Negotiating Colonial and National Politics

Chapter One

Algerian Women in the Public Sphere

Remaking / Her / Story in Assia Djebar's Film La Nouba des Femmes du Mont Chenoua

Postcolonial studies have often examined the nature of visual representations of the female Arab and African "Other" by Western artists, travelers, and writers. The publicity given in the French media to the situation of Algerian women, for instance, can hardly be ignored. The French media, certainly since the early 1990s, tends to report on the patriarchal attitudes among Algerian families and the veil. The focus on these topics indicates that French culture apprehends the gendered subaltern largely through the ubiquitous artifacts and metaphors of photographic technology. By claiming to represent (or speak for) the Algerian woman, thus reducing her cultural life to journalistic headings, accounts, and photographs, the French media are doing her violence, silencing her at the same time that they claim to speak for her. The Algerian woman is projected in the French media as a defenseless and passive witness and victim of both patriarchy and colonialism.

With regard to cinema, little has been produced about the cultural reality and history of the Algerian woman in French cinematic discourse. French film critics like Pierre Jeancolas have pointed out the silence that characterizes French cinema, in general, on the country's colonial history and its past relationship to its former colonies.[1] French films centering on the colonies were often saturated with imperialist representations that frequently rendered the native population mute or invisible. The colonial history of Algeria, in particular, has not often been addressed in French cinema. In her introduction to *Cinema, Colonialism, Postcolonialism*, Dina Sherzer argues that the few French films produced in the 1960s dealt with the Franco-Algerian colonial past only in a subliminal way. Sherzer cites French filmmaker Alain Resnais' two films *Last Year in Marienbad* (1961) and *Muriel* (1963), in which Resnais used rape scenes to represent the crimes that were committed by the French in Algeria.[2] The melding of the Algerian nation with the Algerian woman figures strongly in these two films, as does the filmmaker's use of rape scenes to symbolize the French invasion of Algeria. Such films often misrepresented Algerian women, ignoring their agency and their active participation during the war of liberation. Frantz Fanon represents the Algerian woman as an agent and as an actor in the anticolonial struggle in order to displace the common stereotypical construction of her as submissive and oppressed. The most coherent rendering of his ideas about women's roles during the struggle for independence and the establishment of a postcolonial nation-state comes in his two essays "Algeria Unveiled" and "The Algerian Family." Both of these chapters are from his book *L'an cinq de la Révolution Algérienne*, which translates as *A Dying Colonialism*.[3]

It was in the famous Italian-Algerian *Battle of Algiers* (1966) by Gillo Pontecorvo, who was inspired by Fanon's book *L'an cinq de la guerre en Algérie*, that Algerian women were given credit for their active participation during the war. This film, which, despite its pseudo-documentary form, presents events primarily from the Algerian point of view, represents Algerian women as active agents during the revolution and as objects of nationalism who readily participated in the male sphere of war. In this film, women use their bodies as weapons of war, act as liaisons between male nationalist heroes, and carry bombs. Masquerading as European women, the Algerian women in the film carry explosives in their handbags and navigate the streets of Algiers in their resistance to colonial domination. The film also demonstrates how, in addition to masquerade, the veil served as a mechanism of resistance for Algerian women who hid bombs and guns under their veils, once the French soldiers started to realize that they were posing as European women. Ella Shohat has pointed out that male Algerian fighters have also resorted to masquerade and veiling in their attempt to hide weapons from the colonial gaze.[4]

While *The Battle of Algiers* has been praised for its representation of Algerian women's role in the national struggle, it has also been criticized for ignoring their fight against patriarchy.[5] The issue of Algerian women's social emancipation has been elided and subordinated, obviously, to national struggle and liberation in the film. However, it is worth pointing out that the goal of this film was not just to draw attention to Algerian women. It was also made in the Italian neorealist style, which impacted the messages it represented. Furthermore, the film was made during the time of Third World Movements that fought for social emancipation from fascism. Neorealist cinema critics will argue that it was not Pontecorvo's goal to approach his film through a feminist lens. Nevertheless, femininity as commodity and spectacle figures in *The Battle of Algiers*, where the masqueraded Algerian women are represented as objects of the colonialist's gaze. What is also obvious to the female spectator is the absence of the Algerian woman's perspective, or of any identifiable female voice concerning resistance against colonial control, in the director's visual representations of decolonization, resistance, and colonial war. The film reinscribes the same device of "Othering" that was characteristic of French cinema's representation of Algerian women. The conflation of the nation and the Algerian woman, which is characteristic of French colonial films, also figures here, as illustrated in the final images that show an Algerian woman holding the Algerian flag. This kind of representation of Algerian women in both French and Algerian cinema is the result of a history that has suppressed the presence of Algerian women on the political scene.

This chapter explores another aspect of postcolonial Algerian film by offering an analysis of *La Nouba des femmes du Mont Chenoua* (1978),[6] in which Assia Djebar gives the audience her own representation of colonialism and Algerian women's culture. To film *La Nouba*, Assia Djebar went back to the mountain of Chenoua in order to speak to peasant women in her tribe and to listen to the stories of their own experiences during the war. In the narrative, Lila, the filmmaker's "alter-ego," returns to the tribal village of Cherchell in search of testimonial proof of her brother's disappearance during the war. She is accompanied by her husband, Ali, who is mute and paralyzed as a result of falling from a horse, and her daughter Aicha. Lila is introduced in the narrative as inhabiting a "home" space within which she is experiencing some discomfort as a result of her husband's paralysis. Thus, much of her time is spent outside, in her car, and in other Algerian women's houses. The film is a mixture of documentary, fiction, oral history, and music, as well as multiple cultural codes and languages. Its heterogeneous references are made clear in its multiple dedications, first to the Hungarian musician Bela Bartok, who came to a "silenced Algeria" in 1913 to study popular music, and, second, to the Algerian warrior Zouleikha, who, in 1955 and 1956, coordinated national resistance in both the city and the mountains of Cherchell. The audience is told in the dedication that Lila, the film's protagonist, could be the daughter of Zouleikha. The other six women of Chenoua, who "speak," recount some fragments of their real history. The introduction to the film defines "la nouba des femmes" as "une histoire des femmes (qui parlent 'a leur tour')" [A history of women (who speak 'in their turn')].[7] *Nouba*, in Arabic, the audience is told, signifies a type of symphony in classical, Andalousian music, with specific rhythmic movements. In the Algerian and Moroccan dialects, *nouba* means "turn." The film, as its title indicates, blends Algerian women's speech and history with musical fragments, and French with Arabic. Réda Bensmaia, one of the first critics to write about the film, commented that, in its style, *La Nouba* stands unique as one of Djebar's seminal contributions to consolidating a new way of understanding women's experience and its grounding in Algerian history.[8]

The uniqueness of *La Nouba* stems from its temporal dimensions, which emphasize the importance of history and memory. Djebar's film raises important questions: Whose history is Algeria's? Who speaks it, and to whom? And in what language? These questions are perhaps best answered through the theoretical work of Edward Said. In his book *Orientalism*, Said draws upon Anwar Abdel Malek's argument that orientalism has considered the Oriental as an object of study endowed with a nonhistorical subjectivity.[9] Said has elaborated further on this argument by calling for a kind of revisionist historiography that performs a re-reading of orientalist discourse within the histories of the Oriental. Much like women are constructed in patriarchal films as an image or spectacle that resists narrative, orientalism casts the colonized in a frozen image of otherness without history. Fanon has also drawn attention to the direct and indirect effects of colonialism on the past of the colonized, noting: "Colonialism is not satisfied merely with holding a people in its grip and emptying the native's head of all form and content. By a kind of perverted logic, it turns the past of the oppressed people, and distorts, disfigures and destroys it."[10] Both Said and Fanon, though, fail to draw attention to the historical omissions of female historical agency within discourses of nationalism itself. Nationalism has been and always will be patriarchal and masculinized. In her book *Sexuality and War*, Evelyn Accad, drawing upon Miriam Cooke's definition of patriotism in *War's Other Voices*, explains that while patriotism can be positive because it is "intertwined with male and female images,"[11] nationalism is construed mainly in masculine terms and is never inclusive of feminist sexual politics: "In the Middle East, nationalism and feminism have never mixed very well. Women have been used in national liberation struggles—Algeria, Iran, Palestine to name a few—only to be sent back to their kitchens after 'independence' had been gained."[12]

La Nouba, filmed fifteen years after Algeria won its independence in 1962, and before the violence during the Algerian civil war of the 1990s to early 2000s, responds to both nationalism and patriarchy with a double critique. Djebar's project is to remind the Algerian public of women's roles during Algeria's recent colonial history and to recast the revolutionary subject as female. Women's history is supported in the film by images and sounds of women in war. Although the history of Algerian resistance exists in documented form, as well as in popular imagination, it is a predominantly male history that is not inclusive of the "voices" of Algerian women. Teshome Gabriel points to the "contradictions between official history and collective memory."[13] It is around this idea of popular memory that *La Nouba* would qualify, according to him, as one of the many attempts in Third World cinema wherein "what is repressed in official versions of history is kept alive through collective accounts."[14] Djebar's film aims to recover the Algerian woman's gaze and voice in Algerian history. The film bears strong resemblance to Djebar's novel *La femme sans Sepulture*, which she wrote in 2002 based on *La Nouba*'s story. The novel centers on Zouleikha, the legendary Algerian heroine who fought against the French during the Algerian war for independence between 1954 and 1961. The French title translates as "the woman without a grave," in reference to Zoulikha's unknown grave and her possible murder by French authorities, hence her erasure from public memory. The protagonist goes back to her hometown of Cherchell, also known by the ancient name Césarée, to conduct research and make a documentary about Zoulikha years after her disappearance. Djebar portrays Zoulikha as part of a plural, fragmented Algerian history that has been disrupted not only by colonialism but also by the policies of the postcolonial state. In one of her conversations with Zoulikha's daughters, the protagonist mentions a song she learned as a child: "We have only one language, Arabic / we have only one faith, Islam / we have only one land, Algeria!"[15] She later undermines the song by commenting on "the games of three, on the same earth: three languages, three religions, three heroes of the resistance, isn't that better?"[16] The narrator obviously means that Arabic is not the only language in Algeria and Islam is but one of the three monotheistic religions, thus hinting at the policies of the National Liberation Front, which, in a homogenizing gesture, imposed Arabic as the country's sole official language and Islam as its official religion, in denial of Algeria's cultural plurality.

A FEMINIST FILM?

Djebar has commented upon the filming of *La Nouba* in interviews as well as in the seven chapters entitled "Femme Arabe" (Arab Woman) in her novel *Vaste est la prison.* In speaking about one of the characters of the film, Djebar states: "Je suis ravie. Ferial est la première non seulement à jouer les vedettes, mais à pratiquer du 'féminisme' à sa manière. Ton film, c'est sur les femmes? Me demande-t-elle. Bien sur, je dis."[17] [I am delighted. Feriel is the first one not only to play the role of stars, but also to practice feminism in her own way. Your film, is it on women? She asked me. Of course, I said.] In another interview, Djebar asserts that there is more to her film than its focus on women: "To say that my film is a film about women is meaningless. I will always be drawn to making films. . . . Women's bodies, women, are my subject matter. It's a little like being a sculptor: one uses one material, another different material."[18] *La Nouba* is explicitly feminist if we take into account Djebar's intention to subvert women's subordination in the contexts of patriarchy and colonialism,[19] but it is also the aesthetic aspect of the film that Djebar reminds the viewer not to ignore.

La Nouba is a good example of feminist "cinematic counter-telling,"[20] which characterizes contemporary films produced by Third World women directors. In her essay "Post-Third-Worldist Culture: Gender, Nation, and the Cinema," Ella Shohat states: "Third World feminists, for their part, have participated in these counter-narratives, while insisting that colonialism and national resistance have impinged differently on men and women, and that remapping and renaming is not without its fissures and contradictions."[21] Revolution is, according to Shohat, a recurrent trope in Third World films by women, as it is essential for their feminist projects. *La Nouba* bears some resemblance to Guadaloupean Sarah Maldoror's film *Sambizanga* (1972), for example, in that both films foreground African female subjectivity as it pertains to revolutionary struggles. The feminist and political aspects of *Sambizanga* become explicit to the spectator as the camera follows Maria in her frantic search for her husband, Domingo, who is being interrogated and tortured to death by Portuguese colonialists. As in Assia Djebar's *La Nouba*, *Sambizanga*'s purpose is to give credibility to the African woman's active participation and involvement in revolutionary struggle. Both films also evoke the atmosphere of collectivity and solidarity that exist among women in Africa.

"Third-World feminist histories," Shohat asserts, "can be understood as feminist if seen in conjunction with the resistance work these women have performed within their communities and nations. Any serious discussion of feminist cinema must therefore engage the complex question of the 'national.'"[22] Thus, it would be misleading to read this film in a language devoted to its aesthetic aspects while depriving it of its political and feminist overtones, for "post-Third-Worldist feminist films and videos conduct a struggle on two fronts, at once aesthetic and political, synthesizing revisionist historiography with formal innovation."[23] *La Nouba* was obviously made with a conscious feminist and political sensibility, for it captures the voices of women who shared in the making of Algerian history and culture.

In her book *Femmes Fatales: Feminism, Film Theory, Psychoanalysis* (1991), Mary Ann Doane has argued that contemporary feminist film practice "addresses itself to the activity of uncoding, decoding, deconstructing the given images. It is a project of defamiliarization whose aim is not necessarily that of seeing the female body differently, but of exposing the habitual meanings/values attached to femininity as cultural constructions."[24] In her deconstructions of cultural constructions of femininity in her film, Djebar does exactly what Doane suggests about feminist film practice. What distinguishes Djebar's feminist project from Western feminist film practice, however, is its deconstruction of Algerian women's standard images in both patriarchy and colonialism. While Djebar's project evokes First World feminist film practice in its decoding of the cultural constructions of gender, it allies itself primarily with Third World feminist filmmaking because of the specificity of its ethnic and national positions. Despite the film's Western formal techniques, *La Nouba* enacts a clear decentering of Western feminism in its positioning of an "Algerian feminism" that is conceptualized around a notion of female identity rooted in Algerian culture. The film is clearly marked by nationalist and revolutionary goals, and it privileges an Algerian feminism that is centered on the female collective.

Djebar's reading of Algeria through the female Algerian space has led to a major recasting of modern Algerian history through film. It is commonly agreed upon that the National Liberation Front, the Algerian-led revolution in the 1960s against French colonialism, was the force behind Algerian modernity. It is in the context of Algeria's modernization in the mid-twentieth century that categories like "nation" and "woman" are problematized in the film. The film in its images, for example, dramatizes the divide between the "modern" and the "traditional," which characterizes Western discourse about Algeria. The presence of Lila, the liberated protagonist of the film who is the French-educated daughter of the tribe, as well as other images of Westernized Algerian young women on their way to school, repeatedly emphasizes the point that Westernization is the defining element of Algerian modernity. The contradictions and opposite images that characterize this film (such as the opposing images of veiled women in the city and unveiled women in the villages) are symptomatic of the ambiguities that come up whenever "Algeria" surfaces in contemporary discursive formations. Throughout the film, the image of Lila is posited against images of peasant women and images of old, veiled Algerian women juxtaposed with images of their unveiled and liberated daughters.

The question that we need to ask when evaluating this film is if Westernization is the key to the materiality of Algerian modernity, what then constitutes the reality of the peasant women who were involved in the revolution? In what follows, I examine *La Nouba*'s multiple interventions in the ideologies of modern Algerian history—namely nationalism, colonialism, and patriarchy—through a discussion of female speech, the female gaze, female space, language, translation, and (female) history as materialized in the film.

Djebar's project resonates with themes in postcolonial theory and subaltern studies, for it raises familiar questions concerning the problematic of language, the history of Algeria, and the question of the subaltern. As a film made during the era of Gayatri Spivak's famous theory on the subaltern, it is interesting to note how Djebar's work is a visual representation of the theory. Djebar's representation of Algerian women's speech, for instance, seems to engage Gayatri Spivak's take on subalternity and speech in her essay "Can the Subaltern Speak?" (1988).

Spivak has emphasized the effacement of the subaltern woman by asking the question "Can she speak?" and she answers the question in the negative. Spivak's claim that "the subaltern cannot speak" is spurred by the story of

Bhuvaneswari Bhaduri's suicide. Bhaduri was involved in the resistance movement for India's independence. Unable to carry out the entrusted task of a political assassination, she killed herself.[25] Commenting on Bhuvaneswari's suicide, Spivak states that "the subaltern as female cannot be heard or read."[26] According to her, even the letter that Bhuvaneswari left could not reproduce her as a speaking subject.[27]

Spivak's implication is that within certain discourses of representation, there is no space from which the gendered subaltern can speak. She makes it clear in her interview with Howard Winant that the subaltern woman cannot speak in the place where she is subalternized, but this does not preclude her ability to speak in other contexts for herself. Djebar poses similar questions concerning the Algerian subaltern: Can she speak? Can she gaze? Can she be in Algeria's history? Her film highlights the Algerian woman's speech in the contexts of anti-imperialism and nationalism, as well as in the social field. Assia Djebar is originally from Algeria and is now a professor in the United States at New York University. She was named "Silver Professor of Francophone Studies" in 2002. Her own position as a Westernized Algerian woman who has lived in France and now in the United States puts into question her act of representing the Algerian woman. *La Nouba*, however, makes evident the ways in which Djebar marks the possibility as well as the limits of her representation.

Throughout the film, Lila voices her intention to listen to the voices of the women of Chenoua: "Je ne cherche rien. Je me souviens seulement que je cherchais. Je ne cherche rien, mais j'écoute. Pour vous, que je voudrais écouter."[28] [I am not looking for anything. I just remembered that I was looking. I am not looking for anything, but I listen. It is for you that I would like to listen.] She also describes the silent manner in which she interacts with these women: "Voici que je commence à vous entendre. Vous, les dames de mon Chenoua. Ouvrir une porte, saluer, ne rien dire, laisser parler. Est-ce le passé, est-ce le présent alors qui me reviens?"[29] [I am beginning to listen to you. You, the women of my Chenoua. Open a door, greet, say nothing, let them speak. Is it the past, or the present that is coming back to me?] Here, the film emphasizes the correlation between Lila's looking (gaze) and her strategy of silence in order to be able to listen to Algerian women.

The act of listening to the subaltern speak in Djebar's film enacts Spivak's assertion at the end of her essay that "representation has not withered away" and that "the female intellectual as intellectual has a circumscribed task which she must not disown with a flourish."[30] The act of listening highlights the necessary limits of Djebar's task of representing the Algerian woman, who can only speak in her own language and her own space. Lila, who "would like to listen" to the subaltern woman's speech, is hesitant about her ability to listen. This underlines Djebar's anxiety over representation and her awareness of the near impossibility of even the act of listening, and the interpretation of what the listener hears within the discourse of the representation of the subaltern.

The question is, if women cannot speak (only listen), how can they then create their own narratives? Through Lila's act of listening, *La Nouba* succeeds powerfully in capturing the complexity of the Algerian woman's memory by recording her Arabic speech and transcribing it into French. The film highlights this speech through the female gaze, the female space, the female body, orality, and these women's political agency during the war of liberation.

Djebar's representation of the gaze of the Algerian woman in *La Nouba* resonates with her later critiques of the controlling patriarchal and colonial gaze in the visual representations of Algerian women. In the postscript of her novel *Women of Algiers in Their Apartment* (1992), Djebar draws a comparison between Delacroix's painting "Femmes d'Alger dans leurs Apartments" and Picasso's series of lithographs and canvasses that carry the same title. In comparing the two starkly different artistic renderings of Algerian women by these two artists, Djebar gets at the heart of the disparity between how these women are represented in these paintings and how they might like to represent themselves. Delacroix represents the "colonial night" into which Algerian women are thrust. His privileged glimpse into the harem is associated with the French imperial intrusion into Algeria. By stealing a "forbidden gaze" at these women, Delacroix is characterized as "the thief, the spy, the voyeur."[31] Delacroix's "orientalizing look" objectifies Algerian women and represents them as oppressed, silent, enclosed, and carrying the "perfume of evil haunts."[32]

It takes an artist who is not French to liberate these women in his work. Picasso's "Spanish genius . . . reverses the malediction,"[33] as he fills his depiction of Algerian women with light and "the improvised bursting out into an open space."[34] In Picasso's painting, there is a "glorious liberation of space, the bodies awakening in dance, in a flowing outward, the movement freely offered."[35] The narrator marvels at Picasso's ability to capture women of Algiers during the revolution. His women are seemingly freer than those in Delacroix's work, as symbolized by the "denuding" (to represent the unveiling that was occurring at the time of the revolution). But does "denuding" really indicate freedom? Picasso was a known "objectifier of women," so I do not think he really had in mind Algerian women as "freer" when he painted his nudes.

Djebar abhors the orientalizing gaze of the colonizer, as exemplified by Delacroix's painting, as well as the controlling gaze of patriarchy in Algeria. She laments the double imprisonment of Algerian women and longs for an "unveiling" that allows Algerian women to move, to look, and to speak for themselves. In her reading of *La Nouba*, Mildred Mortimer argues:

> Djebar's deconstruction of the regard orientalisant (the orientalist gaze) points to a dual origin of oppression in both Maghrebian patriarchy and French colonialism. If at first one eye alone existed, the harem master's, it was forced by political events—the conquest of Algeria, to make room for another, the colonizer's. Significantly, Djebar is charting the process of woman's empowerment in the postcolonial era.[36]

La Nouba negates the controlling orientalist and patriarchal gaze by centralizing the female look as an opposition to the male gaze, and as a form of the female collective. The film emphasizes the female collective through the exchange of gazes between Lila and the other Algerian women. Much work in the field of film criticism has been devoted to the idea of the "gaze," and many theories formulated about it have emphasized the scopic drive that propels the male gaze. Enunciation is commonly defined as the filmmaker's desire via organization of the structure of looking at his/her film as articulated to the spectator and as it engages the spectator's voyeurism.[37] One of the most authoritative texts on the discourse of the gaze is Laura Mulvey's essay "Visual Pleasure and Narrative Cinema" (1975), in which she argues that "unchallenged, mainstream film coded the erotic into the language of the dominant patriarchal order,"[38] and that "woman displayed as sexual object is the leitmotif of erotic spectacle, . . . she holds the look, and plays to and signifies male desire."[39] Mulvey's essay appeared over thirty years ago. Some readers might deem her theories old-fashioned, but her arguments are very relevant to Djebar's film. This essay was also published about the same time *La Nouba* was made. After all, the end of the 1970s was when French feminism was maturing. Djebar and Mulvey were both influenced by Hélène Cixous, Simone de Beauvoir, and Julia Kristeva. Mulvey's main argument in this essay is that narrative film has manipulated visual pleasure in such a way that film reproduces a pattern of male looking and female being "looked-at-ness." At the time, her argument focused on defining feminist cinema as necessitating the subversion of this visual pleasure, whereby woman is reproduced as an erotic object for the male hero and male spectator.

The centrality of Lila's gaze in *La Nouba* is subversive of the voyeuristic visual pleasure that characterizes narrative cinema. The image of Ali, the paralyzed and mute husband, who is confined to his wheelchair inside the house, is juxtaposed to the image of Lila, who is in constant movement outside throughout the film. In gazing at the peasant women, the sea, the mountain of Chenoua, and the fields, Lila is liberating herself from the *dakhil* (the inside, the private sphere) as well as from the male gaze. The film, in its structuring of looks, enacts a juxtaposition between the camera's looking at Ali, whose looking at Lila goes unnoticed, and Lila's looking at the women who participated in the war of liberation. The "castration" of Ali puts him in the *dakhil* and enables Lila to envision a more gyno-centric form of nationalism wherein women participate without men. Throughout the film, Lila makes her presence felt through her powerful self-gaze and through the influence of her female observational gaze—as when she looks at her female relatives of Chenoua or listens to their stories. The film captures in images the history of Lila's command of the gaze on others as well as on the outside. In *La Nouba*, the spectator is also made to witness Lila's interaction with the Algerian women of her tribe in a realm that is under the control of the camera but beyond the dominating control of patriarchal and colonial gazes.

Lila's self-gaze is crystallized in scenes where she addresses herself in a poignant tone. In the first sequence of the film, the spectator is presented with an image of the protagonist, her face against the wall, repeating to herself statements that show her strong desire for silence and imprisonment: "Je parle, je parle, je parle. Je ne veux pas que tu me voies; je ne veux pas qu'il vienne me voir en vrai. Prisonnier. Le hasard m'a rendu prisonnière dans le silence et dans l'espace."[40] [I speak, I speak, I speak. I don't want you to see me. I don't want him, indeed, to come to see me. Prisoner. Chance has made me a prisoner within silence and space.] Lila repeats "je parle" (I speak) three times, which underscores the importance of oppositional female speech in the film. Prison, in her statement, is related to silence, as is clear from the allusion to her female imprisonment. The wall against which she stands and the position in which she is standing with her back to the screen gives the viewer the impression that she is confined in a prison. Indeed, Lila is still imprisoned in the memories of a war that she cannot forget.

The film then proceeds from the standpoint of an "I," which the spectator tends to associate with the filmmaker herself. Djebar has admitted in her novel *Vaste est la Prison* that Lila's words at the beginning of the film are hers.[41] The film, however, unfolds in such a way as to merge the autobiographical "I" with the voices of the women who made Algerian history. In the same scene in which Lila expresses her desire to speak, she also voices her longing for silence when she says: "J'avais quinze ans. J'avais cent ans de douleur. Je ne pouvais parler."[42] [I was fifteen, but I had a hundred years of suffering. I could not speak.] Lila's moments of silence in the film, though, seem to be volitional, contrary to the involuntary muteness of Ali following his accident. Her silence is also not to be understood as a result of the dominance of patriarchal speech or the male gaze, both of which are lacking in the film. The patriarchal gaze is subverted in the film through the absence of scenes showing requited gazing between Ali and Lila. In different scenes that portray Ali gazing at Lila, the latter is either asleep or unaware of his gazes, undermining the influence of the patriarchal gaze in the film.

The veil, as portrayed in the film, also serves to subvert male visual pleasure. In the section entitled "Btaihi," there is a scene comprised of whispering sounds and images of veiled women who are helping to bring weapons and ammunition down from the places where they were hidden in the mountain. Frantz Fanon has pointed out that the wearing of the veil by Algerian women was a symbol of active resistance against French colonialism, as he puts it in his "Algeria Unveiled": "In the beginning, the veil was a mechanism of resistance, but its value for the social group remained very strong. The veil was worn because tradition demanded a rigid separation of the sexes, but also because the occupier was bent on unveiling Algeria."[43]

The hidden "looks" of the veiled women in the film resist the gaze of the French male who, despite his looking, is unable to see. The wearing of the veil is not a form of gender-neutral resistance, for it also has a feminist resonance. The scene that portrays veiled women in the film stresses the ability of the veil to reject the gaze of the colonialist as well as the patriarchal male, while allowing the veiled woman to assume the privilege of being the subject of the gaze, the one who looks without being seen. In his close analysis of the Algerian postcards that were sent by French colonialists to France, Malek Alloula remarks:

> The first thing the foreign eye catches about Algerian women is that they are concealed from sight . . . the eye cannot catch hold of her. . . . [T]he Algerian woman discourages the scopic desire (the voyeurism) of the photographer. She is the concrete negation of this desire and thus brings to the photographer confirmation of a triple rejection: the rejection of his desire, of the practice of his "art," and of his place in a milieu that is not his own.[44]

The veil indicates a negation of the "scopic drive" of the French male's gaze as well as of his presence in Algeria. In her book *Picturing the Maghreb*, Mary Vogl examines colonial photographs as symbolic of the colonial gaze and of a history of colonial representations of the Algerian woman. Drawing on Leila Sebbar's musings on North African women and their resistance against such representations, Vogl states: "Reclaiming a heritage that refuses to be co-opted by the 'master' Sebbar looks back to 'the women in graceful folds and complicated drapes' for inspiration on how to face the piercing gaze of the West."[45] Alison Rice argues that colonial postcards and documentary films isolate the "representative" images from context, thus misrepresenting "the pictured subject."[46] Rice summarizes such pictorial representations as part of the colonial and Eurocentric heritage, which project a prejudiced view of the colonized population. In her film, Djebar explicitly rejects the stereotypical image of the colonized.

Within the model set by Edward Said in his book *Orientalism*, for instance, are addressed the politics of the representation of the Arab woman and the enigma that the cultural and religious practice of veiling constitutes for the Western gaze.[47] *La Nouba* challenges this orientalist ideology by emphasizing the ability of the veil to block the gaze of the colonial "Other." Both Lila's self-gaze as well as the hidden "looks" of the veiled women highlight the subversive aspect of *La Nouba* in its double emphasis on Algerian women's physical visibility and the discursive power it signifies, as well as their veiling with its rejection of the patriarchal and the colonial gaze.

FEMALE SPACE

La Nouba's female-centered images make it unique in Algerian cinematographic and cultural production, which has been marked until recently by the absence of images of Algerian women. It is in this figure of the Algerian woman that *La Nouba*'s interventions in Algerian cinematographic productions lie. The female gaze in the film trespasses the spatial boundaries of Algerian society. Through the power of the female gaze, *La Nouba* explores female space, a space not previously represented in Algerian cinema. In doing so, *La Nouba* resonates with Moroccan female director Farida Benlyazid's film *Bab Sma Maftouh* (*A Door to the Sky*) (1988), which deploys female space in the context of liberally interpreted Islam. While the film celebrates the Moroccan, Muslim female collective, it is similar to *La Nouba* in that it also expresses a double critique of both patriarchy as well as European imperialism.

In his critical reading of *La Nouba*, Réda Bensmaïa has gone so far as to characterize this film as a topography of female space. To understand *La Nouba*, he says, is to be able to relate to:

> the different places where women have lived for all time and invested their presence, places that traditional cinema had never been able to reconnoiter. In this sense, *La Nouba* presents not just a simple "(hi)story" of "feminine space," but, one might say, the lay of the land, its topography. It is a matter, above all, of making a topography of feminine places, the map of a continent as yet undiscovered, at the same time as inventing a new chronotope: that of feminine time(s). And this is what makes it possible to understand the mode of construction and the rhythm, or better yet the tempo and cadences, of Djebar's film.[48]

Djebar, we might add, is presenting the Algerian woman in *La Nouba* not as a category, but as an embodiment of female subjectivity. She extends the spectacle of the Algerian woman as image, which figures in earlier films, to her image as female space, occupied by Lila as well as by the peasant women.

Lila has an important function in the film because she is the one who presents the female image through an exiled lens; she embodies the alternative to normative Algerian female subjectivity as she refuses to abide by the gendered expectations that Algerian nationalism imposes on women.[49] This female dimension probably accounts for the absence of any plot or action in the film. Mary Anne Doane has significantly noted how the figure of the woman in film is often associated with spectacle, space, or image, in contrast to the linear flow of the plot: "With respect to a narrativization of the woman, the apparatus strains; but the transformation of the woman into spectacle is easy. Through her forced affinity with the iconic, imagistic aspects of cinema, the woman is constituted as a resistance or impedance to narrativization."[50] Doane is referring here to Mulvey's article, which I cited previously, and particularly to her argument that women are fetishized by the patriarchal structure of mainstream cinema, being turned into a spectacle to be looked at, in order to reassure the spectator who would otherwise see women as symbolic of castration. The narrative of the film stops at such moments, as Djebar focuses on close-ups of women's bodies on display or long exhibitionist musical numbers that do not advance the plot. Femininity, both Doane and Mulvey argue, is not inherently antinarrative, but it is patriarchy that constructs it as such. Within Hollywood cinema, the spectacle of the female figure is set against the narrative. What seems to account for the absence of plot or narrativization in *La Nouba*, however, is not patriarchal structure of the kind represented in Hollywood cinema, but rather the privileging of space over action in the film.

In his essay "Towards a Critical Theory of Third World Films," Teshome Gabriel argues that Third World cinema emphasizes the integrity of space in itself, whereas Western cinema portrays space only as the setting of action. The history of colonialism and the various forms of oppression in the neocolonial era provide the context of these Third World forms of film practice.[51] While Gabriel's argument that all Third World people experience space and time differently from others reveals a certain essentialist and culturalist way of thinking on his part, *La Nouba* happens to endorse his argument that Third World film emphasizes space over action. *La Nouba* privileges the protagonist's constant drifting between places as well as journeys and quests over any central plot or action. Such spaces may symbolize the topographical "erasures" or silences that are imposed on women by Algerian patriarchy and that Lila is trespassing in the film. Lila's physical traversing of spaces in the film is essential to her self-location. It is outside that Lila was able to gaze into a female historical past. Throughout the film, Lila seems to be embarked on a search for an imaginary place, a legitimate space, outside her confining "home" where she can locate herself as a subject. This point is made by the camera's repeated privileging of space over action. Often, the camera lingers for several seconds on the mountain and the plain fields of Chenoua, and all action is suspended. The film ends with an image of Lila lying in a boat on the sea.

The privileging of space in *La Nouba* becomes understandable if we take into account the difficulty of action for Algerian women in the patriarchal and colonized Algeria. But contrary to Gabriel's assertion about the integrity of space in Third World cinema, *La Nouba* emphasizes rather disintegrated space in Algerian society. While space in Moroccan Farida Benlyazid's film *Bab Sma Maftouh* is represented as female and Muslim, *La Nouba* suggests that space is variegated and complex. In one of the shots of the film, Lila, her husband, and their daughter are shown visiting a Christian monument in the region of Chenoua. This scene testifies to Djebar's view that space is heterogeneous in Algeria. In comparing space in *Bab Sma Maftouh* and space in *La Nouba*, I am not suggesting, however, that female Muslim space cannot be complex.

In her book *Writing from the Hearth: Public, Domestic, and Imaginative Space in Francophone Women's Fiction of Africa and the Caribbean*, Mildred Mortimer argues that space is not a simplistic concept because inner and outer space have been defined not only as the division between private and public space, but as the division between the inner worlds of the imagination and memory, and the more graspable worlds of reason and logic. As women have moved to public spaces in search of empowerment, they have also sought alternative spaces for their liberation. This alternative space can function as a site of resistance and performance.[52] In Djebar's film, such alternative, liberating space is manifested in the combination of sounds and images, which highlights the complexity and the heterogeneity of women's experience of space in the film. The gendered space in the film is connected with women's control of the gaze as well as orality, which is rural and not just feminine. The Algerian women imaged in the film occupy emancipatory physical as well as psychological spaces. While the film shows images of veiled women, it also abounds in women's sounds: cries, screams, whispers, songs, and chants. Such psychological female spaces are also enhanced by images of women involved in collective tasks that take place in physical, open spaces, such as harvesting, drawing water, fruit picking, and so on.

LANGUAGE

The film reappropriates and subverts not only the discourse of the patriarchal and colonial gaze on women, but also the discourse of language use in modern Algeria. In the context of postcoloniality, critics are very aware of the essential hurdles associated with writing in the former colonizer's language faced by postcolonial authors. Assia Djebar has always been concerned about the problematic of using the language of the colonizer in her process of rewriting and subverting official French history. Her film, in which the narrator's French speech alternates with Algerian women's testimonies in Arabic that are in turn translated in the French subtitles, allows us to speak of a subversive poetic. Such a subversive poetic permits Djebar to assume a new subject position within postcolonial, Maghrebian cultural and literary production.

Lila's voice-over was first written in French, then translated into Arabic, and then rendered again in French in the French version of the film.[53] By moving from French to Arabic and then back to French, Djebar establishes a juxtaposition between the French voice-over narrator and the Algerian women who speak in the Arabic dialect in the film. The narrator's "French-over" that covers over the Algerian women's Arabic speech (which is in turn translated in French subtitles) forces us to ask whether translation is possible within the act of representation. The peasant woman's story, recounted to Lila about the land that the *gawri* (the Christian man) lent to her, and she cultivated herself, is in turn subtitled in French. The Algerian women's past experiences cannot be narrated outside the French colonial context and its linguistic codes. Lila's voice-over in French carries on with the peasant woman's Arabic speech; it is as if Algerian women must negotiate a specific code of languages in the process of their liberation. All of the women who speak in the film are uneducated Algerian peasants, and every word they say is translated. The film literally lets them speak. Their stories are just as much told in their anguished expressions, tone, pauses, and tears. The French translations alone could not have communicated to the spectators the historical experiences of Algerian women as much as the combination of words and images does. For these peasant women, the "unheard" subalterns, the visual dimension is essential to their stories, and the image further lessens the mediating role of the protagonist.

The fact that the Algerian women's Arabic speech is sometimes mistranslated and interrupted by French subtitles makes us wonder about the loss involved in translation. An Arabic woman who speaks in the film cannot speak French, and even if she could, a foreign language can never represent her experience adequately. In her essay "Diasporas Old and New: Women in the Transnational World," Gayatri Spivak comments on the problematic of translation when she states that "in the unexamined culturalism of academic diasporism, which ignores the urgency of transnationality, there is no one to check uncaring translations that transcode in the interest of dominant, feminist knowledge."[54] According to Spivak, translations of the postcolonial feminist intellectual mark the limits of her representation, for it is impossible for the foreign language to represent the true experience of the subaltern. Lila's hesitant act of listening, her French voice-over, and French subtitles in the film all exemplify the ways in which Djebar marks the limits of representation, and the way in which discourse determines how we hear and how we read the subaltern's speech.

While inadequate translation has often been seen as a limiting act that is conducive to misinterpretation, good translation can be enabling and useful for the postcolonial feminist intellectual in her cultural production. In order to understand Djebar's view of translation, we need first to examine the implications of bilingualism for her, as a Maghrebian intellectual. It is her film, Djebar claims, that has brought her back to writing, mainly because it has made her accept her linguistic bilingualism: "Ce film m'a fait accepter mon bilinguisme culturel avec serenité. Mon rapport avec la langue française est aujourd'hui plus clair. Si j'écris en français, c'est parce que j'ai choisi cette langue et non parce que je suis colonisée. De plus, pour me confronter à la langue arabe, je fais des traductions tous les deux ans."[55] [This film has made me accept my bilingualism with serenity. My rapport with the French language is now clearer to me. Besides, in order to confront the Arabic language, I have been doing translations for the last two years.] Confronting the Arabic language, according to Djebar, necessitates translation.

The nature of Djebar's relationship to Arabic brings to mind Abdelkébir Khatibi's philosophical thoughts on speech and language. For both of these francophone intellectuals, the process of decolonization requires drawing attention to the question of language. For Khatibi, the task of the Maghrebian intellectual lies in bridging the gap between Arabic speech and other languages for "translation requires a plurality of languages and of thoughts inscribed in them. And a 'thought of difference,' is a thought in languages."[56] Djebar's relationship to her mother tongue is equally subversive, for she deploys translation to make the Arabic language express itself in a different language.[57] Translation in the film is also an indication that language and speech are seen under two historical realities: the reality of the colonized and the reality of the colonizer. However, for Djebar, translation is meant to be read outside its history of colonial imperialism. By looking at the two different kinds of speech (French as well as Arabic) "contrapuntally," as constituting "intertwined and overlapping histories," the filmmaker seems also to be propounding a new political vision, one that Edward Said has called "a post-imperial intellectual attitude that might expand the overlapping community between metropolitan and formerly colonized societies."[58]

In his influential essay "The Task of the Translator," Walter Benjamin argues that translation "ultimately serves the purpose of expressing the central reciprocal relationship between languages."[59] Benjamin's argument about the "suprahistorical kinship of languages" or "the relatedness of two languages, apart from historical considerations" confirms his dream of "integrating many tongues into one true language,"[60] and his utopian vision of linguistic as well as cultural interdependencies. Translation in *La Nouba* seems to represent the same utopian vision for Assia Djebar as it did for Benjamin, Said, and Khatibi. What these critics have in common is their search for one common, universal language. While Djebar's feminist, anti-imperialist project foregrounds tension and unequal power balance between French and Arabic, her bilinguism offers her the possibility to bridge the gap between the two languages.

ALGERIAN (FEMALE) HISTORY

In order to fully grasp the historical implications of *La Nouba*, it is important to understand the political context in which it is situated. The film makes constant references to resistance to French conquest in the nineteenth century and colonialism in the twentieth. In 1830, the French army landed in the Bay of Sidi-Ferruch and seized Algiers. Amir Abd el-Kader united Arabs and Berbers, and declared war against the French invaders in 1832. In 1871, the "Great Revolt" in the Kabylia region, against the policy of land confiscation, was violently suppressed and 500,000 hectares of the best land were confiscated. In 1931, L'Association des Oulemas Réformistes d'Algérie (the Reformists of Algeria) was founded with the motto: "Arabic is my language, Algeria is my country, Islam is my religion." In 1954, the Franco-Algerian war began. In 1956, Ferhat Abbas joined the National Liberation Front. In 1962, France recognized Algeria's independence after being defeated following an almost eight-year-long war. In 1976, the new constitution and national charter underscored the positive role played by women during the revolution and the need for their social emancipation. The year 1979 witnessed the foundation of a "Berber cultural movement" in Kabylia.[61] In 1984, the government passed with few amendments the family code, instituting legal discrimination against women. Algerian feminist Marnia Lazreg observes that 1984 "marked the year of the rupture between women and their government and women's radical questioning of the state's legitimacy."[62] In 1990, the Front Islamique du Salut won more than five million votes, which brought the Islamists onto the political scene in Algeria.

The project of locating Algerian women as subjects of a traditional Algerian culture, as well as of a national struggle, requires subverting colonial history in order to highlight the gendered nature of domination. As a response to the objectifying discourse that agents of colonialism and patriarchy had perpetuated about the Algerian woman and her reality, Assia Djebar creates in her film a revolutionary discourse in which she centralizes the Algerian woman as subject of her identity. In her book *Talking Back*, bell hooks argues that "as subjects, people have the right to define their own reality, establish their own identities, name their history."[63] As a historian, Assia Djebar felt it necessary to have documentary evidence of Algerian women's history. Robert A. Rosenstone has pointed out the importance of oral history, interviews, and images as evidence in film. He notes that history on film "is not history in the sense that academics think of it. It is history with different rules of representation, analysis and modes of reading and comprehension that we do not yet fully understand."[64] History as represented in film operates differently from academic history, for the rules normally expected from historical narrative, such as straight chronology, are often manipulated by the filmmaker, and devices like flashbacks and flashforwards often interfere with clear progression of the narrative. The oral transmission of history is made evident in the film, for instance, through repeated images of old women storytellers surrounded by young children. Lila's voice-over comments on these scenes in the following manner: "Ainsi va l'Algérie muette. Toutes les vieilles, chaque nuit, chuchottaient, et l'histoire contée se repète. La merveille dans le songe d'enfants attentifs. Et l'histoire se repète à côté de la braise, avec des mots brisés des voix qui se cherchent."[65] [So goes the silent Algeria. Every night, old women murmured, and the told story repeats itself. Wonder in the dream of attentive children. And history repeats itself beside the embers, with the broken words of inquisitive voices.] Throughout the film, Algerian women's oral history is supported by images and sounds of Algerian women in war.

In its subversion of the historical silencing of subaltern women, the film captures the voices of Algerian women warriors during the revolution. We are told, for instance, that Cherifa saw her brother, Ahmed, a martyr, die in front of her eyes. She spent two nights hiding before she managed to find her brother's body in the river. The image of Cherifa hiding from the French in a tree at the moment when her brother was killed recurs in different scenes in the film. Lila's voice-over in French carries on with the women's story of resistance in Arabic. Lila's identification with Cherifa extends to all the women she listens to, and whom she considers her mothers: "Toutes les femmes errantes du passé deviennent ma mère. Et c'est moi, l'enfant."[66] [All the women from the past are my mothers, and I am the daughter.] *La Nouba* remains, then, an example of feminist films, because it emphasizes the protagonist's identification with Algerian women in her quest for an ethical model of Algerian female identity. In addition to reproducing the stories as told to her by Algerian women, the filmmaker has reorganized that historical evidence. *La Nouba* makes use of flashbacks to record historical events in Algerian women's anticolonial struggle. Their war experiences in the film are at times enacted as nightmares that haunt Lila in her dreams. Lila's dream in the last movement of the film titled *Khlas*, for instance, reenacts Algerian women's resistance in random images and sounds of women in war.

As Lila struggles for identity and wholeness in the film, she also seeks to become "consciously historical,"[67] by connecting her own experience with the collective experience of other Algerian women. As the alter-ego of the filmmaker, Lila allows herself to listen to stories of Algerian women. The personal experiences of these women are evocative of historical suffering and brutal torture: "Ils nous ont descendus au village. Ils nous ont mises dans des tentes. . . . Ils ne nous ont rien donné. Nous croyions que nous allions mourir. Mais nous ne sommes pas morts."[68] [They brought us down to the village. They put us in tents. . . . They did not give us anything to eat. We thought we were going to die, but we are not dead.] In Lila's narrative comment on the story of another woman, we are told: "Elle a eu de la chance.

Elle a tellement risqué d'être jetée dans la cuve! Ces cuves à vin, combien de fois se sont-elles remplies. . . . . De sang et de cris de victimes?"[69] [She was lucky. She almost risked being thrown in a wine barrel. These wine barrels, how many times were they filled . . . with blood and cries of victims?]

Djebar also deploys the medium of cinematic narration to relate the stories of Algerian heroines. The story of Zouleikha comes across in one of the sequences narrated by Lila's French voice-over. We are told that Zouleikha was born in the village of Hatchouk. She was married in 1945 to Hadj Oudai, an illiterate nationalist who was very politically active in the city of Cherchell. After November 1957, Oudai organized clandestine resistance, but he was later executed and his followers arrested. Zouleikha had decided to join the *maquis* at the age of forty. The French ultimately arrested her in the forest amidst the sounds of jeeps and police cars. To the crowd of partisans who were crying, Zouleikha screamed: "Why are you crying? See, all this turmoil is because of a woman."[70] These dialogues also feature in Djebar's novel *La femme sans Sépulture* (2002).[71] In this book, Djebar took the film and committed it to prose. Lila's voice-over carries on with the story of Zouleikha in the following manner: "On parlera de la mort de Zouleikha, et de mes anciens jours de prison. Pour en parler, il faudra en être vraiment sortie, les tirer hors de ma mémoire."[72] [I will speak of the death of Zouleikha, and of my old days in prison. In order to be able to speak, these stories need to really come out—to be extracted from my memory.] Lila later learns about Zouleikha's fate from another woman. When Zouleikha was mutilated, after being tortured, her body disappeared the following night. A man from the *maquis* carried it on his back and buried it in the forest. "Tu vois, il y a bien des façons d'offrir un tombeau à une femme."[73] [You see, there are different ways to offer a tomb to a woman.] Unlike Bhubaneswari in Spivak's story, Zouleikha, in her armed struggle against colonialism and in her act of resistance, was able to *speak* before her death to the agents of colonialism and patriarchy. But like Bhubaneswari, Zouleikha's message is buried; it, too, is lost because it cannot be translated.

WHAT WAS LIBERATION FOR ALGERIAN WOMEN?

Djebar seems to call in *La Nouba* for a kind of liberation for the Algerian woman, which goes beyond her national resistance against colonialism. For her, Algerian women's struggle for emancipation has not yet ended. In one sequence in the film, Lila's memory about her days in prison is followed by her words, "ouvrir de nouvelles prisons" (open new prisons), as the camera pans shots of veiled women. Anne Donadey has pointed out how "Djebar creates a female counter-history that destabilizes the sharp break between colonization and decolonization by foregrounding the process of continual resistance" against patriarchal domination.[74] Djebar's idea of liberation seems to engage Edward Said's concept of liberation as a way beyond nativism. Said has clearly drawn the distinction between independence, nationalism, and autonomy, on the one hand, and liberation, on the other hand.[75] The message of Djebar's film is that the nationalist consciousness that initiated independence must be differentiated from liberation. Decolonization, for Algerian intellectuals like Djebar, involves more than political resistance and liberation movements; it necessitates the decolonization of the mind from ideologies of dominance like patriarchy and imperialism.[76]

The film's implicit critique of the dominant ideologies of modern Algeria also summons forth the philosophy of Moroccan writer Abdelkébir Khatibi, who has often equated the decolonization of thought to "the affirmation of difference and an absolute and free subversion of the mind."[77] Although both are francophone writers, Djebar and Khatibi are different in their backgrounds and academic training, but they come to the same conclusions about the identity crisis experienced by Arab intellectuals. Djebar is a historian, while Khatibi is a philosopher; still, their approach to "double criticism" is an outcome of the crisis of modernization, which has emerged under the guise of double alienation experienced by Arab intellectuals from both Western culture and their own present social and cultural formations.[78] The film, in its images, enacts the double alienation Khatibi referred to when he spoke of the "silent interval between colonization and decolonization," and when he asked people of the Third World to "follow a third way, . . . a subversion that is in a way double, by which, by claiming the power of speech and action, goes to work in the context of a difference that is uncompromising."[79]

La Nouba can be viewed as a double critique of both French colonialism (and its imperialist ideology) and postcolonial (patriarchal) Algeria. The film was made in 1978; that is why there are no allusions in it to the continued unrest and violence throughout Algeria. The Algerian struggle continues after independence in 1962, with the military's tyrannical rule in the name of nationalism and patriarchy. The Arabic song that ends the film reinscribes a pessimistic view of modern Algeria. It is a celebration of the Algerian women who died for the revolution, as well as a plea for the liberation of the Algerian woman of the present, who is still oppressed under patriarchal nationalism:

> O Queens of Chenoua
> Accept my greetings
> Your heart has been distraught
> From the sufferings of the past
> Every evening
> Every morning
> You who understands the symbols
> My song speaks always of freedom

I intercede for all the martyrs
So that others would not be oppressed
The sick woman will recover from her woes
She will say "I am liberated"
To the confined women
We have justified the veil
But now
Begins the day of freedom.

NOTES

1. Pierre Jeancolas, *Le cinéma des Français: la Véme République, 1958-1978* (Paris: Stock, 1979), 156.
2. Dina Sherzer, ed., *Cinema, Colonialism, Postcolonialism: Perspectives from the French and Francophone Worlds* (Austin: University of Texas Press, 1996), 7.
3. Frantz Fanon, *A Dying Colonialism*, trans. Chevalier Haakon (New York: Grove Weidenfeld, 1965).
4. Ella Shohat, "Post-Third-Worldist Culture: Gender, Nation, and the Cinema," in *Feminist Genealogies, Colonial Legacies, Democratic Futures*, eds. M. Jacqui Alexander and Chandra Mohanty (New York: Routledge, 1997), 191.
5. Ibid.
6. Assia Djebar, *La Nouba des femmes du Mont Chenoua*, film (in Arabic with English subtitles), directed by Assia Djebar (Algeria: 1978), distributed in the United States of America by Women Make Movies, New York. In my reading of this film, I am using the version with French subtitles.
7. All translations are my own.
8. Réda Bensmaia, "La Nouba des femmes du Mont Chenoua: Introduction to the Cinematic Fragment," *World Literature Today* 70, no. 4 (1996): 877–884.
9. Edward Said, *Orientalism* (New York: Vintage Books, 1978), 97.
10. Frantz Fanon, *The Wretched of the Earth*, trans. by Constance Farrington (New York: Grove Press, 1968), 161.
11. Evelyn Accad, *Sexuality and War: Literary Masks of the Middle East* (New York: New York University Press, 1990), 15.
12. Ibid., 18.
13. Teshome Gabriel, "Third Cinema as Guardian of Popular Memory: Towards a Third Aesthetics," in *Questions of Third Cinema*, eds. Jim Pines, and Paul Willemen (London: BFI Pub, 1989), 56.
14. Ibid., 56.
15. Ibid., 71.
16. Ibid., 72.
17. Assia Djebar, *Vaste est le prison* (Paris: Albin Michel, 1995), 274.
18. Assia Djebar, Interview by Oussila Tamzali, *Cinéma Arabe* 10/11 (1978), 64.
19. I am taking into account here Assia Djebar's comments on the feminist aspects of her film in her introduction to the English version of *La Nouba* at the annual African Literature Association in East Lansing, Michigan, April 18, 1997.
20. Shohat, "Post-Third-Worldist," 183.
21. Ibid.
22. Ibid., 186.
23. Ibid., 188.
24. Mary Anne Doane, *Femmes Fatales: Feminism, Film Theory, Psychoanalysis* (New York: Routledge, 1991), 166.
25. Gayatri Spivak, "Can the Subaltern Speak?," in *Marxism and the Interpretation of Culture*, eds. C. Nelson and L. Grossberg (Urbana: University of Illinois, 1988), 307.
26. Ibid., 308.

27. Howard Winant, "'Gayatri Spivak on the Politics of the Postcolonial Subject,' Interview with Gayatri Spivak," *Socialist Review* 90, no.3 (1990): 89.
28. Djebar, *La Nouba.*
29. Ibid.
30. Spivak, "Can the Subaltern Speak?" 308.
31. Assia Djebar, *Women of Algiers in Their Apartment*, trans. Marjolijn de Jager (Charlottesville: University Press of Virginia, 1992), 137.
32. Ibid., 149.
33. Ibid.
34. Ibid.
35. Ibid.
36. Mildred Mortimer, "Reappropriating the Gaze in Assia Djebar's Fiction and Film," in *Maghrebian Mosaic: A Literature in Transition*, ed. Mildred Mortimer (Boulder, CO: Lynne Rienner Publishers, 2001), 220.
37. For a detailed definition of such cinematic concepts as "enunciation," "scopic drive," and "gaze," refer to Robert Stam, Robert Burgoyne, and Sandy Flitterman-Lewis, eds., *New Vocabularies in Film Semiotics* (New York: Routledge, 1992).
38. Laura Mulvey, *Visual and Other Pleasures* (Indianapolis: Indiana University Press, 1989), 16.
39. Ibid., 19.
40. Djebar, *La Nouba.*
41. Djebar, *Vaste est la prison*, 297.
42. Djebar, *La Nouba.*
43. Fanon, *A Dying Colonialism*, 63.
44. Malek Alloula, *The Colonial Harem*, trans. Myrna Godzich and Wlad Godzich (Minneapolis: University of Minnesota Press, 1986), 7.
45. Mary B. Vogl, *Picturing the Maghreb: Literature, Photography, (Re)presentation* (Boston: Rowman & Littlefield Publishers, 2003), 77.
46. Alison Rice, *Time Signatures: Contextualizing Contemporary Francophone Autobiographical Writing from the Maghreb* (Lanham, MD: Lexington Books, 2006), 149.
47. Edward Said, *Orientalism* (New York: Vintage Books, 1978).
48. Bensmaia, "La Nouba," 878.
49. For more information on what the National Liberation Front's nationalism was for Algeria and what it expected of women at the time, refer to Marnia Lazreg's *The Eloquence of Silence: Algerian Women in Question* (New York: Routledge, 1994).
50. Doane, *Femme Fatale*, 101.
51. Teshome Gabriel, "Towards a Critical Theory of Third World Films," in *Questions of Third Cinema*, eds. Jim Pines and Paul Willeman (London: BFI Pub, 1989), 44.
52. Mildred Mortimer, *Writing from the Hearth: Public, Domestic, and Imaginative Space in Francophone Women's Fiction of Africa and the Caribbean* (Landham, MD: Lexington Books, 2007), ix–x.
53. I am indebted to Assia Djebar for this information in her comments on *La Nouba* at the African Literature Association in East Lansing, Michigan, April 18, 1997.
54. Gayatri Spivak, "Diasporas Old and New: Women in the Transnational World," in *Revolutionary Pedagogies: Cultural Politics, Instituting Education, and the Discourse of Theory*, ed. Peter Pericles Trifonas (New York: Routledge, 2000), 20.
55. Barrada Smaoui, "Assia Djebar: Comment travaillent les écrivains," *Jeune Afrique* 27 (June 1984): 69.
56. Abdelkébir Khatibi, "Double Criticism: The Decolonization of Arab Sociology," in *Contemporary North Africa: Issues of Development and Integration*, ed. Halim Barakat, (Washington, DC: Center for Contemporary Arab Studies, 1985), 17–18.
57. For a detailed discussion on the nature of the francophone writer's relationship to the French language, refer to Albert Mémmi, *The Colonizer and the Colonized* (Boston: Beacon Press, 1991).
58. Edward Said, *Culture and Imperialism* (New York: Vintage Books, 1993), 18.

59. Walter Benjamin, "The Task of the Translator," in *Illuminations*, ed. Hannah Arendt, trans. Harry John (New York: Schocken, 1969), 75.

60. Ibid., 77.

61. For a detailed listing of the historical events of Algeria, refer to the following sources: Benjamin Stora, *Histoire de l'Algérie coloniale: 1830-1954* (Paris: La Découverte, 1991); and Benjamin Stora, *Histoire de la guerre d'Algérie: 1954-1962* (Paris: La Découverte, 1993).

62. Marnia Lazreg, *The Eloquence of Silence: Algerian Women in Question*, 197.

63. bell hooks, *Talking Back: Thinking Feminist, Thinking Black* (Boston: South End Press, 1989), 42–43.

64. Robert Rosenstone, "History in Images/History in Words: Reflections on the Possibility of Really Putting History onto Film," *American Historical Review* 93, no. 5 (December 1988): 1176.

65. Djebar, *La Nouba*.

66. Ibid.

67. Adrienne Rich, "Resisting Amnesia: History and Personal Life," in *Blood, Bread, and Poetry: 1979-85* (New York: Norton, 1986).

68. Djebar, *La Nouba*.

69. Ibid.

70. Ibid.

71. Assia Djebar, *La femme sans Sépulture* (Paris: Albin Michel, 2002).

72. Ibid.

73. Ibid.

74. Anne Donadey, "Rekindling the Vividness of the Past: Assia Djebar's Films and Fiction," *World Literature Today* 70, no. 4 (1996): 891.

75. Said, *Culture and Imperialism*, 229.

76. In his meditation on the current social crisis in Algeria, Benamar Mediene wonders why the word "independence" substituted for the word "liberation" in 1962. Mediene states that, from the time of its inception, the Algerian state robbed its society of its liberation. Refer to Benamar Mediene, "Algeria: Social Crisis or Crisis of Meanings," trans. Abdel Gaffeur. Conference paper originally entitled "Aujourd'hui l'Algérie: Crise Sociale ou Crise du Sens." Presented at "Algeria: In and Out of French: A Conference on Politics and Culture in Postcolonial Algeria," Ithaca, NY: Cornell University, October 3, 1996.

77. Khatibi, "Double Criticism," 9.

78. This debate reached its zenith in the nineteenth century during the Reformation movement in the Arab world, which came to be called *Nahda*, which means "revival" in Arabic.

79. Khatibi, "Double Criticism," 11.

Chapter Two

Ama Ata Aidoo's Modernism and the Politics of Postcolonialism

Assia Djebar and Ama Ata Aidoo are connected not only through the themes and topics they tackle in their work, but also through a historic timeframe, as they belong to the postindependence era in the 1970s, and they are about the same age. Both authors question postcolonial patriarchy and defend similar feminist issues. And each sees the course of Algeria and Ghana since independence as a promise unfulfilled. Djebar's film *La Nouba* reflects on revolution and women's participation in it, while Aidoo's *Our Sister Killjoy* (1977) questions nationalism and its gendered narratives. Both authors engage with the philosophies of anticolonial thinkers such as Frantz Fanon and Kwame Nkrumah. Indeed, critical Fanonian concepts about racial identity feature strongly in Djebar's and Aidoo's work, as they indirectly draw upon Fanon's insight on racist objectification and how it affects the psychology of African people. Aidoo's understanding of neocolonialism, nationalism, national liberation, and resistance calls for a particular Fanonian analysis.

One of the crucial aspects of Aidoo's work is its critical questioning of the concept of the nation-state. Her work is in constant dialogue with Fanon's and also with Kwame Nkrumah's official brand of nationalism. Fanon wrote *The Wretched of the Earth* after taking part in Algeria's anticolonial liberation movement in the 1950s. In this book, he foresees that the problem of colonialism will be replaced by the twin problems of neocolonialism and native bourgeois elites who have internalized the values of colonial power: "If nationalism is not enriched and deepened by a very rapid transformation into a consciousness of social and political needs, in other words, into humanism, it leads up a blind alley."[1] We may take Fanon's observation back to Aidoo, whose choice to reject nationalism offers, in Anthony Appiah's words, an instance of "post-nativist politics . . . a transnational rather than a national solidarity."[2]

In 1957, Ghana became the first African country to achieve independence from its colonial ruler. At the outset of *Our Sister Killjoy*, Aidoo questions the fictive parade of national independence when she alludes to Ghana as being the first colony to achieve independence in Africa, "since Ghana opened a dance of masquerades called Independence, for Africa."[3] Since then, Ghana has suffered major political and economic crises. Written in the 1970s, Aidoo's novel *Our Sister Killjoy* emerges out of a crisis in postcolonial Ghana when the Eurocentric narrative of colonial modernity and the gendered narrative of nationalism began to be questioned by a new generation of African writers. Aidoo's critique embodies an African modernism that questions neocolonialism and its capitalist legacy; her writing also reveals a Nkrumahian nationalism that is marked by the urge to reclaim an African past that has been repressed under colonialism. Exploring the relationship of Aidoo's novel to the colonial metropolis in which it is set, and the Ghanaian nation that was emerging from colonialism, enables us to uncover her perspective on postcolonial modernism. Literary critic Anuradha Needham labels Aidoo's anticolonial positions as "inversions of colonial ideology . . . representations and narrative forms."[4] Needham further argues that Aidoo's position resonates with Benita Parry's claim for a "counter-hegemonic" and a "combative subject position that stands in unmitigated antagonism to [colonialism]."[5]

One way to reclaim Aidoo's *Our Sister Killjoy* in these terms is to approach the text as a narrative of Ghana's independence and as a novel preoccupied with both the means by which colonized communities fight for independence as well as the potential pitfalls of nationalism. The radical break of the novel from realist narrative techniques, through its mixture of prose and poetry, is an initiation into a new understanding of modern Ghana. Aidoo's postcolonial feminist views on both colonialism and nationalism, and the political context in which she writes, are emphasized through such techniques. This is not to argue for modernism as the key to understanding postcolonial African literature, but it is worth exploring the points that some postcolonial African writers like Aidoo have in common with modernism. This group of writers has undoubtedly borrowed from the techniques of literary modernism in order to produce a sense of crisis in the same way Euro-American modernists helped produce a sense of crisis in the aftermath of World War I. African novels are all produced during or after what these works help to define as a series of localized crises and ruptures evidenced in colonialism, the national liberation movement, apartheid, neocolonialism, immigration, and global capitalism. All of these events have much to do with the shared African experience of colonialism and imperialism, and the persistence of neocolonial relationships of power and domination in Africa today.

The major crises Aidoo evokes in her novel, namely neocolonialism, brain drain, the posturing of the African elite, and global capitalism, are shared crises throughout Africa. Aidoo redirects her readers' attention away from the event of national independence toward the more poignant reality of neocolonialism:

> Nigeria. Nigeria our love. Nigeria our grief. Of Africa's offspring her likeness—O Nigeria. More of everything we all are, more of our heat, our naïveté, our humanity, our beastliness, our ugliness, our wealth, our beauty. A big mirror to our problems. Our tragedies. Our glories. Ghana? Just a tiny piece of beautiful territory in Africa had greatness thrust upon her once. . . . Now she picks tiny bits of undigested food from the offal of the industrial world.[6]

Ghana and Nigeria are both equally emblematic of this crisis. Both countries represent fundamentally African problems that transcend the artificial European-drawn borders now regulated by the different African states. Ghana and Nigeria signify major neocolonial problems and the failure to modernize as independent nation-states. This implies that the African project to modernize, as a whole, is seen as a failure. In contesting notions of universal history, Aidoo's assessment of modernism emphasizes Africa's developmental complexity. The nationalists' project to bring economic development to the nation—which may have seemed possible at the moment of political independence—now looks less and less possible in the current configuration of global capitalism.

The novel offers a trenchant critique of Nkrumahism. While she embraces Nkrumah's appraisal of neocolonialism, Aidoo is aware of the dangers and contradictions of his brand of nationalism, which seeks to combine modernization and tradition through gendered narratives. A staunch advocate of Pan-Africanism and the founder of the Organization of African Unity, Nkrumah negotiated Ghana's independence from British colonial rule in 1957 and became the first President of Ghana. Among Nkrumah's ideas is the concept of "the African Personality," which "expresses identification not only with [the] African historical past, but with the struggle of the African people in the African revolution to liberate and unify the continent and to build a just society."[7] As a student of philosophy, Nkrumah developed a new social and political philosophy that he called "consciencism," which he deemed relevant to Africa's cultural reality. Through this concept, he strove to harmonize the three constituents of African society, namely African indigenous traditions, Islam, and Western influence, in order to create one African culture.[8] Certainly, his view of nationalism, as being inclusive of Western and Islamic traditions, is not common. According to Abiola Irele, Nkrumah's philosophy of consciencism represents "a focused endeavor to negotiate a mode of accommodation between Africa and the West,"[9] as it not only sought to achieve modernization in the Western sense, but also aimed to assert traditional African culture. While it defines itself in opposition to European nationalism, Nkrumah's anticolonial nationalism simultaneously remains implicated in European nationalism's gendered narrative that often associates the nation with the "motherland." Aidoo's feminist perspective on nationalism runs counter to Nkrumah's masculinist narrative, which views women as "the mothers of the nation."[10] Nkrumah insists upon a unified national and patriarchal identity[11] (although he repeatedly emphasizes that it is not ready-made, but instead has to be constructed), while Aidoo radically calls into question his idea of a static African identity. Aidoo's novel brings a feminist view of nationalism that does not discount the female protagonist's agency and her own imaginings of nation. Though Aidoo is critical of Nkrumah's essentialist discourse of cultural authenticity, which views women as symbols of indigenous traditions, her work nevertheless shares his commitment to Africa and his position on anticolonial resistance.

The novel is divided into four parts: "Into a Bad Dream," "The Plums," "From Our Sister Killjoy," and "A Love Letter." The title of the novel is significant in relation to the female protagonist because "Killjoy" refers to someone who is critical and always sees the glass half empty. Using the framework of a journey, Aidoo traces the transcontinental journey and transcultural experience of the protagonist Sissie as she travels through Germany and England and returns home to her native country, Ghana. The novel combines free indirect speech and a letter Sissie wrote to her lover while on a plane ride back to Ghana. Free indirect speech allows Aidoo to enter and speak from within the mind of the protagonist, but also to leave that internal space in order to reflect externally upon the relationship between Africa and Europe. The overall narrative consists of a number of sub-narratives. While one narrative evokes the failed hopes of African nationalism, another one engages with the European neocolonial legacy. The neocolonial situation often found in Africa, which generated a sort of dumping ground for industrialized nations, is the legacy of the colonial period, when Europeans exploited Africa's resources. The neocolonial legacy makes Africa dependent on exports, while its industrialization and modernization lag behind. This narrative also calls attention to the past European slave trade, of which vestiges in the form of castles and forts still stand along the African coastline. A related narrative is that of capitalism and globalization, which help the author understand the imperial bases of European success. Yet another sub-narrative speaks to the position of Africa's pseudo-intellectuals, who signal a break from the past and establish their new foundation on the individual, far less than on traditional authority. For them, knowledge is something to be created and continuously pursued, even if it means abandoning Africa and immigrating to Europe. The story of pseudo-intellectuals points to a change in temporal orientation, because they symbolize the future and the possibility of "progress." Their problem, however, is that they mimic Western ways and values, and believe that Western culture is superior to an African one. Finally, there is the sub-narrative of African womanhood, which consists of a radical questioning of the corrupt authority of neocolonialism, racism, and nationalism, reclaiming instead the black diaspora. Sissie becomes the champion of the freedom of conscience, asserting the inevitable progress of freedom and enlightenment, and espousing a certain type of "womanism."

Aidoo's questioning of nationalism is mediated through Sissie, who constitutes a political voice for the author's critique of national politics. In her travels to Europe, Sissie has a unique vantage point as a commentator on both European and African politics. Through her experience, she quickly develops insights into the contradictions between so-called European democracies and the poverty of the African masses. She is shocked by the European lifestyle and its emphasis on consumerism, instant gratification, and even hedonism, which she feels are symptoms of late industrial era capitalism. In line with this lifestyle is the black Mercedes-Benz in which her hosts pick her up and which is emblematic of transnational capitalism. The abundance of food consumed by members of the Involou group conjures up in her mind images of starving people in Africa who have to "pick tiny bits of undigested food from the offal of the industrial world."[12] When she meets the lonely German housewife Marija, she is all the more disillusioned by "the West's societal degeneration," the "breakdown of the family,"[13] and the oppression of women by a universal patriarchy. Identification with and disavowal of Marija are almost simultaneous. Marija's homosexual advances push Sissie to moralize against the dilemma of identification these advances evoke: "Sissie thought of home. . . . What strings . . . drew her into those pinelands . . . where now a young Aryan housewife kisses a young black woman with such desperation."[14] Empathizing with Marija, Sissie's feminist consciousness[15] begins to develop only to be eroded by what she later realizes are irreconcilable cultural and historical differences between them. Nevertheless, the text signifies common grounds of solidarity between European and African women. Both are marginalized Others of European modernity, and both share common interests in rejecting masculinist nationalist structures. Yet, the author is all too aware that they occupy different positions in capitalist structures: "Marija could have passed for a soul sister. But for her colour—and our history."[16] The novel insinuates that African women have been subject to neocolonial exploitation and unfairly targeted by multinational corporations, which subject them to violence for the purpose of scientific research. Aidoo has noted elsewhere that "when people ask me rather bluntly every now and then whether I am a feminist, I not only answer yes, but I go on to insist that every woman and every man should be a feminist—especially if they believe that Africans should take charge of African land, African wealth, African lives and the burden of African development."[17]

Some critics have interpreted Aidoo's commitment to Africa as anti-Western. Chris Dunton dismisses Sissie's confidence as "anti-Western nationalism."[18] Brenda Cooper contends that Aidoo's critique of Europe's neocolonial exploitation of Africa embodies "a right-wing black exclusivist position"[19] and "a resurgence of a modern version of Negritude"[20] that stereotypes Europe and promotes the myth of a national culture. According to Cooper, the beliefs and perceptions of Aidoo and her protagonist are the same. One can chart the course of Sissie's development by assessing the way in which her own perspective comes gradually into a near perfect convergence with that of Aidoo. Their perceptions "include derogatory (retaliatory) descriptions of white skins, the genetic unsoundness of Europeans, their love of dogs . . . their eating habits."[21] Both Cooper and Dunton accuse Aidoo of some version of a Negritudist notion of Africa. Contrary to what Cooper and Dunton presume, however, Aidoo assumes such nationalist positions in the novel, not as mythical essence but as a political strategy against common experiences of colonial and neocolonial exploitation. Aidoo is not taking a racist position; she simply points to the danger and damage inflicted on Africa and its people.[22] Her investment in Africa is strategic in Gayatri Spivak's sense of the word. She makes "strategic use of a positive essentialism in a scrupulously visible political interest."[23] The concept of "strategic essentialism" suggests that it is possible to postulate an African identity for the purpose of contesting hegemonic discourses that exclude Africans. It also enables the author to critique the contradictions of narrow concepts of nationalism that exclude Africans in the diaspora. Such a strategy is used in Aidoo's work as a discursive measure to conceptualize a version of African political agency. Thus, she strategically draws upon the Nkrumahian discourse of African political unity and its problematic inscription of the nation-state as uncritically borrowed from Europe in order to reveal the existential tragedy of power-brokering in African politics. She also recognizes a priority of nationalist allegiance, evident in comments made during her interview with Anuradha Needham:

> All these issues are related. I mean, how are you going to be able to say as an African that you are a feminist if you are not a nationalist? Or how can you claim to be aware of Pan-Africanism if you are not aware of our concerns as women? Or how are you going to say that you are an African nationalist if you are not a feminist?[24]

In the same interview, Aidoo revises her earlier nationalist position and substitutes it with what she terms "African identification": "We need a kind of rallying point around which we can cohere to stop this endless exploitation of ourselves, our resources, our environment . . . we need an African identification for there surely are an African people."[25] Aidoo's espousal of what she terms "African identification" as resistance to European imperialism needs to be distinguished from what Edward Said calls "nativist" positions within nationalism. Said rejects nativism as an essentializing form of nationalism when he asserts that "to accept nativism is to accept the consequences of imperialism, the racial, religious, and political divisions imposed by imperialism itself."[26] This understanding is very similar to Wole Soyinka's attitude toward the philosophy of Negritude. In his book, *Myth, Literature and the African World*, Soyinka rejects Senghor's negritude, which is based on the "very foundations of Eurocentric epistemology," and professes to establish a neo-negritude on the basis of purely African categories.[27] Edward Said responds to the question, "How does a culture seeking to become independent of imperialism imagine its own past?" by listing three choices, and he negatively criticizes the third choice because it embodies nativism of the "Caliban who sheds his current servitude and physical disfigurements in the process of discovering his essential, pre-colonial self."[28] In the same vein, Fanon argues that decolonization should give way to a new order that rejects not only nativism or racialism but also assimilation to European culture by the African elite, who merely mimic the old colonial model.[29] Along the same lines, Neil Lazarus distinguishes between Fanon's critique of "bourgeois anti-colonial nationalism, an ideology aimed at the (re)attainment of nationhood through means of the capture and subsequent 'occupation' of the colonial state," and his advocacy of "another would-be hegemonic form of national consciousness—a liberationist, anti-imperialist, nationalist internationalism."[30] The distinction between nationalism and national consciousness is fundamental to Aidoo as she follows a similar ideology. Like Fanon, Aidoo appeals for a type of international consciousness beyond nationalist consciousness, which would secure a better future for the African masses.

Aidoo's "African identification" differs from Nkrumah's Pan-Africanism not only in ideological disjunctures but also in terms of language, given her consideration of the African diaspora. Aidoo's novel blends Standard English and the local Ghanaian dialect Akan, thus reproducing local and global identities. The impetus for Aidoo's modernist experimentation with language and form has less to do with aesthetic innovation for its own sake than with her subversion of Nkrumah's static ideas to narrate Africa's cultural past and future. Nkrumah was misguided to use the African Personality in the service of a past that is divorced from the urgent problems of the moment. Aidoo's modernist novel is thus less about narrative experimentation than it is with overthrowing novelistic forms and structures, and by extension forms engendered by Nkrumahian nationalism that are outmoded and repressive. Thus, by blending Akan and Standard English, she creates a work of fiction that corresponds with her new understanding of African and global politics. Aidoo explores interlocking connections between Africa and its diaspora in all her fiction, including her most recently published collection of short stories

Diplomatic Pounds (2012). The stories, though rooted in African consciousness and Africa's historical reality, depict encounters between Africa and its diaspora, converging on the global scene. They thus describe different types of relationships (friendship, romance, family, and the workplace) in a global context.[31]

In *Our Sister Killjoy*, language variety adds more depth to the novel's global connections. The author, however, is aware of the essential problem of anti-imperialist writers like herself who have to address imperialism in English, the language of the former colonizer. Sissie explains to her lover: "I have only been able to use a language that enslaved me, and therefore, the messengers of my mind always come shackled."[32] Sissie's "voyage in" from the periphery to question imperialism, using the tools and discourses of that same addressed center, is problematic. So it is not surprising that the author should seek to reconcile her art and political commitment by fusing English with local Akan. Aidoo's subversion of language entails a political critique of European imperialism and of Nkrumah's Pan-Africanism, which attempted to elide difference in the process of defining a unitary African subject. Nkrumah's aim for a greater national unity failed precisely because of the illusory nature of a static African subject.

Aidoo's novel, which speaks to the African masses everywhere who are engaged in struggles to reclaim their human rights on an international scale, overwrites Nkrumah's exclusive continental Pan-Africanism, thus emphasizing the links between Africa and its diaspora. The author uses a transnational framework to show how Africans experience capitalist exploitation in Africa and also in the diaspora. When Sissie arrives in London, she sees "so many black people there."[33] African immigrants in London are shown struggling and bearing the brunt of poverty and racism: "The women especially were pitiful. . . . They smothered their bodies in raiments of diverse lengths, hues, and quality—in a desperate effort to keep warm."[34] Here, the novel alludes to a common "African" experience that is characterized by exclusion, alienation, and nonbelonging. Frantz Fanon has pointed out that "the effective disalienation of black people entails an immediate recognition of social and economic realities."[35] Aidoo obviously shares Fanon's social and materialist conception of Africans in the diaspora. Her project might be seen as tracing the interchange between black identity and socioeconomic factors with regards to the African diaspora.

Furthermore, the novel suggests that there is a disconnect between such African masses and Africa's elites who have betrayed the African cause and become agents for the exploitation of the masses. The novel's critique of Nkrumahian nationalism and transnational capitalism is compounded by its questioning of the African elite, who, in Fanon's words, would act as a "transmission line between the nation and a capitalism, rampant though camouflaged, which today puts on the masque of neocolonialism."[36] Their greed, spurred by the greed of multinational capitalism, leads them to embezzle money and resources from their African citizenry. The novel also denounces the "brain drain" phenomenon that disconnects African intellectuals from Africa's masses and causes them to take a different path, reinvesting themselves in Europe instead. The author exhorts African exiles to return home and connect themselves to grassroots Africa and end their alienation. Upon meeting Sammy—"her fellow countryman"— at the German embassy dinner, Sissie realizes that he is completely dissociated from Africa: "He spoke the German language well and was familiar with them in a way that made her feel uneasy."[37] The problem with Africans like Sammy rests in their alienation from Africa and their easy adoption of European lifestyles and values, which is the price they have to pay for their colonial education. The author denounces self-exile as "only a younger version of the old bankruptcy" that causes us "to lose our identity quickly in order to join the great family of man"[38] in the name of universal art, culture, and literature. Aidoo questions this notion of the universal as well as the African intellectual who "in the face of a reality that is more tangible than the massive walls of the slave forts standing among our beaches, still talks of universal truth, universal art, universal literature and the gross national product."[39] Here, she joins African writers like Chinua Achebe who are adamant in their critique of universalism. Achebe has been critical of the false universalism of Eurocentric intellectuals who narrowly label European values and achievements "universal": "It would never occur to them to doubt the universality of their own literature. In the nature of things, the work of a Western writer is automatically informed by universality."[40] Achebe hopes "to see the word 'universal' banned altogether from discussions of African literature until such a time as people cease to use it as a synonym for the narrow, self-serving parochialism of Europe, until their horizon extends to include all the world."[41] The "until such times" clause in Achebe's critique makes it clear that he, like Aidoo, is a firm believer in a genuine universalism, that is "a universal universalism" that bears fruit in its uncompromising rejection of imperialism.

Such astute rewritings by Aidoo not only challenge the history and the narrative of Nkrumah's nationalist project, which is confronted on various levels in the novel, but directly attack neocolonial relations of power and domination in which African people still find themselves caught up today. If the Westernized intellectual elite like Sammy are deluded and confused, and African people are not united, how is one to overcome this tragic loss of self and the ghettoization of a whole continent? What then constitutes a viable solution for Africa? Fanon proposes a new order that rejects both assimilation and nativism. Like Fanon, Aidoo suggests that Africa will be modified and changed only when bourgeois assimilation as well as regressive nativism are rejected. Sissie writes to her lover: "'In any case, the question is not just the past or the present, but which factors out of both the past and present represent for us the most dynamic forces for the future. . . . That is why, above all, we have to have our secret language.'"[42] She asserts the necessity of a secret language to maintain contact with one's community. In the same letter, she proceeds to inform her lover that:

> [M]other and father had not been to school at all. So no one could accuse them of having got acculturated. . . . they definitely have not been overseas and therefore were not westernized. . . . Given all of that, if they didn't know how I should have been brought up as an African woman, then who does?[43]

Here, Aidoo seems to imply that the solution to Eurocentricity must be sought in Africa's indigenous culture and communal values.[44] In the letter, Sissie views her medical student lover and his friends as being selfish in their desire to follow their careers in Europe and not return to Africa to rebuild its future. Nevertheless, it could also be argued that their decision to stay in London for career purposes is sensible, rather than a rejection of Africa. They are, after all, research scientists and cannot practice their academic pursuits in Ghana. The argument, obviously, is between individualism and communalism, or Western versus African values, but this dichotomy can be a simplistic understanding of the novel. Sissie's return to Ghana, in hopes of reinventing a better future there, can nevertheless represent a refusal to engage with modernity. It can also represent a way to stave off Africa's brain drain, or a romantic retreat to the kind of nativism Aidoo is herself critiquing in the novel. For some critics, however, Sissie's return to Africa is not only a change of geography but also a change of cultural and political perspective. Anthony Appiah has pointed out that for postcolonial African novelists, like Aidoo, undue emphasis is put on Africa: "What they have chosen instead of the nation is . . . Africa—the continent and its people,"[45] and for this they might seem "misleadingly postmodern."[46] Their project, however, is not a postmodernist one because it is "grounded in an appeal to an ethical universal . . . in the name of humanism. . . . And on that ground it is not an ally for Western postmodernism but an agonist, from which I believe postmodernism may have something to learn."[47] Aidoo's literary modernism diverges from postmodernism because Africa is still the poor continent, being plundered by multinational corporations and multilateral agencies—and further oppressed by foreign debt servicing.

In rewriting neocolonialism and in rejecting Nkrumahian Pan-Africanism, Ama Ata Aidoo's literary modernism looks toward some alternative future. While her novel endorses some views advocated by Nkrumah, such as his positions on anticolonial resistance and brain drain, it also rejects what is narrow, patriarchal, and nativist in his theories. Her work constitutes a critique of Nkrumah's political discourse, which, in an attempt to unify Africa, has essentialized the continent in a way that excludes the problems and complexity of African consciousness and history. For Aidoo to suggest that Nkrumah's work is narrow, or for her to critique the project of a nationalist patriarchy, implies that there has to be the recovery of an existential project of freedom and a true understanding of agency involved in African intellectual subjectivity, history, and culture. Aidoo's Fanonian clarity about the consequences of European imperialism and nationalist oligarchy are especially important. We should remember that Fanon was also a psychiatrist who was very invested in the psychological damage people of African descent have endured. This being said, Sissie's writing back to her lover in Europe is an attempt to free the complexity of African subjectivity from the essentialist representations of a European colonial gaze and a reductive form of African politics that misunderstands African people.

NOTES

1. Frantz Fanon, *The Wretched of the Earth*, trans. Constance Farrington (New York: Grove Press, 1968), 204.
2. Anthony Kwame Appiah, *In My Father's House*: *Africa in the Philosophy of Culture* (New York: Oxford University Press, 1992), 155.
3. Ama Ata Aidoo, *Our Sister Killjoy: Or, Reflections from a Black-Eyed Squint* (Harlow, Essex: Longman Drumbeat, 1977), 95.
4. Anuradha Dingwaney Needham, "Reversing Europe's Gaze: Ama Ata Aidoo's Oppositional Art," in *Using the Master's Tools: Resistance and the Literature of the African and South-Asian Diasporas* (London: Macmillan Press LTD, 2000), 77.
5. Ibid., 76.
6. Ibid., 52–53.
7. Basil Davidson, *Black Star: A View of the Life and Times of Kwame Nkrumah* (London: Lane, 1973), 205.
8. Kwame Nkrumah, *Consciencism* (New York: Monthly Review Press, 1970), 68.
9. Abiola Irele, *The African Imagination: Literature in Africa and the Black Diaspora* (New York: Oxford University Press, 2001), 79.
10. Takyiwah Manuh, "Women and Their Organizations during the Convention Peoples' Party Period," in *The Life and Work of Kwame Nkrumah: Papers of a Symposium Organized by the Institute of African Studies*, ed. Arhin Kwame (Trenton, NJ: Africa World Press, 1993), 113.
11. See Elizabeth Willey, "National Identities, Tradition and Feminism," in *Interventions: Feminist Dialogues on Third World Women's Literature and Film*, eds. Bishnupriya Ghosh and Brinda Bose (New York: Garland Publishing, Inc., 1997), 12.
12. Ibid., 35.
13. Gay Wilentz, "The Politics of Exile: Reflections of a Black-Eyed Squint in *Our Sister Killjoy*," in *Emerging Perspectives on Ama Ata Aidoo*, eds. Ada Uzoamaka Azodo and Gay Alden Wilentz (Trenton, NJ: Africa World Press, 1999), 83.
14. Aidoo, *Our Sister Killjoy*, 64.
15. While some critics like Wilentz have asserted that Sissie rejects Marija's homosexual advances because she is heterosexual, Angeleta Gourdine argues that Sissie harbors homosexual desire for Marija but remains ambivalent. Her ambivalence, however, is "related to notions of race and family, and . . . as an attempt to reconcile the role of nationalist women with their identities as female homosexuals." See Angeletta K. M. Gourdine, *Difference Place Makes: Gender, Sexuality, and Diaspora Identity* (Columbus: Ohio State University Press, 2002), 97.
16. Aidoo, *Our Sister Killjoy*, 63.

17. Ama Ata Aidoo, "The African Woman Today," in *Sisterhood, Feminisms and Power: From African to the Diaspora*, ed. Obioma Nnaemeka (Trenton, NJ: Africa World Press, 1998), 47.

18. Chris Dunton, "'Wheyting Be Dat': The Treatment of Homosexuality in African Literature," *Research in African Literature*, 20, no. 3 (1989): 422–448.

19. Brenda Cooper, "*Chaiba the Algerian* versus *Our Sister Killjoy*: The Case for a Materialist Black Aesthetic," *English in Africa* 12, no. 2 (1985): 27.

20. Ibid., 31.

21. Ibid.

22. Ranu Samantrai defends Aidoo against allegations of racism and argues that the latter's Pan-Africanism stems from a nonracialist impulse. She points out that her novel *Our Sister Killjoy* "provides an example of how a non-racialist, non-foundational African identity might lead to Pan-African solidarity." See Ranu Samantrai, "Caught at the Confluence of History: Ama Ata Aidoo's Necessary Nationalism," *Research in African Literature* 26, no. 2 (1995): 140–157.

23. Gayatri Spivak, *Outside in the Teaching Machine* (New York: Routledge, 1993), 205.

24. Anuradha Dingwaney Needham, "An Interview with Ama Ata Aidoo," *The Massachusetts Review* 36, no.1 (1995): 124.

25. Ibid., 127.

26. Ibid., 292.

27. Wole Soyinka, *Myth, Literature and the African World* (New York: Cambridge University Press, 1990 [1976]), 127.

28. Said, *Culture and Imperialism*, 292.

29. Fanon, *Wretched*, 94.

30. Neil Lazarus, "Disavowing Decolonization: Nationalism, Intellectuals and the Problematic of Representation in Current Theories of Colonial Discourse," in *Nationalism and Cultural Practice in the Postcolonial World* (Cambridge: Cambridge University Press, 1999), 78–79.

31. Ama Ata Aidoo, *Diplomatic Pounds and Other Stories* (Oxfordshire: Ayebia Clarke Publishing Limited, 2012).

32. Ibid., 112.

33. Aidoo, *Our Sister Killjoy*, 85.

34. Ibid., 88–89.

35. See Frantz Fanon, *Black Skin, White Masks* (New York: Grove Press, 1968), 12–13.

36. Fanon, *Wretched*, 122.

37. Aidoo, *Our Sister Killjoy*, 9.

38. Ibid., 121.

39. Ibid., 6.

40. Chinua Achebe, *Hopes and Impediments: Selected Essays 1965-1987* (London: Heinemann, 1988), 11.

41. Ibid.

42. Aidoo, *Our Sister Killjoy*, 116.

43. Ibid, 117.

44. Elizabeth Willey has pointed out that Aidoo's novel *Our Sister Killjoy* replicates Nkrumah's plea for an "African personality," one that is not "Westernized" or "acculturated." See Willey, "National Identities, Tradition and Feminism," 9.

45. Anthony Kwame Appiah, *In My Father's House*, 150.

46. Ibid., 152.

47. Ibid., 155.

Chapter Three

Rewriting Power

Bessie Head's Revolutionary Politics

Bessie Head (born in 1937) is of the same generation as Assia Djebar (born in 1936) and Ama Ata Aidoo (born in 1942). They all started writing their first novels around the same time (in the 1960s and 1970s). Unlike Djebar and Aidoo, however, Head did not write in a postcolonial era because South Africa was still colonized at the time. The colonial situation undoubtedly shaped her voice and what it meant for her to be an African woman writer. Given that Head led an essentially truncated life, rife with challenges, based on her gender and her status as a colored woman under apartheid, she was well ahead of her time in tackling issues such as globality and ecofeminism—subjects that require an amazing amount of imagination. While Djebar's and Aidoo's writings are equally rooted in the tradition of liberal humanism, Head advocates an inclusive type of universal humanism that is pluralistic, heterogeneous, and reaches beyond the African continent. Summarizing the difference between Bessie Head and Ama Ata Aidoo in their attitude toward universal humanism, literary critic Caroline Rooney points out that their definition of universalism is different: "In Aidoo's book, 'universal' pertains to the pseudo-universal: a universality that is European, and so on, and so not universal. In Head's book, 'universal' pertains [to] ordinary people."[1]

Bessie Head's discourse of liberation appears to go beyond the African framework and thus aspires to the universal. This radical aspiration is reflected in her human-centered approach to Africa's problems, putting humanity above the exclusivity of nationalism and racism. Head is often recognized as an international writer whose views on writing and politics place her among international women writers such as Sylvia Plath, Virginia Woolf, and Alice Walker. Along with African writers like Wole Soyinka and Chinua Achebe, Head is a globally known writer from Africa in a modern sense in that she sees Africa's values as important for the rest of the world. Her transition from writing for a purely local audience at the time she was a journalist to addressing a global readership was rapid because of her sensitivity to global politics and her vision of political change. Head's ideas, with respect to thinking about Africa in global terms, were very innovative for the time. It can be said that she is one of the first global and environmentally conscious African authors of the postcolonial era.

Despite the fact that her writing is shaped by colonialism and well-grounded in the resistance tradition of South African writers, critics have judged Head's work as not sufficiently *engagé* (committed politically). She was condemned by Pan-Africanists for her resolve not to identify with their cause and was viewed by feminists as not sufficiently feminist. She responded to such criticisms in an interview quoted by her biographer, Craig McKenzie: "[A] writer automatically feels pressurized into taking a political stand of some kind or identifying with a camp. . . . It was important to my development to choose a broader platform for my work, so I have avoided political camps because they falsify truth."[2] Head perceives politics as selfish power-mongering that has led people to stray away from values and has distorted Africa's humanity and richness of culture. For her, politics has become a question of power instead of a collective effort to identify and solve issues.[3]

It is indeed quite understandable why Head denounces politics in general. Her own life was marred by the abuses of power carried out by both Afrikaner and black nationalisms. In 1948, when the Afrikaner National Party assumed power in South Africa, blacks were automatically stripped of their citizenship. Refugees like Bessie Head, who escaped apartheid, were also deprived of their citizenship. In addition to the citizenship law, the National Party instituted a number of laws that were at their core based on racial segregation. One such law was the Immorality Act, which outlawed interracial marriage and sex, with the aim to control sexuality within apartheid's colonial context. In an article that appeared in *Ms. Magazine* in 1975, Head narrates the story of her mother who gave birth at a mental hospital, where she was confined as punishment for having sex with a black "stable boy."[4] This story, however, has been contradicted by two of Head's biographers, Susan Gardner and Gillian Stead Eilerson, who found that Head's mother was hospitalized because of mental illness.[5] As an infant girl, Head was rejected by her mother's family because of her illegitimate status as colored. She was shuffled from one orphanage to another before she finally joined St. Monica's School in Durban. Escaping racism in what she calls "the unholiest place on Earth," Head exiled herself to Botswana in 1964 on an exit permit, thus losing her South African citizenship. She taught at a school in Serowe, but was refused citizenship by Botswana authorities, instead remaining a refugee.

THE FEMINIST POLITICAL IN BESSIE HEAD'S WRITING

Despite her refusal to openly identify with official political and feminist movements, Bessie Head's work is indeed feminist and highly political in its attack on patriarchy—colonial and nationalistic—and its exploration of questions of power, resistance, and freedom. Through the blending of politics and feminism, Head's novels position her alongside Assia Djebar and Ama Ata Aidoo as a critic of gender injustice, colonialism, decolonization, and nationalism. In one of her letters to Alice Walker, Head admits her noncommitment to the women's liberation movement: "I think, like my attitude towards politics, I'd not do so well in woman's lib."[6] African women like her have always been hesitant to identify with mainstream feminism because the lives and concerns of white, middle-class women were the main focus of the women's liberation movement. In order to read Head's work as feminist, we need to understand feminism in a broader view, steering the discourse of feminism away from its traditional linear history and toward a global perspective that recognizes the diversity of women's experiences and ever-changing perceptions of feminism. In the 1970s, there was only one version of feminism, primarily the Anglo-American one. Even African-American feminism at the time was obfuscated within other movements such as that of the Black Panthers (about which Head was fascinated) and Malcolm X's brand of Marxism.

Head's feminism, avant-garde for its time, demonstrates a transnational critique of power rather than association with a particular category of feminists. Hers is a global feminist consciousness that uses writing to contest power politics and challenge oppressive patriarchal, capitalist, and racist structures. Head is committed to political, feminist, and ecological causes; she writes against people in power to articulate what is unconventional and potentially revolutionary. Her novels should be read as writings of revolution that stem from her radical feminist critique of all institutions and structures of power. According to Head, the oppression of women and minorities is rooted in legal, economic, political, social, and cultural abuses of power. While several critics have written about Head's political involvement, my particular contribution lies in reading her critique of power in light of different strands of feminist theory: radical feminism, African feminism, ecofeminism, and antinationalist and global feminism.

HEAD'S RADICAL FEMINIST AGENDA

Living under the dictatorship of apartheid in South Africa and then as a refugee in Botswana, Bessie Head deploys writing tactics in response to authoritarian regimes and their abuses of power. Power is a feminist issue because it lies at the core of the hierarchical political and social structures that dominate South African culture. Michel Foucault has defined power as a nexus between power and knowledge, or what he calls each society's "regime of truth."[7] Foucault, however, makes no mention of gender in his analysis of power, and neither do Marx, Lenin, Nietzsche, nor any male theorist of power before the advent of feminism. Head's feminism testifies to the different and gendered nature of women's relationship to power. Cellestine Ware, a self-identified black radical feminist, argues in her book *Woman Power: The Movement for Women's Liberation* that changing the face of power has been a basic tenet in the development of radical feminism in its struggle against male dominance: "Radical feminism . . . postulates that the domination of one human being by another is the basic evil in society. Dominance in human relationships is the target of their opposition."[8]

Bessie Head comes into her own power through writing, using it not only in a therapeutic way, but also to resist the disempowerment of women. Writing, therefore, constitutes a form of taking power and of testing what it means to speak power in the feminine. Her writing and rewriting of power is an attempt to construct women's agency while deconstructing patriarchal and racist discourses. She demonstrates in her writings that women's creativity has the potential to unsettle power structures and that women's power resides in the feminine, is spiritual in nature, and is creative and transforming. Head conceives of writing as a way of "doing" feminism, given its power as a medium for tangibly articulating the painful experiences of women in a meaningful way. Head's pain is only resolved through autobiographical writing and her farm work. Her positive work on the farming commune in Botswana was also a source of comfort for her during her exile. She confides to Alice Walker that in Botswana she was able to transform the obscenity and terror she was subjected to into "a creative work of art (Power) simply because the obscenity had a desperate explanation."[9] This "obscenity" is real but also partially imaginary, which is a sign of her incipient madness. Thus, through writing, she forges an alternative definition of power as self-fulfillment, creativity, and energy. This new kind of power lies in an everyday reality and experience that is far removed from the speechmaking and powermongering of male politicians.

Head's attempt to draw on female power and subvert male abuse of power, through her writing, is closely connected to theories of *l'écriture féminine* developed by Hélène Cixous and Luce Irigaray, who both espouse a feminist aesthetic outside the symbolic patriarchal order. Cixous, though educated in France, was born and raised in Algeria, and was familiar with the liberation struggles of "the colonized . . . the workers, the nations, the species off whose backs the history of men has made its gold."[10] Because of her concern with the exclusionary dynamics of institutionalized forms of power, Cixous suggests a strategy that implies the disruption of dominant institutions and forms of power. Such a strategy can be realized through the revolutionary practice of writing, which is embodied in the feminine text: "A feminine text cannot fail to be more than subversive. It is volcanic. . . . If she's a her-she, it's in order to smash everything, to shatter the framework of institutions, to blow up the law, to break up the 'truth' with laughter."[11] Such subversive feminine writing "is precisely the very possibility of change,"[12] because it dares to change conventions and norms. Head's novels follow Cixous' dictum as her female protagonists use their art and writing as a means to effect change within their community.

Literary critic Anthony O'Brien argues that the basis for Bessie Head's feminism lies in her "displacement of the question about power toward the 'private' sphere, traditionally coded female."[13] By grounding the political in the private sphere, Head is following a feminist line of thought that "rethinks Marxism and nationalism by shifting the terrain of power from state . . . to the private sphere of 'ordinary daily lives.'"[14] O'Brien is mistaken, however, in assuming that just because Head assigns her female characters power—which is traditionally considered outside and antithetical to women's nature—she is transferring power inward, to the private realm. On the contrary, by giving her female characters agency, and letting them find their political voices, Head is thrusting them into the public sphere where they can effect change within their communities. In Head's novel *Maru* (1971), Margaret's art and writing help to break down social barriers and provide solutions intended to alleviate racism against the Masarwa minority in Botswana. Akin to the oral tradition, art is a means of binding the community together despite differences. Margaret is an artist, and her paintings serve as a means for bringing people together, thereby facilitating more meaningful social interaction between the Basarwa majority and Masarwa minority. So, it is through the public manifestation of Margaret's art that Head can fulfill her utopian vision of a unified community: "I see something as it looks, but it looks better when it reappears as a picture in my own mind."[15] The paintings depict images of racism and foresee the marriage between Maru, the future Botswana chief, and Margaret, a Masarwa. Head believes that marriage between a Masarwa and a Basarwa is the only way to transcend color differences and conflicts among people in Botswana. By postulating that art is transformative, Head shows that art, along with language, is capable of intervening in society in a powerful way. However, the transformation never actually happens because the Masarwa do not accept the marriage between Maru and Margaret, so the couple is obliged to leave the village.

THE AFRICAN FEMINIST

Head's work is rooted in the African community that sustains and nurtures her feminist activism. Her African feminist consciousness is especially revealed in her collection of short stories *The Collector of Treasures and Other Botswana Village Tales* (1977). The collection draws attention to the unique experiences of African women who are circumscribed differently by environment, race, nation, and gender relations. In these stories, which are based on folktales selected from the southern African oral tradition, Head focuses on portraits of African women (girls, wives, and mothers) from the community who are broken by life and depicted as always suffering. Her female characters bear the brunt of the crises of their nation-states: colonialism, the failure of male-dominated nationalist politics, and absence of liberation in the aftermath of independence. The author shows a remarkable ability to identify with these women and enter into their situations, exposing male violence, the abuse of power, and injustices against them. Specifically, she depicts her women characters as relying on the African feminist tenets of community, orality, networking, and survival strategies. In the title story, "The Collector of Treasures," Dikeledi, the female protagonist, discloses her husband's pattern of abusiveness to her neighbor, who, with sympathy and support, offers to "loan" Dikeledi her loving husband. Her act of generosity and kindness speaks to a deep connectedness in a community where "neighbors are the center of the universe to each other. They help each other at all times."[16] Dikeledi declines the offer and ends up killing her husband to exact revenge. While in prison, Dikeledi explains to her prison mate Kebonye that she is there because she killed her husband, which prompts a sympathetic response from Kebonye, who replies, "We are all here for the same crime."[17] In the face of depression and despair, Dikeledi finds nurturing and love through her friendship with Kebonye. Their solidarity may even be created and nurtured through the painful experience they share: "And so the woman Dikeledi began phase three of a life that had been ashen in its loneliness and its unhappiness. And yet she had always found gold amidst the ash, deep loves that had joined her heart to the hearts of others."[18] Thus, female communalism is one marker of African feminism in Head's story, which demonstrates that, despite their suffering, African women find strength in their communal solidarity and determination to overcome structures of male oppression.

In her book *The Dynamics of African Feminism*, Susan Arndt identifies three types of African feminism: reformist, transformative, and radical feminism. Reformist African feminism condemns patriarchy but tries to negotiate with the patriarchal foundations of African society. Transformative feminism criticizes men more harshly than reformist feminism, but also assumes men's ability to change. Radical African feminism, on the other hand, believes that men are inherently sexist and that violence is the only means of putting an end to male dominance, thus ensuring women's liberation.[19] According to Susan Arndt, Head's short story "The Collector of Treasures" is situated between transformative and radical African feminisms, exemplifying work that reflects the multiple subjective positions occupied by women who are both victims and agents. In the narrative, Head uses the stories of Dikeledi and her neighbor and friend Kenalepe to underscore male abuse of the female body as well as possibilities for female agency. The author's representation of Dikeledi's husband, Garesego, who typifies man's violent, sexist, and narcissistic nature, and Kenalepe's husband, Paul, who typifies deep love and respect for women, makes for a representation that is both disturbing and reassuring.

THE ECOFEMINIST

A major theme of Head's writing is the connection between abuse of power, the domination of women, and ecological degradation. Ecofeminist critic Starhawk (born Miriam Simos) defines ecofeminism as a spiritual movement rooted in a nature-based religion that venerates nature and views the earth as alive and worthy of human efforts to preserve it.[20] For Starhawk, ecofeminism and environmental issues only matter to the extent that they are put into practice via ethical action that challenges all relations of domination and seeks to subvert the structure of power, while also recognizing the perspectives of women, the poor, and members of other races and cultural communities.[21] Ecofeminism is clearly manifested in most of Head's writings, namely *When Rain Clouds Gather* (1968), *Serowe: Village of the Rain Wind* (1981), and *A Question of Power* (1974), which provide lengthy descriptions of community projects involving garden work, local grassroots projects for sustainable agriculture, and the development of poor, rural communities. As a pioneer African ecofeminist, Bessie Head sought to address the crises of poverty, environmental degradation, violence, and human rights abuses. Head's ecofeminism is evident in her ethnographic study *Serowe: Village of the Rain Wind*, which provides a detailed history of Serowe, the village where she lived as an exile in Botswana. The study is an account of three leaders who have influenced Serowe's history, namely Khama the Great (1875–1923), who helped transition Serowe from tribalism to Christianity, and Khama the Great's son Tshekedi Khama (1926–1959), whose era "was famed for educational progress, and the ideal of self-help [that] was introduced into Serowe life long before it became an international byword."[22] Tshekedi Khama's progressive educational experiments paved the way for the work of white South African refugee Patrick Van Regensburg, who started Swaneng Hill Secondary School, based on the tradition of community service formerly established by Tshekedi Khama. Head gives a thorough description of the Swaneng project, which "engages many local people and foreign volunteers; the volunteers have tended to make Serowe one of the most international villages in Africa."[23] When Van Regensburg felt that the school was becoming too elite, he resigned from his position as principal and became involved "with rural development and the poor and the ordinary 'have-nots.'"[24] Van Regensburg was also the founder of the Brigades, consumers' cooperatives in education, farming, tannery, gardening, building, textiles, weaving, and printing. He initiated Boiteko, a village, self-help, local production project, which originated from a store the members had built and stocked with goods they produced themselves. Van Regensburg appears in Head's novel *A Question of Power* as Eugene, a refugee from South Africa, who is involved in a voluntary agricultural project. The pamphlets he writes about the project "conjured up in the minds of the poor and starving a day when every table would overflow with good food. . . . They felt in every way like food and opportunities for everyone."[25]

Ecofeminism also figures strongly in Head's novel *When Rain Clouds Gather*, which draws connections between the environment and gender dynamics in traditional African society. The narrative is set in the village of Golema Mmidi, where the protagonist, Makhaya, is involved in an agricultural project along with his neighbors Gilbert and Paulina. The project will lead to a new agrarian community and economic development opportunities for its inhabitants. The result is a kind of modern farm based on the new values of sustainable agriculture and animal husbandry. Head's message is that Botswana's inherently tribal and patriarchal social structure has clearly contributed to the breakdown of the sustainable use of Earth's resources, a problem colonialism has also contributed to. The agricultural plan is initially opposed by the tribal chiefdom led by Matenge, a member of the Botswana National Liberation Party that fought for independence, which is ironic because he abuses power and intends to prevent the creation of economic development opportunities for farmers. Head's underlying message is that colonialism, nationalism, the tribal system, and patriarchy have all contributed to Africa's poverty and dispossession, and that the only way toward progress and modernization is to give up backward tribal beliefs and hierarchical gender roles. She imparts her critique of tribalism and patriarchy through her protagonist, Makhaya, who detests any form of ethnic or tribal identity: "I am no tribalist. My parents are."[26] Makhaya's worldview is marked by his own discomfort with the shackles of African society, such as tribalism, chiefdoms, and the oppression of women. He is adamant about leaving his tribal affiliations behind by rejecting his own name: "That tribal name is the wrong one for me. It is for one who stays home."[27] He is now convinced that nationalism and tribalism are not compatible with the modern economy, as they hinder development plans and do not guarantee freedom, citizenship, or empowerment. In Head's ecofeminist worldview, tribalism and nationalism are being superseded by universalism. Golema Mmidi is represented as an ecologically sustainable community that has evolved from tribalism toward the heterogeneity of its members, who are men and women, black and white. Head envisions an ideal community based on what Paul Gilroy, writing in a different context, has subsequently called the "politics of transfiguration," which emphasizes "the emergence of qualitatively new desires, social relations, and modes of association within the . . . community of interpretation and resistance and between that group and its erstwhile oppressors."[28] Head's use of Golema Mmidi, Serowe, and Motabeng as models for community development puts her work in dialogue with ecofeminism in its emphasis on sustainable development and its advocacy for social justice. Her ecofeminism cuts to the heart of power relationships in African society, as it promotes heterogeneous communities that encourage civic engagement and equal treatment of all members of society. While nationalism, as a game of power, leaves the individual vulnerable to fragmentation, ecofeminism is what gives meaning to the self as a socialized being.

THE ANTINATIONALIST FEMINIST

In her novels, Head targets in radical terms, not only Afrikaner nationalism, but also black nationalism and postindependence Botswana with respect to discourses on women and the colored. Head's experience with black nationalism began when she became involved in Robert Sobukwe's anti-apartheid, Pan-Africanist movement in the early 1950s.[29] Sobukwe relied on Pan-Africanism as a global movement that viewed Africa and black Africans as a unit. Head's decision to break ties with the movement was spurred by the racism and sexism she found to be rampant within the movement.[30] In one of her letters to Randolph Vigne, she writes: "I was such a hot rod Black nationalist. I very soon got over that phase because many people pointed out to me that I was not black enough. . . . Some people can hog the black skin for themselves but I have to opt for mankind as a whole."[31]

Head's novel *A Question of Power* (1974) explores, through the protagonist's internal consciousness, the destructive workings of black nationalist power and the forces that embody it. Power in the novel is explored in all its manifestations, not just as something related to politics and government. Elizabeth is driven into madness by black nationalists represented by the characters of Dan, Medusa, and Sello, who torment her in her dreams. Head insists that her novel is autobiographical: "Elizabeth and I are one."[32] The novel is a voyage into Elizabeth's subjective consciousness as she sinks into madness because of the harsh reality surrounding her. But beyond the narrative innovation of this novel, Head is preoccupied with disseminating a political message about evil and power. The growing madness in Elizabeth mirrors the growing madness in Head as she faced the taunts she suffered as an exile in Botswana. Head, who has power over her narrative world, enters into the protagonist's consciousness and reports to the reader the inner workings of Elizabeth's mind with understanding and sensitivity. In various phases of her madness, Elizabeth is a shattered, fragmented self that exists only in the projections of her tormentors.

Philippe Le Jeune's definition of autobiography as a pact between author, narrator, and protagonist suggests coherence and fixity of subjectivity through writing.[33] This was because the conventions of autobiographical writing were put in place during the Enlightenment when the genre emerged.[34] Poststructuralist theory of autobiography has questioned the Enlightenment coherence of self, suggested by traditional autobiographical writing, positing instead a fragmented, unstable self that contests and deconstructs hegemonic discourses. Head's protagonist is the embodiment of fragmentation in an unstable and fragmented environment. The narrative unfolds as a poignant account of the female protagonist's coming to agency in the face of her debilitating psychological trauma. Autobiography becomes Head's vehicle for transforming the self and for creatively inventing new kinds of subjectivity for her protagonist. It should be noted that both ethnic and feminist contributions to the history of autobiography represent movement away from the telling of a single, individual story and toward the telling of the stories of others in the community. Elizabeth's eventual agency involves the development of a meaningful social role in the community through involvement in gardening and farm work.

The characters, Sello, Medusa, and Dan, who embody the forces of black power, taunt Elizabeth, reappearing again and again in her dreams and paranoid delusions. These fictional characters are based on real people Head knew in Botswana.[35] Elizabeth's tormentors have proven unable to conceive any paradigm that is not patriarchal, which shows the extent of their desire to assert hierarchical control and power. Sello is introduced as a monk whose teachings are similar to those of Buddha and other remarkable spiritual figures Head venerates in her narrative. Through his preaching, he becomes seductive, and Elizabeth is mesmerized by his power. At this point, any motive other than his selfless service would be too early to admit. As a spiritual leader, Sello is able to enchant Elizabeth in the atmosphere of intimacy and trust he has carefully built. In his presence, she experiences an impaired sense of self, relinquishing any sense of critical thinking. She has "no distinct personality apart from Sello."[36] Sello becomes entranced by his own charisma, for Elizabeth's compliance and hero-worship nourishes in him a type of insidious narcissism. The "poor," who have lost trust in him, admonish Elizabeth: "He is controlling your life in the wrong way."[37] Because his grandiosity is falsely posed as sainthood, he morally stunts himself and compromises Elizabeth's trust. Ultimately, it is a woman who gives

Elizabeth the warning—an example of the communalism addressed earlier as part of Head's African feminism.

In one of Elizabeth's nightmarish visions, Sello is preaching to her that with the darker side of his holiness come moral lapses: "There are so many lessons you have to learn this time; that the title God, in its absolute, all-powerful form, is a disaster to its holder, the all-seeing eye is the greatest temptation."[38] Sello challenges Elizabeth to name his "height of goodness" and "depth of evil." His is a spiritual power that allows him to invade her mind, and the link between him and God makes it seem as if God is the abuser. Sello's power allows him to persecute "fellow men" and masquerade as a spiritual leader with authority. His power is thus spiritually sanctioned, thereby making it hard for the "superficial reader" to discern his control and authority. However, Elizabeth is soon able to see Sello as a sham "deliberately manipulating the words and gestures of the people who approached her."[39] In another of Elizabeth's nightmarish visions, Sello the monk is replaced by Sello in the brown suit, as someone "who had no contact with the Sello in the monk's robes."[40] Sello in the brown suit is a nationalist who believes in the brotherhood and equality of man: "A part of my present evolution is African, and I hear the beginnings of a great symphony, a complete statement for the future about the dignity of man, where none is high and none is low but all are equal."[41] His words, though grounded in the humanist tradition, resonate with the rhetoric of the Black Power Movement that had its roots in a racist perception of reality, even though some claim that the seemingly "racist" mantra of the Black Power Movement was necessary.

To Elizabeth, Sello's idea of the evolution of African culture is marked by "relentless cruelty and hatred."[42] When Sello speaks of African evolution, when he dons the garb of Africa, he assumes that black suffering is going to be alleviated, that there will be no more evil, and that Africans will be saved. His rhetorical excesses offer people like Elizabeth a glimpse of paradise, a way of seeing beyond evil. However, such rhetoric suppresses differences among Africans. Nationalists like Sello in the brown suit often hide their bourgeois interests behind the totalizing tropes of Africanness and Blackness. Sello tries to lay down the terms of Africa's future as being good, without seeing into the nature of the evil that Elizabeth is able to experience and see: "He had defined the future, in African terms, as one of unpromising goodness. It had been fixed for her securely in his earlier attitudes. Then he had tried to weave Medusa into this structure. . . . Why had he occupied himself all the time with evil?"[43]

The failure of Sello, the nationalist, to bring about liberation is thus exacerbated by his inability to control the evil embodied in Medusa. Medusa is introduced as the wife of Sello the monk, who only stares at her "without any censure."[44] When Sello reappears as Sello in the brown suit, Medusa is metamorphosed into the "wild-eyed Medusa."[45] In the Ancient Greek myth,

Medusa has a duplicitous role. In appearance, she is a wife or a mother, but this façade hides her true, and inherently evil, nature. In the myth, she is a representation of binaries, such as good/bad, conscious/unconscious, woman-as-reality/woman-as-image. Medusa is also a projection of the anxiety and fears of men: "When a man finds himself in the embrace of Medusa, she is really the direct and tangible form of his own evils, his power lusts, his greeds, his self-importance, and these dominate him totally and bring him to the death of the soul."[46] Medusa's power over Elizabeth's mind gains strength as Sello's power wanes. She reappears in Elizabeth's visions as the latter slips further into madness. Medusa projects her racism and racist motivations onto Elizabeth as a way to feel good about herself and avoid responsibility. Through Medusa, Head challenges the feminist view that power is mostly white, patriarchal, and male, as women too can abuse power. Medusa's accusations are infused with notions of racial purity: "You hate Africans. You don't like the African hair. You don't like the African nose."[47] Her taunts give Elizabeth insight into the rigidity, conformity, and segregated nature of African society: "'We don't want you here. This is my land. These are my people. We keep our things to ourselves.' . . . The wild-eye Medusa was expressing the surface reality of African society. It was shut in and exclusive."[48] Medusa appears in another one of Elizabeth's visions and warns her that she will kill both her and homosexuals. Such visions are indicative of Elizabeth's sexual anxiety about her status as a colored woman in South African society. Head represents coloreds and homosexuals as victims of apartheid in its rigid, oppressive categorizations.[49] To Medusa, Elizabeth is fixed in an identity that renders her invisible. However, such fixed identity depends on Medusa's visual observation and scrutiny of Elizabeth's body.

The idea of Medusa is also very Freudian. Elizabeth's confrontation with her evokes Sigmund Freud's essay, "Medusa Head," which has implications for gender identity and sexuality. Freud states: "The terror of Medusa is thus a terror of castration that is linked to the sight of something."[50] To him, Medusa's head corresponds to a female's "castrated" genitals, which evoke in the male spectator the fear of castration. He also equates the terrifying effect of looking at Medusa with an erection. In her re-reading of the Medusa myth, Hélène Cixous argues that it is female subjectivity and desire that horrify the spectator, who expects only female "objectivity," as Medusa represents female desire.[51] Medusa flaunts her sexuality in an attempt to hamper Elizabeth's sexual expression and coerce her into erasing her erotic side in a society that is oppressive of women. The sexual constraints placed on Elizabeth go hand-in-hand with her rejection by society for being a woman and a colored: "She had some top secret information to impart to Elizabeth. It was about her vagina. Without any bother for decencies she sprawled her long black legs in the air, and the most exquisite sensation travelled out of her towards Elizabeth. . . . Then she looked at Elizabeth and smiled . . . : 'You haven't got anything near that, have you?'"[52]

In line with Freud's and Hélène Cixous' interpretations of the myth, Head seems to imply, from Medusa's interaction with Elizabeth, that sexuality is an object of knowledge, and hence domination. Literary critic Huma Ibrahim argues that Elizabeth's sexuality relegates her to a space of exile in a discourse wherein race, sexuality, and access to language form part of the discourse of power: "When Elizabeth's psyche experiences Medusa's rejection at a sexual-lingual level the whole process of an exile's reclamation begins. . . . Medusa forces Elizabeth into the process of an exile's urgent need to reclaim her body through language in order to seek her lost, primary fundamental 'home.'"[53] Ibrahim further argues that Medusa's flaunting of her sexuality is a way of exposing an aspect of Elizabeth's sexuality that has been "shell-shocked" by the sexual taboos surrounding her birth in apartheid South Africa.[54] The Medusa myth makes discernible society's control over the threat of female sexuality. Her falsity corresponds to that of the fetish; she exposes the fictional about herself so as to make way for the reality of male dominance. Medusa's banishment is the price she must pay for her exposure of what must remain hidden. Thus, her hypersexuality cannot survive in light of masculine control, which renders woman absent and invisible.

In the second section of the novel, Medusa's power is displaced by that of Dan, who represents the black nationalists, who seek their own interests and power more than the interests of the people: "When someone says 'my people' with a specific stress on the blackness of those people, they are after kingdoms and permanently child-like slaves. 'The people' are never going to rise above the status of 'the people.' They are going to be told what is good for them by the 'mother' and the 'father.'"[55] In Elizabeth's nightmarish visions, Dan appears as a powerful and violent figure who torments her by putting phonograph records in her head and bringing a group of women to her bed who serve as markers of his masculinity. Dan's sexual relationships take the form of staged acts. The major theme of his encounters with women is male power, which takes different forms: physical power over women, the symbolic power of naming others, the power of possession as a signifier of masculinity, the power of money, and the power of sex. With all his power, "Dan was not over. He had not yet told his story to the whole of mankind about his ambitions, like Hitler and Napoleon, to rule the world."[56] The relationship Dan has with each of his lovers is a symptom of disequilibrium in social, economic, and political power relations. By telling the story of Dan and his lovers, Bessie Head forces the reader to recognize that the dynamics of gender relations in Botswana are analogous to the political relations of colonialism and black nationalism. Here, she explores the dynamics of gender and power inequality most powerfully as she begins to question the ideological assumptions underlying Dan's violence. Head distances herself from Dan's nationalism because she views his politically motivated domination of women as yet another aspect of colonial and nationalist violence.

Frantz Fanon argues in *The Wretched of the Earth* that nationalist leaders, who abuse power over common people, provoke the continuation of violence in the postcolonial period.[57] African postcolonial critic Achille Mmembe argues that violence and the show of power are defining characteristics of Africa. The exercise of power by African dictators manifests in festivities that "constitute the pre-eminent means by which *the commandment* speaks and the way in which it dramatizes its magnificence and prodigality."[58] The exercise of power manifests not only in everyday routines, but also in the grotesque and the vulgar, which constitute forms of control and power.[59] For his part, Nigerian scholar Denis Ekpo writes: "Excessive stage shows, pomp extravaganza, megalomania, and so on characterize rulership in most of Black Africa."[60] Ekpo feels these leaders turn out this way not because they are born monsters, but because they have been influenced by colonial models and ambition.

THE GLOBAL FEMINIST

Power politics is what compelled Head to break ties with the black nationalist movement and to create, through her writing, a global-level feminism that was autonomous, revolutionary, and not attached to any nationalist political party or feminist movement.[61] In condemning national politics, Head's novel *A Question of Power* reaches out on a more universal plane of meaning. Jacqueline Rose sees such universality emerging out of Elizabeth's madness: "Inside the head is the place where you can make the links or points of connection—of universal potential."[62] The autobiographical narrative functions as a means of drawing the reader's focus to what is communal and universal as Elizabeth moves from a state of fragmentation to a world of "community and language."[63] As she recovers from her state of madness, Elizabeth is able to achieve subjectivity and wholeness through writing and farm work that both contribute to her self-discovery and empowerment. She soon "fall[s] into the warm embrace of the brotherhood of man,"[64] as she becomes more and more involved in the gardening project with her friend Kenosi and an international group of workers that includes refugees from South Africa. Like Head, Elizabeth is now a writer who chronicles her experience of redemption in her autobiographical story: "She refuses to remain an object; she becomes a subject, an 'I.'"[65] The notebook, within which she inscribes her thoughts about gardening, constitutes her "coming to writing."[66] Her newfound power echoes Margaret's ability, in *Maru*, to inscribe her thoughts about the racism she experiences in Botswana through her paintings. Elizabeth "[begins] to jot down fragmentary notes such as a shipwrecked sailor might make on a warm sandy beach as he stared back at the stormy sea that had almost taken his life."[67] Writing thus becomes her tactic for survival and recovery from the nightmares. The compassionate energy within Elizabeth's new community marks the aspiration of Head's representational ethics. Through its representation of an emerging transnational community that is primarily composed of women, Head takes part in a vast history of gender-based internationalism. Through such a community, she implies that the exclusion of women from national politics can eventually become a kind of national advantage in the world of global politics. Altogether, Head's international vision of solidarity bears hope for a utopian world, where oppression, marginalization, and hierarchy no longer exist.

NOTES

1. Caroline Rooney, "Dangerous Knowledge and the Poetics of Survival: A Reading of *Our Sister Killjoy* and *A Question of Power*," in *Motherlands: Black Women's Writing from Africa, the Caribbean, and South Asia*, ed. Susheila Nasta (New Brunswick, NJ: Rutgers University Press, 1992), 120.
2. Craig Mackenzie, *Bessie Head* (New York: Twayne Publishers, 1999), 63.
3. In a letter addressed to Robert Sobukwe in 1972, Head expresses her discomfort with politics, though she admits that "circumstances in South Africa make one some kind of political thinker." Bessie Head, Personal letters, KMM372BHP3, January 6, 1972, Khama Memorial Museum, Serowe, Botswana.
4. Bessie Head, "Autobiographical Essay," *Ms. Magazine*, November 1975, 72–75.
5. Dobrota Pucherova, *The Ethics of Dissident Desire in Southern African Writing* (Trier, Germany: Wissenschaftlicher Verlag Trier, 2011), 53.
6. Bessie Head, KMM76BHP5, January 6, 1972.
7. Michel Foucault, *Power and Knowledge* (New York: Pantheon Books, 1980), 131.
8. Cellestine Ware, *Woman Power: The Movement for Women's Liberation* (New York: Tower Publications, 1970), 11.
9. Ibid.
10. Hélène Cixous, "The Laugh of the Medusa," trans. Keith Cohen and Paula Cohen, *Signs* 1 (1976): 888.
11. Ibid.
12. Ibid., 879.
13. Anthony O'Brien, *Against Normalization Writing Radical Democracy in South Africa* (Durham, NC: Duke University Press, 2001), 52.
14. Ibid., 54.
15. Bessie Head, *Maru*, (London: Heinemann, 1995 [1972]), 104.
16. Bessie Head, "The Collector of Treasures," in *The Collector of Treasures and Other Botswana Village Tales* (London: Heinemann Educational, 1977), 93.
17. Ibid., 89.
18. Ibid., 91.
19. Susan Arndt, *The Dynamics of African Feminism: Defining and Classifying African-Feminist Literatures* (Trenton, NJ: Africa World Press, 2002), 82–86.
20. Starhawk, "Power, Authority and Mystery: Earth-Based Spirituality and Ecofeminism," in *Reweaving the World: The Emergence of Ecofeminism*, eds. Irene Diamond and Gloria Feman Orenstein (San Francisco: Sierra Club Books, 1990), 74.
21. Ibid., 77.
22. Bessie Head, *Serowe: Village of the Rain Wind* (London: Heinemann, 1981), 76.

23. Ibid., 138.
24. Ibid.
25. Bessie Head, *A Question of Power* (London: Heinemann, 1974), 56–57.
26. Bessie Head, *When Rain Clouds Gather* (London: Heinemann, 1995 [1969]), 9.
27. Ibid.
28. Paul Gilroy, *The Black Atlantic: Modernity and Double Consciousness* (Cambridge, MA: Harvard University Press, 1993), 37.
29. Gillian Stead Eilerson, *Bessie Head: Thunder Behind Her Ears* (Portsmouth, NH: Heinemann, 1995), 62.
30. Dorobta Pucherova deals with this double exclusion at length in her essay, "A Romance that Failed: Bessie Head and Black Nationalism in 1960's South Africa," *Research in African Literatures* 42, no. 2 (Summer 2011): 106.
31. Randolph Vigne, ed., *A Gesture of Belonging: Letters from Bessie Head, 1965-1979* (Portsmouth, NH: Heinemann, 1991), 64.
32. Michelle Adler, "Bessie Head," in *Between the Lines: Interviews with Bessie Head, Sheila Roberts, Ellen Kuzwayo, Miriam Tlatli*, ed. Craig Machenzie and Cherry Clayton (South Africa: National English Library Museum, 1989), 25.
33. Philippe Le Jeune, *Le Pacte Autobiographique* (Paris: Seuil, 1975).
34. Sidonie Smith and Julia Watson, eds., *Women, Autobiography, Theory: A Reader* (Madison: University of Wisconsin Press, 1998), 35.
35. Ibid., 120.
36. Ibid., 32, 35.
37. Ibid., 32.
38. Ibid., 36–37.
39. Ibid., 62.
40. Ibid., 39.
41. Ibid., 62–63.
42. Ibid., 92.
43. Ibid., 95–96.
44. Ibid., 62.
45. Ibid., 38.
46. Ibid., 40.
47. Ibid., 48.
48. Ibid., 38.
49. For more information about Head's depiction of homosexuality in her novel, refer to Rosemary Jolly, "Nadine Gordimer, Bessie Head and Homophobia," in *Cross-Addressing: Resistance Literature and Cultural Border*, ed. John C. Hawley (Albany, NY: SUNY Press, 1996); and Femi Ojo-Ade, "Bessie Head's Alienated Heroine: Victim or Villain?" *Ba Shiru: A Journal of African Languages and Literature* 8, no. 2 (1977): 13–21.
50. Sigmund Freud, *Medusa's Head* (London: Hogarth Press, 1955), 46.
51. Hélène Cixous, "Laugh," 888.
52. Ibid., 44.
53. Huma Ibrahim, *Subversive Identities in Exile* (Charlottesville: University Press of Virginia, 1996), 130.
54. Ibid., 131.
55. Bessie Head, *A Question of Power*, 63.
56. Ibid., 14.
57. Frantz Fanon, *The Wretched of the Earth*, trans. Constance Farrington (New York: Grove Press, 1968).
58. Achille Mmembe, "The Banality of Power and the Aesthetics of Vulgarity in the Postcolony," *Public Culture* 4, no. 2 (1992), 9.
59. Mmembe, "Banality," 1–2.
60. Denis Ekpo, "The Aporia of Post-Colonial Anger: Dissidence and Difference in Africa's Contemporary Literary Discourse," *Social Semiotics* 9, no. 1 (1999), 17–18.
61. In 1990, the National Executive Committee of the African National Congress issued a "Statement on the Emancipation of Women," which states the terms of women's liberation

outside the nationalist movement. See "Statement of the National Executive Committee of the African National Congress on the Emancipation of Women in South Africa," *Agenda (Durban)* 8 (May 2, 1990): 19–23.

62. Ibid., 415.

63. Margaret Tucker, "A Nice-Time Girl Strikes Back: An Essay on Bessie Head's *A Question of Power*," *Research in African Literatures* 19, no. 2 (1988): 170–181.

64. Bessie Head, *A Question of Power*, 206.

65. Margaret Tucker, "Nice-Time Girl," 173.

66. Bessie Head, *A Question of Power*, 204.

67. Ibid.

II

Postcolonial Injustices

Chapter Four

National Reconciliation through Narrative

Malika Oufkir's Stolen Lives

In Morocco, as well as elsewhere in Africa, women since the end of colonialism have engaged in the sociopolitics of their home countries. Where Djebar, Aidoo, and Head marked the first wave of women who began thinking about Africa and women's place and role in it through a postcolonial lens, a later generation of women writers, such as Malika Oufkir, began to more fervently criticize their home governments as repressive and undemocratic. Use of testimony as critical inquiry into the inadequacies of postcolonial governments has been a form of writing particularly valuable to women. Moroccan authors like Fatna El Bouih, Saida Menebhi, Aicha Channa, and Houria Boussejra, among others, have made the case for compelling narratives that recount the egregious human rights violations of the past. In this chapter, I chose Malika Oufkir and not another one of these women writers because of Oufkir's international appeal to different audiences.

In her book *The Body in Pain* (1985), Elaine Scarry states that "physical pain has no voice, but when it at last finds a voice, it begins to tell a story."[1] Physical pain, she adds, is experienced with certainty by the people feeling the pain, but for those who are not, "it is so elusive that 'hearing about pain' may exist as the primary model of what it is 'to have doubt.'"[2] Despite the fact that physical and psychological pain cannot be shared, the victims of torture are able to transcend pain and "enter a realm of shared discourse,"[3] as they record their experience and speak on behalf of those who have been too traumatized to recount their experiences. Physical pain destroys language, for "to be present when a person moves up out of that pre-language and projects the facts of sentience into speech is almost to have been permitted to be present at the birth of language itself."[4] With this hypothesis, Malika Oufkir gives voice to her experience of pain and imprisonment in her book *La Prisonnière* (1999), published in translation as *Stolen Lives* in 2001. Malika Oufkir is the daughter of General Muhammad Oufkir, who was the second-in-command to King Hassan II and a known torturer. She was adopted in 1958 at age five by King Muhammad V to be raised as a companion to his daughter, Princess Lala Amina, also age five. As punishment for his attempted coup against King Hassan II, General Oufkir was executed in 1972 and Malika, together with her siblings, her mother, and two other female relatives were made to "disappear." How they were held in various prisons for twenty years, and finally gained their internationally broadcast release, is the main substance of Malika Oufkir's autobiographical account.

The nagging questions therefore remain: Whose pain does Oufkir relate in her narrative? Does other people's pain matter to her? Does she ever come to understand that her father was a torturer who inflicted pain on others? Oufkir never fully explains her father's rise to power or the motives that made him seek that power. She does not probe her father's crimes, what he did to protect the monarchy, and how he betrayed the king. There are two forms of pain: pain suffered and pain inflicted. Pain can also be manipulated aesthetically. There have been questions in reception studies about who feels what kind of pain. The reader sometimes does not know who really suffers, because there are mechanisms of denial, distancing, and blame. Though Oufkir has testified to the pain inflicted on her and her family, it has been impossible for her to make Moroccan audiences, haunted by memories of the crimes committed by her father, understand the extent of her suffering. The obstacle in sharing pain is what Jean-François Lyotard called a "differend," the difference between cognition of injustice and the suffering of the victims. In his book *Differend: Phrases of Dispute*, Lyotard argues that it is impossible for the victim to make his damage known to others.[5] Thus, Lyotard calls this double bind a "differend," a case in which the victim does not have the means to prove his damage:

> This is the case if the victim is deprived of life, or of all liberties, or of the freedom to make his or her ideas or opinions public, or simply of the right to testify to the damage. . . . Should the victim seek to bypass this impossibility and testify to the wrong done to her, she comes up against the following argumentation, either the damages you complain about never took place, and your testimony is false; or else they took place and, since you are able to testify to them, it is not a wrong that has been done to you, but merely a damage, and your testimony is still false.[6]

Oufkir only partially understands how the privileges of her youth were negotiated and only belatedly empathizes with the sufferings of oppressed others.

Her inability therefore to convey to the Moroccan reader a sense of gross personal injustice, and to tell the whole truth, constitutes a "differend." The question is whether Moroccans' failure to receive Oufkir's memoir sympathetically discredits her work. Oufkir's account is not significantly discredited. An application of Lyotard's notion of the "differend" to her situation, with respect to her Moroccan readership/audience, allows us to rescue Oufkir's memoir and make a case for its importance to the work of truth, justice, reconciliation, and healing that the nation of Morocco is undertaking.

In expounding on the "Lead Years" and public memory, Moroccans have moved from the private experience of pain to a sharing of experiences that coincides with recovery from collective traumas and subsequent questions of justice. In Morocco, Hassan II maintained power through a period known as "Sanawat Arasas," "les années de Plomb," in French, and in English as "the Lead Years," a time of coups, political trials, torture, rebellion, and severe repression lasting from 1963 to 1999. The torture of prisoners was for a long time kept hidden and secret from Moroccans. Now awareness is taking hold and people prepare to confront the institutions of imprisonment and torture that in many ways sustained their society in the past. Narratives by liberated prisoners and survivors of torture serve as a focus for a community able to recognize its traumas and find new coherence in a postdictatorial world. As the pain is shared, so too is recovery, and the populace gradually comes to terms with suppressed pain and questions of justice, revenge, and forgiveness.

In the last two decades of Moroccan history, a culture of remembrance has emerged within the growing debate about past human rights abuses. Occulted history—pain and torture—has been revealed to Moroccans via a series of testimonies.[7] In her memoir *Stolen Lives*, Malika Oufkir elaborates various techniques for testimony and reinvention in the shadow of a history full of torture and violence.[8] Her autobiography illustrates in multiple ways Walter Benjamin's work on memory and remembrance. For Benjamin, "history is not only a science but also a form of remembrance."[9] Remembrance of past suffering and injustice gives impetus for revolution. In this sense, Oufkir's autobiography, as a work of remembrance, resurrects the memory of the tortured and disappeared victims who require truth, justice, and reconciliation. When the author uncovers information buried in old memories, disseminating it to a larger audience, she establishes a form of solidarity with those who endured similar fates in Morocco. International publicity put pressure on Hassan II to free her family, and world opinion would likewise influence change in the treatment of political prisoners. Circulation of their family story as a news item helped to shed light, as well, on many oppressed victims under the dictatorship of Hassan II. These victims were placed outside official history. The process of truth-telling and reconciliation is now linked to Malika Oufkir's narration of her privileged education and extreme suffering, and to criticism of the political regime that first subsidized luxury, then subjected her and her family to incarceration and torture. Her testimony becomes part of an ongoing national process of searching for truth. With a growing body of facts, reinterpretation becomes necessary for healing and for the opening up of new alternatives for the future.

Malika Oukfir's memoir is a tantalizing example of a whole category of memoirs and films contributing to a new national consciousness. Autobiographies, memoirs, and films that document violence in Moroccan prisons during the Lead Years give impetus to this emergent culture of remembrance. Khalid Zekri's book *Fictions du réel: Modernité romanesque et écriture du réel au Maroc, 1990-2006* provides an excellent discussion of such Moroccan *littérature carcérale* (prison literature) in both French and Arabic. Such literature, he notes, has challenged "taboos that for a long time have weighed on Moroccan society."[10] Jellali Ferhati, Saad Chraibi, Hassan Benjelloun, and Lahcen Zinoun are among the many Moroccan filmmakers who have documented this history of violence. Authors of novels have either used fictitious stories to relate past human rights violations (Tahar Benjelloun and Abdelhak Serhane) or relied on their own experience with imprisonment and torture in autobiographical accounts (Abdellatif Laabi, Ahmed Marzouki, Abraham Serfaty, Abdelfettah Fakihani, Jawad Mdidech, Fatna El Bouih, and Malika Oufkir). Their texts bear witness to severe deprivation and infliction of physical and psychological pain, and commemorate those who cannot speak for themselves—for some bodies disappeared with no known burial site.

It is important to situate these texts within the larger political context of the conflict between the state and opposition groups in the postindependence period. Tensions between the state, the leftists, and the Islamic nationalists persisted during this period, as did intraethnic tension between Berbers and Arabs. King Hassan II himself faced a considerable political challenge, not only from the Berbers who were dissatisfied with the new Arabization policy, but also from the left under Moroccan intellectual Mehdi Ben Barka. The conflict between the state and the leftists culminated in the authorities' decision to assassinate Ben Barka,[11] a member of the Istiqlal (Independence) Party, which played a key role in the struggle for Morocco's independence from French colonialism. Ben Barka broke from the Istiqlal Party in 1958 and formed The National Union of Popular Forces (*L'Union National des Forces Populaires*). Hassan II accused him of plotting against the government and exiled the leftist politician to France. Ben Barka had an interesting international profile as he worked with the Third World Movement and with Che Guevera in the months prior to his death in October of 1965, organizing the meeting of Third World "revolutionary" countries at the Three Continents (or Tricontinental) Conference that took place in Cuba in 1966. Ben Barka was twice sentenced to death in absentia by the Moroccan courts.[12]

When he was offered amnesty to return to Morocco, one of the conditions he posed was the resignation of General Oufkir, who was abhorred by Moroccan leftists. During the early postindependence period, Oufkir, serving as interior minister, emerged as a member of the Westernized elite who spoke and wrote in French and endorsed capitalist regimes. In contrast, Ben Barka was part of the Westernized intellectual elites conversant with socialism and communism. These conflicts were symptomatic of the contention between the ruling elites, the leftists, and the regional rural Berbers over control of the state. There were also the Islamists who resisted the French civilizing mission.

The task of nation-building became the project of urban elites like the Fassis (represented by nationalist leader Allal Al Fassi), who were resented by the Berbers. Two coups d'état against Hassan II in the postindependence period had fomented tensions between Arabs and Berbers. Medbouh, the coup leader of the 1971 assassination attempt of Hassan II at Skhirat, was a Berber, as was General Oufkir, who was behind the 1972 coup. Ernest Gellner has hinted at the ambivalence that characterized the relationship between King Hassan II and the Berbers, an ambivalence that led to the coup d'état in Skhirat, and in which Oufkir, it was later revealed, played a key role.[13] On the matter of ethnicity, both General Oufkir and his wife, Fatima Chenna, came from wealthy Berber families, and during incarceration the family clung to their identity as Berbers. There was constant tension between ethnic Berbers and the monarchy, as demonstrated by the Tafilalt revolt of 1957, the Rif rebellion of 1958, the High Atlas uprising of 1960, the two coup d'états of 1971 and 1972, and the army revolt that took place in the Middle Atlas in 1973.[14] The state, which depended mainly on the use of violence to repress the left, the Islamists, and intermittent Berber rebellions, tried to compromise between the legitimization of violence against political dissidents and its justice and democracy propaganda. This also helped endorse the state's violence against opponents of the regime as a legitimate political means.

Neither the first nor the last of the testimonies on state violence,[15] but certainly one of the most widely translated and publicized, is Malika Oufkir's *Stolen Lives*. The author is the eldest daughter of General Muhammed Oufkir and his famously beautiful wife Fatima Chenna. When Hassan II succeeded his father, he brought up his own children along with Malika Oufkir and Princess Lala Amina, and for eleven years Malika lived not with her natural parents and siblings, but in the seclusion of the harem—a luxurious and privileged environment. The author's life as a companion to Princess Lala Amina was a fairytale, yet it meant confinement. She learned the rituals and manners, how the concubines sat at the feet of the king and surrounded the nearby table of the queen mother, partaking of food cooked by slaves. Concubines lived in their own private quarters. Once trained, they were married to the king and then vied for his favor. Being torn between "East and

West,"[16] Malika yearned to escape, and she did when at age fifteen she began her three years as a member of Morocco's *jeunesse dorée* (young men and women of privilege from the most elitist families).

Oufkir's narrative brings out gendered themes dealing with mother and father figures. The author senses an inner conflict over her "two fathers" without probing its cause or her own gendered position in a context that includes both: the most powerful man in all the land and the second most powerful man who serves him. A photograph between the two parts of the book shows her father, the general, kissing the hand of her "father" the king. She pleases both, but is, in effect, a victim of the system. Hassan II is depicted as an absolute and patriarchal tyrant. If displeased by Malika's grades, he would himself administer a cruel whipping. She comes to resent, from a beating she received at age fifteen, the oppressive power of Hassan II, but she never reproaches her father, General Oufkir, for having left her so vulnerable to it. She will also agonize over consequences she has had no role in precipitating: "My own father had tried to kill my adoptive father."[17]

Against the backdrop of the palace, the author foregrounds her mother as an all-powerful and influential figure in her life. Her refusal to categorize her mother in the patriarchal manner arises from the author's close identification with her. From the very outset, the text positions itself within the author's fears and anxiety over her separation from her mother. Growing up in the palace, Malika felt a void in her motherless world and blamed her woes on the absence of her mother. Fatima was also left motherless at a young age, and, though of Muslim parentage, was placed by her soldier-father in a Christian convent run by nuns. Later reclaimed by her father, she was again shut away, as was "traditional for girls."[18] The narrative foregrounds the mother figure as a speaking subject, who refuses to submit to patriarchal constraints, rather than a passive sufferer. Beautiful and with claim to a fortune, she escaped at age fifteen by marrying a man sixteen years her senior, whose family was the army.[19] There came a time, however, when Fatima, rejecting her husband's infidelities, took a lover, rented a villa, opened a boutique, and consorted with intellectuals and artists.[20] Malika justifies these acts and resents the king for arranging another marriage for her father. The parental divorce was followed by their remarriage and another child. In the case of Malika, the context of her speech and actions is clear. It was fear of marriage arranged by the king that made her insist on returning to the home, also luxurious, of her family in Rabat. Malika's highly privileged and sequestered years were followed by years of vulnerable freedom. As punishment for his attempted coup against King Hassan II, General Oufkir was executed and his family was put under house arrest. Ordered to pack for two weeks, Malika foresees banishment.

Stolen Lives can be situated not only among Moroccan women's prison narratives such as Fatna El Bouih's *Hadit Al Atama* (2002), translated by

Mustapha Kamal and Susan Slyomovics as *Talk of Darkness* (2008), and Saida Menebhi's *Poèmes, lettres, écrits du prison* (2000), but also among Arab women's autobiography in general and the genre of Arab women's prison narratives in particular. Oufkir's memoir stands unique among Arab women's autobiography, for no Arab woman writer has created the stir that Malika Oufkir did when she published *La Prisonnière* (*Stolen Lives*) in 1999. The memoir generated widespread international attention and great commercial appeal because of the author's association with the Moroccan king and the tragedy of her torture and imprisonment. Being viewed as an inverted Cinderella tale (from riches to rags), an account of a bold and well-reported escape, an overture to confession and redemption, and an introduction to her "new life," the memoir caused the author instant on-stage fame in Paris, the United States, and elsewhere. *Stolen Lives* remains an important work in the genre of Arab women's autobiography not only because of the sensation it has created and the instant fame it gave its author, but also because it is the first Arab woman's autobiography to give an inside portrait and intimate details about the life and family of an Arab king, thus breaking the sacred aura surrounding the Arab monarchy. Oufkir's act of writing becomes a means of intervening in public spaces, allowing her to respond to the patriarchal discourse that oppressed her and her family. Resistance to such discourse is embodied in the text itself, which either overtly rejects or implicitly undermines the patriarchal structures of the monarchy and Moroccan society.

Oufkir's memoir shares many characteristics with Arab women's autobiographical prison accounts. Narratives such as Nawal El Saadawi's *Memoirs from the Women's Prison*, Farida Al-Naqqash's *Al-Sijn: Dam'atan wa Warda* (*Prison: Two Tears and a Rose*), and Safinaz Kazim's *Al-Sijn wa al-Hurriya* (*Prison and Freedom*) typically begin by narrating the trauma of initial prison formalities, recount details about conditions and deprivations, and describe the writer's strategies for psychological survival. Miriam Cooke has noted that Arab women write autobiography as a means for political and social empowerment and in subservience to a master-/male-oriented narrative.[21] Similarly, Nawar Al-Hassan Golley argues that writing for Arab women is a means of "subverting dominant hegemonies and asserting agency."[22] It is also a way to voice their "silenced" narrative:

> Autobiography, therefore, is often an informed choice, one used as a political tool with the object of exposing problems within Arab society. . . . It is therefore all the more powerful as a tool of indictment of a social system when the autobiography entails the narration of the trauma of imprisonment and torture.[23]

Fatna El Bouih admits that her first-person narration in *Talk of Darkness* is a means of speaking on behalf of all the women who were imprisoned and tortured during the Lead Years, including Saida Menebhi, who was tortured and died in prison on December 11, 1977. The posthumous publication of her poems titled *Poèmes, lettres, écrits de prison* in 2000 became part of the historical discourse and testimonial literature of the "disappeared."[24]

That *Stolen Lives* has been translated into several languages attests to its popularity. By 2003, there were versions of the French original in English, Arabic, German, Italian, Spanish, Japanese, and other languages. Further popularized by newspaper and television reviews and interviews, the book has been read in a variety of ways by different audiences in different countries. Such readings often show responses not reflective of the book's historical and political context, and they therefore warrant a study of the book's audiences. Reviews of the book have focused on the different ways audiences in Morocco, the United States, and France have responded to the book. While both France and the United States had long ago thrown off autocrats, become nation-states, and largely separated constitutional law and civil-rights amendments from religion, Morocco under Hassan II was a patriarchal Islamic autocracy where religion was used to support an absolutist regime. France has been a more open society since the overthrow of a monarch who proclaimed "l'état, c'est moi." Torture, however, remains an ongoing issue all over the world. For the United States, there are Guantanamo Bay, Abu Ghraib, "extreme rendition," and the US Army's School of the Americas that taught torture.

Susan Slyomovics' review of the book is particularly astute and noteworthy for comments about the varying ways in which Oufkir's autobiography has been received. Slyomovics explains that reception of the book in France differed from its American response. She argues that while the French were quite familiar with such testimonial literature about political repression during the reign of Hassan II given their colonial history in Morocco, Americans were, on the whole, ignorant of this historical and political context.[25] American audiences, she argues, were remote from the political context and more attracted by the exoticism the text evoked. Slyomovics identified General Muhammad Oufkir as "the brutal and much-feared Minister of the Interior for King Hassan II." Further along, as an American, she notes: "The bloody family drama of a man who built a system of secret prisons and torture centers—only to have it consume his own family—lies outside our collective imagination and interest, as does his daughter's steadfast loyalty and love for her father."[26] American audiences' fascination over Malika Oufkir's presence on the Oprah Winfrey Show, or on 60 Minutes, as well as other television programs, were likely to identify with innocence (and beauty too) emerging from torture. One important aspect of Slyomovics' review is to show that just as Malika had to see through her "innocence," so too should American audiences give up their identification with innocence, which is a form of ignorance. Elaine Scarry's theorizing about "doubt" in narratives of pain may not apply to Americans, who do not have to deal with the pain. American white, middle-class audiences reading Oufkir's book locate the suffering far away, in "another country," and maybe they are all too ready to believe in the self-congratulatory basis that "it cannot happen here."

In Morocco, where the book was banned, *Stolen Lives* never circulated in bookshops or libraries. Around the time when it was published, the country was still witnessing book-banning, suppression of intellectual freedom, and other forms of censorship. The journal *L'Hebdomadaire* faced censorship when it published an interview with Malika Oufkir in March of 1997. In the same year, Oufkir appeared briefly in Nabil Ayouch's film *Mektoub* (*Destiny*), in which she was dressed in red and green, the colors of Morocco's national flag, and holding a rifle. Restrictions on writing in Morocco were combined with sexual and political taboos to suppress certain topics. Conditioned in this way, Moroccan readers unconsciously read over anything that was politically taboo. The publication of the interview with Malika Oufkir in *L'Hebdomadaire* broke a political taboo because mystery and rumor had surrounded the name "Oufkir." The breaking of these taboos stimulated public discussion about the political past. Moroccans were aware of the coup d'état staged by General Oufkir in 1972 against Hassan II but had been left in the dark about what happened to him and his family. The author notes that the name "Oufkir" "aroused fear. . . . Our resurrection perturbed them."[27]

The author's discussion of religion might also be another reason why the book was banned in Morocco. Some Moroccan critics were shocked by certain authorial statements, which undermine an Arabic Muslim tradition that forms the cultural and religious memory of Moroccan society. Mokhtar Ghambou, who criticized the author's conversion to Catholicism, objected to what he considered the author's undermining of the Muslim Arabic tradition, thus insulting "the spiritual, cultural, and psychological sensibilities of an entire people."[28] The Moroccan reception of the book was also negative due to the author's deliberate omission of her father's murderous history and lack of reflection on his abuse of power as Minister of the Interior. The political formulation of "whoever lives by the sword dies by the sword" frames the Moroccan response to Oufkir's narrative. Critics have accused her of mythologizing her experience and not telling the full truth. In his review of the book, Mokhtar Ghambou clearly admires some of the features of Oufkir's autobiography, including "its powerful language, dramatic tone, suspense, and vivid imagery,"[29] but objects to the author's "naiveté" regarding her father's murderous past. He invokes not only General Oufkir's coup d'état against Hassan II but the role he played in the assassination of Moroccan intellectual Mehdi Ben Barka in France in 1965. He states:

> Malika's naiveté and obsession with luxury . . . might explain her disinterest in political details, but never to the extent of ignoring the fact that her father had

> absolute power over the Moroccan secret service. . . . Most importantly, by the time Malika conceived and wrote down her story she was a mature woman and a responsible public figure that could no longer hide the truth under the excuse of naiveté.[30]

Ghambou also harshly criticizes the author for allocating the assassination of Ben Barka, a major event in Moroccan history, to a footnote in her book.[31] Thus, he accuses Oufkir of not telling the whole truth to her audiences.

Two fundamental questions come to the forefront when analyzing Oufkir's book: How reliable is she in presenting her coauthored first-person narrative? And does the reader have access to accurate information with respect to the abuses she and her family suffered under Hassan II? The political context of her autobiography makes any version of experience subject to ideological manipulation. Malika Oufkir asserts pride in her storytelling skills and in having played the role of Scheherazade[32] by writing this text. Moreover, the facts themselves have aspects of fairytale and nightmare. Yet the issue of truth would also seem to have important implications for how the audience receives and evaluates her story. Additionally, the book was coauthored by Michele Fitoussi, who may have empathetically recreated some parts of Oufkir's story. There are verifiable names, dates, and places, and confirmation in memoirs by her mother, Fatima, and her brother.[33] Possible imaginative interventions by Fitoussi may have abetted the narrative flow. However, whether they might have impinged on Malika Oufkir's obligation to tell the truth cannot be ascertained. It is just as likely that other events may have been omitted lest they strain their readers' credulity. In sum, for some Moroccan readers, Oufkir's account remains too unintelligible and untenable to comprehend. Thus, pointing to General Oufkir's past crimes and accusing his daughter of omitting them from the text become a ploy to distract from the horrors of her imprisonment and torture.

A close reading is required to determine how much Malika Oufkir knew about her father's role in palace affairs. The author makes many references to her father, but rarely does she transcribe their conversations or attempt to probe his private thoughts and feelings. She also avoids passing judgment on his words and deeds. However, she does feel guilty for having been unable to prevent her father's death: "I swung between humiliation, pain and rage."[34] Her father remains the victim, just as she and her family remain persecuted innocents. She does not analyze, even retrospectively, the brutalities that supported their former privileged lives. The author's desperate need, as victim/survivor, to keep the reader fixed on her story of imprisonment and pain makes for disruptions in the narrative and avoidance of facts about her father's past.

References to her father's story are merely the prelude to the main plot. The reader learns early in the narrative that her father was an officer in

Indochina, boasting "a chestful of medals" during the French-Indochinese war.[35] He enlisted as "reserve second lieutenant" in the French army, and was later appointed aide-de-camp to General Duval, commander of the French troops in Morocco. He negotiated King Mohammed V's return from exile, and by 1955, he became the king's chief aide-de-camp.[36] The author brushes aside, though she does note, certain allusions made about her father's career: "People feared and criticized him."[37] Casually she notes her brother Raouf's fears for their father because of the 1971 coup, during which several people were killed during King Hassan II's birthday.[38] She declares, though, that her father's role in this first coup "was never proven, but . . . the clemency he showed toward the rebels gave rise to speculation."[39]

The 1971 coup d'état at Skhirat was a turning point in Malika Oufkir's relationship to the palace. Following this event, she observed growing tension between her father and the king. Resolving conflicted loyalties, Malika at last declares a political stance: "I no longer supported the monarchy."[40] Malika left Morocco to enroll in a Paris *lycée* under her mother's maiden name and, in a rented apartment, she adopts a bohemian lifestyle. When she has a serious car accident, her father is unable to come to France to be with her, because he has been convicted of murder at the Ben Barka trial.[41] There is no hint, however, that she ever confronted her father about what he had done or the charges against him. Concerned for her safety, her father called her immediately after his failed 1972 coup d'état. That same day he was executed, and the palace ruled his death a suicide. Malika insisted on seeing her father's body, needing in this way to "lay bare the truth": "I counted the bullet marks on his body. There were five. The last one, on his neck, sent me into a frenzy of pain."[42] The author must force herself to believe facts. Though, she notes, it is forbidden for a Muslim woman to see the body of a dead man, she insists not just on seeing but on being left alone with her father's body. She counts the five bullet marks and feels justified in her anger against the king.

Reading Oufkir's autobiography as an act of bearing witness might constitute an option to resolve the crisis of truth in her narrative. No matter how much one testifies, some truth(s) will remain unknown. Oufkir herself sometimes resorts to speculation. Nevertheless, the reader who is interested in figuring out where the truth is also knows that "the plausible" is not necessarily "the factual," and is at times persuaded and even swept away by vivid fiction. If we read Oufkir's work as a testimony, then it cannot be held to any other standard. The question is: What makes this book a testimony, rather than a life narrative, or just a sensationalized autobiography to make money? In the tradition of testimony, the act of bearing witness is received as "true" because the narrator contributes to a collective truth. According to Shoshana Felman, to testify is "to vow to tell, to promise and produce one's own speech as material evidence for truth."[43] Along the same lines of argument,

Susan Slyomovics points out in her book *The Performance of Human Rights in Morocco* that the act of witnessing is a public performance which is legally binding, and thus judged as just and truthful.[44] Slyomovics also emphasizes the idea of "testimonio" as a personal obligation to bear witness to an event experienced collectively. Fatna El Bouih's *Talk of Darkness*, in which she narrates her experiences as a political prisoner from 1974 to 1982, is one example of such collective endeavors to speak for the collective experiences of voiceless Moroccan women and female activists who were too marred by their horrific experiences to tell their stories.[45] Slyomovics further argues that *shahada*, the Arabic word for testimony (témoignages, in French) is the equivalent of testimonio in Latin American literature:

> The word testimonio translates literally as testimony, as in the act of testifying or bearing witness in a legal and religious sense. . . . In testimonio, it is the intentionality of the narrator that is paramount. . . . The position of the reader of testimonio is akin to that of a jury member in a courtroom. Unlike the novel, testimonio promises by definition to be primarily concerned with sincerity rather than literariness. [46]

In Islamic jurisprudence, Moroccan women are banned from giving testimony in certain cases such as criminal law (*hudud*). When a woman is allowed to give testimony in court, she counts only as half a witness. The testimony of two women is equal to that of one man. Slyomovics credits Moroccan human rights discourse with extending "the legally binding, political term shahada outside the court to public space and beyond male-female inequities to gender-neutral acts of narration by men and women. . . . Shahada is a performance-based mode deployed to express female suffering publicly."[47] Similarly, Oufkir uses the collective framework of Moroccan human rights discourse as backdrop to her experience, which is in turn recognized by that collectivity. In Oufkir's negotiation of autobiography, she positions herself within the masculine-constructed tradition of shahada yet disrupts this tradition by representing the agential female subject as witness.

The author gives her shahada outside the scope of the Muslim tradition. Boldly and provocatively, she states that she and her family, with the exception of her mother, converted to Catholicism while in prison. For the author, this does not represent a radical disjunction for she has noted that "in our family, Christmas had always been sacred. Even at the Palace, where Islam was dominant, Christmas was still Christmas."[48] This revelation shows the different ways religion is observed in the different strata of Moroccan society—a topic that is treated deftly in Leila Merrakshi's film *Marock* (2005). Grueling privations and acute suffering that drove the author and members of her family to attempt suicide eroded whatever reverence she might once have had for her father-monarch, "God's representative on earth," and even for the God he represented. She had been physically close to the king, with reciprocated affection. The same king gave orders to "subdue" her family (three women and six children).[49] Torn between respecting Hassan II and hating "the despot he had become,"[50] she fails to recognize that he was a despot all along. The three women (two female relatives voluntarily accompanied the family) and six children were at the mercy of a masculine power structure.

Determined to retain "the name that the monarch wanted to exterminate,"[51] and not to be crushed by his punishment of those who bore that name, she gradually intuited why Hassan II did not have the Oufkirs killed outright: "The two successive coups d'état had shaken his power. He was being challenged, he the leader of the faithful, God's representative on earth."[52] With Hassan II as "God's representative on earth," Islam had failed her. Moreover, bereft of male protection, persecuted by a powerful male ruler, constrained to age without social or sexual companionship, she and her family turned for comfort and inspiration to a female figure: "We were convinced the Virgin was protecting us. . . . We had rejected Islam . . . and opted for Catholicism instead."[53] Malika's sister Maria chose her name "in homage to the Virgin," and in rejection of the name given her by Hassan II. The comforts of conversion are only superficially theological, for Malika has lived secular years in both Morocco and France. "The radio made me aware of feminism and sexual liberation," she says, and she cherishes aspirations for publishing a successful novel and being part of a theatrical company.[54] In addition, keeping her family's tribulations in perspective, she asks how belief in God can be sustained after such horrors as the Jewish Holocaust.[55]

Oufkir provides testimony to the story of her torture and imprisonment within collective human rights discourse and against the patriarchal, collective tradition that would silence her. She admits her loss of words whenever she wants to describe the horrifying prison Bir El Jdid, where she and her family spent ten years: "In this death camp . . . we had been pariahs, cast out by the world."[56] The author, who not only suffered the death of her father, but also permanent removal from her community through imprisonment, metaphorically tells the story of her death: "I had mourned the death of my father. Now I was mourning my own life."[57] She later realizes that death is being forced upon her against her will: "All the time we were being pushed back down towards the dead."[58] The initial journey from Rabat to the mayor's house in Goulimine is cursorily described, but as they move closer to the desert, more details and scenery are revealed. The family was left totally in the dark about their final destination: "We were entering the realm of the irrational. . . . This was a country where they locked up young children for their fathers' crimes."[59] The author uses the light and dark division to dramatize complications in their ordeal. As subsequent journeys to other prisons unfold, the environment and the other guards begin to occupy more narrative space. During their journey to Agdz, their treatment became harsh, as they were stuffed in blacked-out vans and were not allowed to move for eighteen hours straight. After their four-year stay in Tamattaght, the family was transported blindfolded for twenty-four hours to Bir-Jdid prison where they were to spend the next ten years of their incarceration. In Bir-Jdid, Colonel Benaich authorized a harsher treatment for the family. They were stripped bare of all necessities, separated, punished with solitary confinement, and subject to severe privations. It was against the rules to keep a radio, to own a book or a writing pad, to send or receive letters from relatives, or have a newspaper or a magazine. Food reduction would become a standard form of punishment. They were rationed meager portions of bread, rotten meat, and rotten vegetables. By malnourishment, the authorities, in fact, condemned them to death by hunger. Maltreatment unmade their world and destroyed their identity.

In a similar fashion to Fatna El Bouih's prison memoir *Talk of Darkness*, Oufkir's memoir underlines the tension between the feminine and masculine realms in Moroccan prisons. Both Oufkir and El Bouih reflect on the gender constraints of their imprisonment. Oufkir describes how seven women prisoners found their menstrual periods synchronized: "We had no cotton wool or sanitary towels, so we cut hand towels into strips and used them over and over again."[60] Synchronization of menstrual periods also happens when other groups of women share a common dwelling, such as in a harem. Menstrual blood becomes a gender marker of their bodies. Given the fact that Malika, her mother, her sisters, and their two female companions are not implicated in the political activities that led to their imprisonment, they become marked not so much by politics but by menstrual blood. Their blood signifies the relevance of their gender within the male-dominant structure of the prison system. During her interview with Susan Slyomovics, Fatna El Bouih remarked on the significance of menstrual blood while in prison: "We used to suffer a great deal, we women, for example during our period, because we couldn't change."[61] Slyomovics further comments that "allowing the women to soil themselves with their menstrual blood was part of a system of humiliation and worse, specific to women detainees, that included being treated as prostitutes, forced nakedness, rape threats and rape."[62] Sexual difference became important in prison, given the tactics of torture played by the prison guards. The torturers used their "masculinity" to exercise absolute power and inflict pain on the female victims. They reinforced such power by giving their female victims male names, which served to deny them their femininity. El Bouih's prison memoir *Hadit Al Atama* was translated into French as *Une femme nommée Rachid* (*A Woman Named Rashid*), and into English as *Talk of Darkness*. She recounts how her jailors assigned her a male name to deny her identity as a woman: "I couldn't believe I was in front of the man in charge, the chief himself, the teacher, the government authority. My God, were these the men in power in my country? They gave me a number and a name: 'From now on your name is Rashid.' . . . It was the beginning of the destruction of my identity."[63] While female prisoners were masculinized, male prisoners were feminized, humiliated, and emasculated. Oufkir describes how her elder brother, Raouf, was deliberately taunted and feminized. He insisted on reminding the prison guards of his shared masculinity when he pleaded with them not to shave his goatee.[64]

As the author details survival through twenty years of incarceration, all of it harsh and brutal, she also reveals strong family bonds and tremendous resourcefulness. The author recounts that after multiple suicide attempts failed to hail the attention of the authorities, she and her family devised a plan to escape as well as strategies to overcome danger and outwit their jailors. First, they learned how to manipulate the guards. Raouf was able to hide the radio and use amplifiers he hid from the guards to create a transmission from cell to cell, which allowed the others to communicate with each other and listen to radio programs broadcast from his cell. Next, they devised a plan to escape. Having tunneled themselves out of the prison in Bir-Jdid, Malika, her sister Maria, and their two brothers headed first to Casablanca and then on to Rabat where they were to find out that Hassan II had ordered their house to be razed to the ground.[65] During their two-day stay in a hotel in Tangier where they were not able to book rooms, they managed to call the French channel France Inter and inform the broadcaster about their fifteen-year imprisonment in Moroccan prisons and their dramatic escape. Soon after, they were captured by the Moroccan police, who stopped short of treating them as prisoners when the story of their escape became international news. Under international pressure, the Oufkirs were released from prison but placed under house arrest for another five years. It was only in 1991 that they were able to secure their passports and leave Morocco. The author went on to become a celebrity with further ambitions.

Oufkir's memoir has become, thus, a means to remake her world,[66] to transcend the suffering she endured and to fashion a new identity through freedom of expression. Her discourse of identity shows the extent to which she wants to reveal her experience. She states that the act of narrating her story places her in the position of someone who has survived the story of her death: "Pain gave me new life. . . . I've gained an identity. . . . And that is priceless."[67] Malika Oufkir's autobiography exemplifies creative remaking of her world both in literature and life. The narrator's awareness of the importance of narrative in the production of identity and freedom can be found in different instances in *Stolen Lives*. She retained that identity and sense of freedom even in captivity when she invented stories and play-acting to keep up the morale of the younger children. This narrative subjectivism is apparent in the narrator's identification with the characters in the stories she invented. Oufkir was a good storyteller from early on, and she used storytelling to distract her family from their torments during incarceration. A tale set in Russia, replete with Cossack raids, sleigh rides, and passionate love affairs (which she called The Story), helped keep the family sane while beset by torrential rains and infestations of roaches, fleas, mice, and rats.[68] Identity therefore becomes a role play, as the narrator experiments with different narrative identities.

In her rhetorical construction of identity, the author frames her experience as a story of collective agency triumphing over suffering and pain. Because she frames her experience as one of triumph over pain, she is thus able to experience forgiveness. Drawing on Jacques Derrida's model of mourning in the context of forgiveness allows description of Oufkir's autobiography as a "work of mourning" linked to processes of public and private forgiveness and reconciliation. Derrida writes that "forgiveness forgives only the unforgivable."[69] For the philosopher, forgiveness is an impossible dream as long as one is engaged in the process of mourning and of working through resentment. Forgiveness is also unconditional: "I forgive regardless of the attitude of the guilty party. . . . I forgive him insofar as he (or she) is guilty or even insofar as he (or she) remains guilty."[70] Malika Oufkir admits her willingness to forgive "those whom I once loved at the palace."[71] Because Oufkir's working through of pain allows her to forgive and let go of resentment, her narrative has thus contributed to reconciliation and brought change to the Moroccan political scene.[72]

The story of the Oufkirs exists at the heart of an emerging Moroccan democracy. Bouabid, a Moroccan official who came to see the Oufkirs while they remained under house arrest in Marrakesh in 1991, commended the family for the stir they had created since their escape. This evolution in human rights has in turn generated a new body of literature. Telling the truth about past injustices, individually and collectively, is the first step toward attempted reconciliation. Also, the emergence of more documents and new forms of life-writing makes denial and refuge in blame all the more harder for Moroccan authorities. It is no coincidence that it was only after the international outcry stirred by the Oufkirs' imprisonment and their dramatic escape that Hassan II established an Advisory Committee on Human Rights in 1990. When his son Mohammed VI took power after the death of his father in 1999, he promised to address the human rights abuses committed during the Lead Years era. The Moroccan Justice and Reconciliation Commission,[73] instituted on January 7, 2004, by Mohammed VI, is so far the only official truth seeking commission in North Africa and the Middle East. Because of the new contexts of upheaval in the region, Morocco's present king is going to have to recognize how to avoid internal revolt by extending democracy in Morocco. Learning a lesson from Hassan II's intransigence, he has tried, through recent constitutional reforms,[74] to meet the challenge of maintaining stability while democratizing and emerging as a modern multiethnic state, according rights of citizenship to women as well as men, having women represented in government, and respecting human rights.

NOTES

1. Elaine Scarry, *The Body in Pain: The Making and the Unmaking of the World* (New York: Oxford University Press, 1985), 3.

2. Ibid., 4.

3. Ibid., 9.

4. Ibid., 6.

5. Jean-Francois Lyotard, *Differend: Phrases in Dispute (Theory and History of Literature)*, trans. George Van Den Abeele (Minneapolis: University of Minnesota Press, 1988), 5.

6. Ibid.

7. Freed political prisoners have enacted testimony to their imprisonment through autobiographies, comics, poems, novels, and films. Among these former prisoners is the Marxist-Leninist Abraham Serfaty, who served seventeen years of a life sentence in the Kenitra Prison before he was deported to France in 1991. Prior to Malika Oufkir, Fatna El Bouih was the first female prisoner to recount her incarceration and torture in Moroccan prisons. Former political detainees also used film to document their horrific experiences. One such film is *Derb Moulay Ali Cherif*, in reference to the Derb Moulay Ali Cherif torture center.

8. Both Malika's mother, Fatima Oufkir, and her brother, Raouf Oufkir, have published autobiographical accounts of their imprisonment. Fatima Oufkir wrote *Les jardins du roi: Oufkir, Hassan II et nous* (*The King's Gardens: Oufkir, Hassan II and Us*). Raouf Oufkir wrote *Les invités: vingt ans dans les prisons du roi* (*The Guests: Twenty Years in the King's Prisons*). Fatima's title, *Les jardins du roi*, is provocative, evoking what Stephen Hughes notes is the paradox existing in the persona of the king: "The king's 'secret garden' was a euphemism for a very private place in his life and mind. In this inner sanctum are state secrets and answers to enigmas he hoped would die with him. He considered that he could not be held accountable for them once they were planted in the garden." Stephen Hughes, *Morocco Under King Hassan* (New York: Ithaca Press, 2006), 187.

9. Walter Benjamin, *Arcade Project*, trans. Howard Eiland and Kevin Mclaughlin (Cambridge, MA: Belknap Press of Harvard University, 1999), 471.

10. Khalid Zekri, *Fictions du Réel. Modernité Romanesque et Écriture du Réel au Maroc: 1990-2006* (Paris: L'Harmattan, 2006), 199.

11. In November 1999, Bachir Ben Barka was interviewed by a Marxist journal in which he revealed the horrible details surrounding the kidnapping and assassination of his father, and his tireless efforts to discover the truth. Bachir ponders the question of complicity between General Oufkir, who engineered Ben Barka's abduction, and different foreign agents such as French intelligence agents, the Central Intelligence Agency, and the Mossad. Speculations abound about what happened to the body, which was never found. Collaboration by French agents was not surprising, given the major preoccupation of Western Europe in the post-World War period to force newly independent African states into pro-Western policies and eliminate socialist tendencies. A 1994 *New York Times* article quotes a European diplomat as saying that human rights abuse in Morocco "is one where amnesia rather suits the West. There are diplomatic priorities." Roger Cohen, "King's Wrath: Morocco Family Tale of Two Decades," *New York Times*, January 25, 1994, http://www.nytimes.com/1994/01/25/world/king-s-wrath-morocco-family-tale-of-2decades.html (accessed January 2, 2011).

12. Thomas Park and Aomar Boum, *Historical Dictionary of Morocco*, 2nd ed. (Oxford: The Scarecrow Press, 2005), 60.

13. Ernest Gellner, "Introduction," in *Arabs and Berbers: From Tribe to Nation in North Africa*, eds. Ernest Gellner and Charles Micaud (Lexington, MA: Lexington Books, 1972), 19.

14. Mordechai Nisan, *Minorities in the Middle East : A History of Struggle and Self-Expression* (London: McFarland & Company, Inc., 2002), 70.

15. Examples of such testimonials include Tahar Ben Jelloun's novel *Cette Aveuglante Absence de Lumière* (*The Blinding Absence of Light*) (2001); Abdelhak Serhane's novel about Tazmamart Prison, *The Bitch of Tazmamart* (2001); Midhat Bourequat's *Mort Vivant* (*Living Dead*) (2000); Abdelfettah Fakihani's *Le Couloir: Bribes de Vérités Sur les Années de Plomb* (*The Hall: Fragments of Truth about the Lead Years*) (2005).

16. Ibid., 57.

17. Ibid., 114.
18. Ibid., 13.
19. Ibid., 14.
20. Ibid., 59.
21. Miriam Cooke, *Women Claim Islam: Creating Islamic Feminism through Literature* (New York: Routledge, 2001), 29.
22. Nawar Al-Hassan Golley, ed., *Arab Women's Lives Retold: Exploring Identity through Writing* (Syracuse, NY: Syracuse University Press, 2007), 185.
23. Ibid.
24. Valerie Orlando, *Francophone Voices of a "New" Morocco: Representing a Society in Transition* (New York: Palgrave Macmillan, 2009), 88–89.
25. Susan Slyomovics, "Review of *Stolen Lives: Twenty Years in a Desert Jail*," by Malika Oufkir and Michele Fitoussi, *Boston Review* 26.6, January 2002, http://bostonreview.net/BR26.6/slyomovics.html (accessed September 28, 2010).
26. Ibid.
27. Malika Oufkir, *Stolen Lives*, 281.
28. Mokhtar Ghambou, "Malika Oufkir and the American Making of a Moroccan Star," http://www.wafin.com/oufkir.phtml (September 25, 2010).
29. Ibid.
30. Ibid.
31. For more information on the Ben Barka affair, refer to Stephen Hughes' book *Morocco Under King Hassan* (New York: Ithaca Press, 2006). For a full discussion of the films and novels produced on the Ben Barka affair, refer to Valerie Orlando's *Francophone Voices of a "New" Morocco: Representing a Society in Transition* (New York: Palgrave Macmillan, 2009).
32. Malika Oufkir, *Stolen Lives*, 155.
33. See note 8 for the titles of both Fatima Oufkir's and Raouf Oufkir's memoirs.
34. Malika Oufkir, *Stolen Lives*, 168.
35. Ibid., 15.
36. Ibid.
37. Ibid., 66.
38. Ibid., 68.
39. Ibid.
40. Ibid.
41. Ibid., 87.
42. Ibid., 93–94.
43. Shoshana Felman and Dori Laub, *Testimony: Crises of Witnessing in Literature, Psychoanalysis, and History* (New York: Routledge, 1992), 5.
44. Susan Slyomovics, *The Performance of Human Rights in Morocco* (Philadelphia: University of Pennsylvania Press, 2005), 146.
45. Ibid., 144.
46. Ibid., 146.
47. Ibid., 147.
48. Malika Oufkir, *Stolen Lives*, 153.
49. Ibid., 105.
50. Ibid., 114.
51. Ibid., 168.
52. Ibid., 169.
53. Ibid., 188.
54. Ibid., 167.
55. Ibid., 168.
56. Ibid., 197.
57. Ibid.
58. Ibid., 150.
59. Ibid., 103.
60. Ibid., 149.

61. Fatna El Bouih, "This Time I Choose When to Leave," Interview, *Middle East Report* 218, Spring 2001, http://www.merip.org/mer/mer218/time-i-choose-when-leave (September 30, 2010).

62. Slyomovics, *Performance*, 135.

63. Fatna El Bouih, *Talk of Darkness*, trans. Mustapha Kamal and Susan Slyomovics (Austin: University of Texas Press, 2008), 14–15.

64. Ibid., 150.

65. Ibid., 213.

66. Elaine Scarry has explained how violence exercised on prisoners unmakes their world, destroying patterns of behavior and mental structures. See her book *The Body in Pain: The Making and Unmaking of the World* (1985).

67. Malika Oufkir, *Stolen Lives*, 79.

68. Ibid., 155–159.

69. Jacques Derrida, *On Cosmopolitanism and Forgiveness* (New York: Routledge, 2001), 32.

70. Jacques Derrida and Elizabeth Roudinesco, *For What Tomorrow: A Dialogue*, trans. Jeff Fort (San Francisco: Stanford University Press, 2004), 161.

71. Malika Oufkir, *Stolen Lives*, 149.

72. Toward the end of the narrative, the author notes that even though the European Parliament and Amnesty International mediated the release of over 670 political prisoners between 1987 and 1991, "there are still hundreds of political prisoners . . . many of whom died in Tazmamart, a prison camp in the High Atlas." Malika Oufkir, *Stolen Lives*, 291.

73. The main role of the Moroccan Justice and Reconciliation Commission is to uncover serious human rights violations committed between the years 1956 and 1999, and to decide on claims of damages and reparations to the victims. Susan Slyomovics has noted that not all victims of human rights abuses benefited from the reparations instituted by Mohammed V's 1999 Indemnity Commission. See Susan Slyomovics, "Reparations in Morocco: The Symbolic Dirham," in *Waging War, Making Peace: Reparations and Human Rights*, eds. Susan Slyomovics and Barbara Rose Johnston (Vancouver, BC: University of British Columbia Press, 2008), 105.

74. In July 2011, King Mohammed instituted a new constitution under which the prime minister becomes the head of the executive branch. See Kenneth M. Pollack, Daniel L. Byman, Akram Al-Turk, et al., *The Arab Awakening: America and the Transformation of the Middle East* (Washington, DC: Brookings Institution Press, 2011).

Chapter Five

National Violence and Male Crisis Discourse in Yvonne Vera's *The Stone Virgins*

A fictional narrative can have an important testimonial function by recognizing and making public past experiences of violence. Yvonne Vera's novel *The Stone Virgins*,[1] published in 2002, three years before her death, conveys as much pain as Malika Oufkir's personal memoir *Stolen Lives* (2001). Oufkir had left Morocco and wrote her book in exile and thus did not run the risk of being censored or persecuted for telling her story; Vera, however, remained in Zimbabwe and risked persecution due to confronting her government. In fact, had Vera published her novel *Obedience*—which she did not complete prior to her death in 2005—she would certainly have been persecuted by Robert Mugabe's repressive regime. *Obedience*, which is set in the city of Bulawayo in the week before the 2002 presidential election,[2] deals with Mugabe's regime's intimidation of the disloyal population. My analysis of Vera's novel *The Stone Virgins* is grounded in the following questions: How does Vera express pain in her narrative? Using language and plot, how does she convey suffering—from political violence and also from such experiences as alienation and racial discrimination? How does a nation in pain affect gender relationships? How can pain, as fictionalized in her narrative, affect public opinion and perhaps prevent future violence? As much as Vera's narrative aims to convey pain, it also reveals the limits of language to express pain. This chapter addresses these complex questions, while taking into account the historical context of the novel.

Born in Matabeleland's capital city Bulawayo, Vera is one of Zimbabwe's and Africa's most prolific women writers.[3] Along with Zimbabwean writers Shimmer Chinodya, Charles Samupindi, Alexander Kanengoni, and

Chenjerai Hove, she is among the few authors who have addressed Zimbabwe's colonial and national violence. Vera wrote *The Stone Virgins* in response to the violence that the Zimbabwe Africa National Union (ZANU) government of Robert Mugabe committed against the Ndebele people in the region of Matabeleland, subsequently inciting genocide. The plot centers on Thenjiwe and Nonceba, two sisters who live alone in Kezi after the death of their parents. In 1983, Sibaso, an ex-Zimbabwe People's Revolutionary Army (ZIPRA) guerrilla fighter, resurfaces in Kezi after hiding out in the Gulati Hills following independence. He murders Thenjiwe and rapes her sister Nonceba before cutting off her lips with a razor. Following the attacks against the two sisters, the military forces of Robert Mugabe arrive in rural Kezi and conduct a massacre against its inhabitants.

Much of the action in the novel takes place in Kezi, where the landscape contains ancient caves and Bushmen San paintings. The setting embodies the timeless cultural heritage of Zimbabweans. It also stands for Vera's vision of what colonial modernity and war threaten to destroy. However, literary critic Arlene Elder has warned that it would be premature to conclude that the novel is based on contrasts between the modern and traditional, or the urban and rural.[4] If anything, the narrative offers evidence of breaking down colonialist divisions between the urban and the rural. This is evidenced in the Kezi-Bulawayo bus service being used as an interface between the colonial city of Bulawayo and Kezi. The divisions in the novel are not between rural and urban but are rather ideological and political.

The chronology of the novel follows two phases: the preindependence period from 1950 to 1980 and the postindependence period from 1981 to 1986. It is in this latter period that the national violence known as *Gukurahundi* took place. The civil war, followed by the Gukurahundi state of emergency, is rooted in the liberation war, in which the two nationalist parties ZANU and Zimbabwe African People's Union (ZAPU), and their military wings ZIPRA and Zimbabwe African National Liberation Army were involved. The war of liberation against the Rhodesian government, led by Ian Smith, began in the 1960s and came to an end in 1980 with Zimbabwe's negotiated independence. ZAPU's loss to ZANU in the elections of 1980 led to continued political conflict between the two nationalist parties. Army recruitment gave rise to a growing association between ZAPU and its ZIPRA military wing with the Ndebele people. Likewise, there was a strong, increased identification of ZANU and its Zimbabwe African National Liberation Army military wing with Shona speakers.[5] ZIPRA guerrillas took up arms in a rebellion against the newly elected Shona government of Robert Mugabe. In response to the rebellion, Mugabe formed a new army brigade called the Fifth Brigade, had it trained in Korea, and deployed it in a violent campaign against the Ndebele inhabitants of Matabeleland, who were accused of harboring and protecting dissidents. After an estimated twenty thousand civilians were killed, Mugabe and Joshua Nkomo, the ZIPRA party leader, signed the 1987 Unity Accord, which led to the merging of ZAPU into the nationalist majority party ZANU, and put an end to the violence.[6]

Records about the violence have not been disclosed to the public, and those responsible for murder, rape of women, and destruction of property have not been charged or tried. According to historian Terence Ranger, Yvonne Vera's depiction of "real" history "shows great restraint," because what she describes are just a few of the many examples of the government's horrific acts of violence.[7] Ranger further argues that the novel constitutes a change in attitude toward history as it describes the impact of a large-scale crime on private lives and how that event can be a catalyst for change. It is, after all, "a book that confronts the reality of History and which transcends that reality by means of confrontation."[8]

BEARING WITNESS TO "HISTORY"

With its public distanced from a painful past, the novel *The Stone Virgins* creates a space where trauma and pain can be articulated. The construction of such a narrative is all the more urgent given the current government's failure to bear witness to its history of violence. Shoshana Felman's view of literature as testimony stresses the connection between narrative, history, violence, and healing—topics that are central to Vera's narrative.[9] According to Jacques Derrida, a secret testimony is impossible, as "in principle, to testify—not being a witness, but testifying, attesting, 'bearing witness'—is always to render public."[10] The performance of oral history, with its emphasis on re-memory, functions in the novel to inscribe the violence against the Ndebele people in public space as a way of grounding the Ndebele community through its past. Vera's goal is to rewrite Robert Mugabe's "official" history, which denies that crimes against humanity were committed in Zimbabwe during his regime. Her focus on such rewriting of official history is the subject of much of the criticism that has appeared since the publication of *The Stone Virgins*. For example, Lene Bull-Christiansen argues that the novel constitutes "an opening of the discursive space of national identity by forming a counter discourse to Zanu (PF)'s appropriation of national history."[11]

The dialogic relationships between the different perspectives of what happened to civilians in Matabeleland expose Vera's strategy of questioning official historical discourse and reinventing an open process for constructing new versions of the past. Linda Hutcheon uses the term "historiographic metafiction" to describe novels that draw on official historiography but undermine its authority by using individual experiences of the characters in the text.[12] Because Zimbabwean history is made up of a multiplicity of voices, an accurate depiction of reality must involve a dialogic representation of these diverse points of view, including Mugabe's. The story is told by an omniscient narrator, but most events are seen through the eyes of each one of the four major characters: the two sisters, Thenjiwe and Nonceba, the former guerrilla fighter Sibaso, and Thenjiwe's ex-lover Cephas. The author's unconventional use of narration and multiple points of view characterize *The Stone Virgins* as a postmodern novel. The multiplicity of the novel's space and time dimensions is also consistent with Vera's postmodernist strategy to deconstruct the univocal and unilateral view of history, consequently asserting the complexity of Zimbabwe and the plurality of its contending voices.

FEMALE VOICES OF RESISTANCE

An analysis of the narrative strategies in *The Stone Virgins* demonstrates that the novel is not just an attempt at revisionist history. It also problematizes the way history is presented to the public by reconceptualizing and rewriting it from a feminist perspective. According to Joan Scott, it is this rewriting of official history that makes postmodernism appealing to a feminist who questions the epistemological status of history itself, which ignores the voices of the excluded and marginalized, such as women.[13] Vera's search for women's voices is intended to do justice to their true role in Zimbabwe's history. Her first novel, *Nehanda* (1993), tells the story of the historical heroine of the First Chirumenga, the war of resistance against British colonialism between 1895 and 1898.[14] Nehanda, a spirit medium, was tried in court and hanged in 1897 for inciting her countrymen to fight against the British.[15] The oral mystical tradition says that at her burial Nehanda predicted that "my bones will rise again" to fight against the Europeans. Thus, her living spirit inspired the Second Chirumenga—the liberation wars of the 1960s and 1970s. Through Nehanda, Vera establishes that there is such a thing as female leadership, but women's leadership role in public versions of history is almost nonexistent.

In *The Stone Virgins*, Vera narrates the war of liberation, which took place from 1972 to 1979, from the point of view of female ZIPRA guerrilla fighters, thus inserting female voices to speak for women's experiences within the larger narrative of national history. The use of flashbacks constitutes an important narrative structure and foregrounds the centrality of female representation. When the female liberation fighters returned to rural Kezi at the end of the war, they wanted to claim the land and "forget the . . . death, the years of deafness and struggle."[16] These women, who are now "the freest women on earth" and "have no desire to be owned, hedged in, or claimed,"[17] have taken men's places in the Thandabantu store ("the veranda"). This is a sign of liberation and change in gender relationships: "This veranda was their adobe, they transformed it, and they became the ultimate embodiment of freedom."[18] The occupation of a male space by these revolutionary heroines causes a crisis in male identity that has already been weakened by colonialism. The feminization of male space signifies the symbolic loss of male identity—an identity upon which Zimbabwe's patriarchal tradition constructed its cultural values.

There are notable differences between the male and female guerrilla fighters who return from the war. The women "arrive with a superior claim of their own. They define the world differently."[19] Where the women are purposeful and independent, the men are insecure and lack a purpose. The novel depicts the returning male guerrilla fighters as betraying a lack of self-containment around women and an instability, which contradicts the certainties of masculine machismo exhibited during the war of liberation: "These men wear lonely and lost looks . . . [and] walk awkward . . . not at all like what the women imagine heroes to be."[20] According to Jane Parpart, the legacy of racism and violence in Zimbabwe, dating from precolonial conflicts over land and colonial/settler rule to postcolonial struggles over majority rule, have influenced "the way men and women have understood their place in an often violent and unpredictable world. It has pitted competing notions of manhood and womanhood together in a complicated and often unforgiving history."[21]

BLACK MASCULINITY IN CRISIS

Vera views both colonialism and the civil war that broke out in the aftermath of independence as manifestations of gender crisis. Under colonialism, men suffered atrocious brutality, humiliation, and ruthless economic exploitation. Colonial rule contributed to the emasculation of colonized men by depriving them of social markers of manhood, such as land and other sources of wealth. Frantz Fanon points to the emasculation of colonized men in Algeria as an example. He argues that the aim of colonialism was to destabilize the authority of indigenous men. To reinforce control over them, colonialism produced a dichotomy between the "civilized" European, who had a mission to liberate the colonized woman, and the colonized man, who was viewed as "savage."[22] The image of black men as savage brutes who failed to be civilized set them apart from British men, and that was used to justify taking away their land, keeping them powerless. Grace Musila argues that black manhood was undermined in the urban colonial space. While the colonial city might have affected a crisis in black manhood, women might have had more autonomy in the urban space. The city provided a negotiable space for redefining womanhood outside the constraints of indigenous patriarchy.[23]

From Vera's description of the colonial city of Bulawayo, where both men and women were relegated to the margins, it is clear that she wants to depict colonialism as a perverted system that produces the failure of black men. The *Stone Virgins* explores the conflicted vision of Bulawayo as an urban colonial space inhabited by white political and economic elites, as well as the black urban poor. The central forces of control and authority are concentrated in Bulawayo, which is the locus of British colonial power. The city represents an affluent enclave of residential and recreational areas, while in its shadows exists a marginal zone of interstitial spaces. The space of marginalization in the city, where blacks reside, is also the space of oppression and dehumanization. Black men are excluded from work in Bulawayo, as they have to travel to Johannesburg to work in gold mines. Praise Zenenga has pointed out that colonialism caused black men to lose their "public honour and private mastery."[24] It did so through forcing them to leave their rural communities in search of employment in cities, thus stripping them of authority, in public spaces and also in the private spaces of their homes and communities. As one result, the colonial identity of the black man as "an eternal boy" led to "the incorporation of the term 'boy' into the indigenous Shona and Ndebele languages as '*boyi*.'"[25]

In Vera's novel, black men are depicted not only as nomadic workers who have to "voyage back and forth between Bulawayo and Johannesburg,"[26] but also as consumers of modernity. The image of temporary workers and modern consumers in the representation of black men is important to the construction of black identities in the colonial city: "They attend soccer matches. . . . Their readiness is buoyed by . . . their portable radios, their double-doored wardrobes."[27] Part of black engagement with the modern, and their motivation to integrate into the city, includes their involvement in commercialized leisure. Their crisis, however, lies in the need to adjust within a colonial context that impedes their attempts to claim their share of urban colonial space and find their place in a society that is deeply racist. In Bulawayo, Blacks live on the periphery of the city. As lovers, they meet only at the edge of buildings, *ekoneni*, because they are barred from the city: "Ekoneni is . . . a place to meet. You cannot meet inside any of the buildings because . . . entry is forbidden to black men and women."[28] Ekoneni is the space of tension between the European city center and its black margins. As a liminal space, it is also the space of resistance against colonialism.

Early in the novel, Vera describes independence as the reason for joy and celebrations among young men, who as "the van drives off in a cloud, they chase after it . . . just to show they are neither quiet nor defeated."[29] Their misbehaving is a politically subversive act that works to undermine the hegemony of colonialist discourse about black men as "passive," "humble," and "ignorant." Vera's description of ekoneni as a liminal space of resistance provides the starting point for her narration of gender and decolonization in postcolonial Zimbabwe.

RESCUING BLACK MASCULINITY

As Zimbabwean men forged their anticolonial resistance, they incorporated some of the colonizer's values, internalizing the colonizer's image of them. Furthermore, they adopted the European model of nationalism as a male-centered and patriarchal ideology. In the process of developing anticolonial nationalism—the object of which was to rescue black masculinity—women were doubly oppressed by colonial and nationalist discourses. Gloria Jean Watkins, better known as bell hooks, observes that in addition to colonialism, women "were tyrannized by the imperialism of patriarchy which makes oppression of women a cultural necessity."[30] Using the example of black nationalism, hooks argues that the black man tries to assimilate into the cultural world of white men in order to regain his masculinity. The black man mimics the values of white patriarchy and thus oppresses women to prove his masculinity to the extent that he can resort to violence against them in order to "lessen [his] anxiety and fear that [his] masculine power will be usurped."[31] In order to shed the "emasculated" image produced by colonial logic, black nationalists associated anticolonial resistance with hypermasculinity. Such patriarchal "hypermasculine" practices continue to manifest in the postcolonial period.

Gender politics has been given an interesting twist by the masculinist politics of Mugabe's government.[32] During the war, the media generated propaganda about women that supported women's equality and liberation from traditional roles due to their participation in the war of liberation. It is a known fact, though, that women endured gender discrimination and sexual violence during the war.[33] While the new government granted civil rights to women, it also endorsed patriarchal practices. Passage of the Legal Marriage Act in 1982 gave women the right to guardianship and custody laws, inheritance rights, and property rights. At the same time, through incorporation of the Victorian code of morality established by British colonialism, anticolonialist discourse began eroding the sexual rights of women traditionally guaranteed in Zimbabwean society. In 1983, the government launched "Operation Clean Up," targeting female ex-guerrilla fighters whom it accused of prostitution. In addition to omitting from public versions of history the role these women played during the struggle for independence, the government targeted them through its campaigns and subjected them to imprisonment. Any woman found on the streets alone at night, without being able to provide proof of marriage, was arrested. As a result, around six thousand women were detained and placed in a detention center in the Zambezi valley.[34] One female ex-guerilla fighter describes outrage and anger over such detentions: "Zimbabwean women were subjected to the shameless, degrading and totally unjustifiable humiliation at the hands of the police and soldiers who forced, beat and generally mishandled women on the dubious allegations of being prostitutes."[35] With the "new" Zimbabwean government, the status and liberation that women gained during the revolutionary phase of the war of liberation came to a halt. Female war veterans were designated as refugees and were underrepresented in the new government. They continue to face discrimination with regard to education, property rights, and the right to own farming land, even if they are heads of households.[36]

THE CIVIL WAR AS A CRISIS IN GENDER

By subordinating women's causes and turning the entire nation into masculine fighters during the 1981 to 1986 civil war period, Mugabe's government tried to restore patriarchal concepts of nation and renew its masculine identity. The macho rhetoric of military propaganda celebrated militant manhood as the symbol of nationhood. Jane Parpart has pointed out that violence in Zimbabwean history served to reinforce the masculinity of the perpetrator: "The hyper-masculine, warrior imagery used to fuel the struggle" between the Rhodesian government and nationalist resistance fighters "fostered a vision of masculinity that prized physical toughness. . . . Enemies were feminized while success in war and the ability to kill became the litmus test of successful manhood."[37] Black ex-guerrilla fighters, caught between the emasculating effects of colonialism and the liberation war, struggled to maintain a masculine identity. In the novel, Sibaso, the former ZIPRA guerrilla fighter, who commits acts of unspeakable violence against Thenjiwi and her sister Nonceba, is a dissident. He is, therefore, excluded from victorious manhood.

In her essay "Male Hysteria," Elaine Showalter attributes the phenomena known as shell shock and male hysteria to "the social expectations of the masculine role in war," which views "emotional repression as an essential aspect of the . . . masculine ideal."[38] Shell-shocked by colonialism and the effects of war, men attempt to regain their masculinity by embracing extreme violence. Indeed, Vera's novel is not just about the victimization of women and the effects of violence on the female survivor's body; it is also about male trauma, identity crisis, and how violence against women is a result of wounded male identity. The narrative brings to light such male crises by tracing both the trajectory of Sibaso's perpetuation of extreme violence against two women and the Shona government's war on women and the inhabitants of Matabeleland. Women were subjected to brutality by the government's Fifth Brigade, as well as by individual male guerrilla fighters returning from the war traumatized and violent. They brutalized women with the same weapons they brought back from the fighting. It was not just women who were being murdered by the dissidents and the Fifth Brigade, however. Gender violence was part of the general violence in which they killed and tortured male and female civilians and destroyed their property.

Through a series of flashbacks, the novel revisits Sibaso's war experience and subsequent traumatization that led to his attack on the sisters. His narrative of violence is driven by the logic of a revelation—to disclose the truth of what lies behind his acts. Thus, through his stream of thoughts, he ultimately comes to blame the war for creating an emptiness in him that threatens to destroy his identity: "In a war, you discard names like old resemblances."[39] The war zone is a place that renders humans nameless. The forgetting of his name in the throes of war condemns him to a deathlike absence, thereby creating through him a metaphor for the disintegration of identity and loss of collective memory. Sibaso loses his individuality during the war, instead becoming part of a collective, the liberation army. But war also gives him an identity that he values. He is a liberator and a nationalist, until he realizes his sacrifice was for naught. It is at this moment that he remembers his name.

The underlying current of symbolism is strongly felt in the novel. Sibaso's streams of thought dwell on the image of the spider, which is posited as a metaphor for his masculine identity. Like Sibaso, spiders are described as hollow. Like him, they also change "color" and identity: "There is a type of spider that changes color when mating. It devours its own partner."[40] Because of its carnivorous nature and its connection with its natural enemies, the spider is metaphoric for the predatory nature of men who are involved in war. The spider's sexual relations are also a metaphor for gender relationships and the predatory nature of men like Sibaso. According to Terrence Ranger, the spider may also symbolize history, thus suggesting the illicit and perverted nature of Sibaso's version of history and war.[41] As he remembers the war, Sibaso is filled with a sense of personal annihilation, death and deprivation, which leaves no room for prewar existence so crucial to the construction of memory and identity.

Sibaso's violence against the sisters is based not only on his war experience, but also on his disillusionment with the government's false idealism in which he previously believed. The interpretation of Sibaso's actions, based solely on the violent displacement of his identity dislocation and misogyny onto the sisters, undermines the complication of his disillusionment and the complexity of his response to his dashed idealism about the war. Sibaso does not go off on a murderous rampage until he comes face-to-face with the irony in receiving a copy of Solomon Mutswairo's idealistic and nationalistic Shona novel, *Feso*, from the skeptical tenant of his family's home. He soon realizes that he read the novel during his first year at university before abandoning his studies. *Feso*, published in 1957, was censored a few years later by the Rhodesian colonial government because of its nationalist undertones. The novel is based on oral and rural Shona tradition, with its moral and social framework, and underlying narrative of anticolonial resistance. It also incorporates a poem that evokes the spirit of Nehanda, leading some critics to read it as an allegory of colonial oppression. The novel has a symbolic significance for the nationalists and may have inspired Sibaso to join the armed struggle for independence. Inside the novel's pages, Sibaso finds a map and a crushed spider "weighed down by time."[42] The crushed spider metaphorically symbolizes his dashed hopes about the war of liberation. Having been dehumanized by his experiences, Sibaso sees himself as a mere "instrument of war."[43] He is also in a state of denial, because "Independence is the compromise to which [he] could not belong."[44] Being so out of touch with reality allows him to embrace a certain type of freedom, although the concept of liberty is abstract and not specific to his country or the continent's situation: "Independence . . . has proved us a tenuous species."[45] Thus, realization of his past misinterpretation of the war, and his "noble" participation in it, are catalysts for his murderous rampage against the sisters.

Sibaso's rape of Nonceba mimics lovemaking, as "he . . . places her across both his knees, like a bride."[46] For Sibaso, rape represents an attempt to find a coercive kind of "intimacy," to establish power and dominance over his female victim. The rape scene dramatizes the thoughts of each one of the two characters as they engage in subjective reflections about one another. The subversion of dialogue brings to light the impossibility for men like Sibaso to accommodate or incorporate women's speech without silencing them. In her stream of thought, Nonceba describes Sibaso as "a predator,"[47] for whom rape becomes a means of asserting his dominance and boosting his fragile masculinity: "He commands. She dares not contradict him."[48] As he reflects on the rape, Sibaso draws provocative correspondences between Nonceba and the sacrificial virgins, young girls sacrificed at a king's burial during one of Zimbabwe's ancient kingdoms: "She is a woman from . . . the naked caves in the hills of Gulati . . . a dead past."[49] His thoughts about Nonceba resonate with his reflections on the rock paintings of San's sacrificial virgins during his time in the Gulati Hills: "I place my hand on the rocks where . . . long-breasted women stand together. . . . They are the virgins who walk into their own graves before the burial of a king."[50] Sibaso's original identification with the virgins in the cave explains his subsequent realization that he has been sacrificed for an ignoble cause. Out of this realization comes a self-hatred he seems to vent on the sisters. He appears to identify with the sacrificial virgins in their subordination and powerlessness, just as he was subordinated and rendered powerless by the army. Sibaso's experience of fighting for a cause, only to realize that it was all for nothing, parallels that of the stone virgins who walked to their deaths for a fruitless cause. The result of his sacrifice was the rise to power of Robert Mugabe, and he hates seeing himself in such a "feminine" role, manipulated by Mugabe's emasculating power structure. His violence against the two sisters, representative of his own powerlessness, is thus a form of retribution, considered in his mind as necessary for both individual and national rebirth. In referring to the sacrificial virgins, Vera is indirectly criticizing the cultural idealization of female self-sacrifice. This serves, in Sibaso's case, to compensate for the military and political defeat of Ndebele men by the Shona government.

NARRATIVE RECONSTRUCTION

Vera doubts Sibaso's ability to share in the construction of a collective memory of the war. According to Maurice Vambe, "associating Sibaso's war narrative with a 'cracked' mirror, 'broken face' and 'fragile' dreams is Vera's way of casting doubt on the authenticity of that narrative."[51] Hence, his inability to articulate the memory of destruction is compounded by a feeling of emptiness, a void that his imagination tries to fill with monstrous images. Sibaso's failure to construct a narrative may be interpreted as the author exploiting the potential for distancing herself from his narrative in order to put her own voice and those of the women in the novel into the foreground.

The author's attempt to construct such a narrative is reflected in Nonceba's struggle as she works through the traumatic experiences of her rape and her sister's murder, and strives to verbally express her pain. According to Judith Herrmann, narratives of recovery play an important part in the process of reconstructing a sense of self after trauma. The victim's ability to access traumatic memories mediates elements that facilitate healing.[52] Nonceba's experience of trauma impinges on her body and her surroundings, yet cannot be articulated in language: "She watches as stone dissolves like salt. . . . There are no words to describe this lack."[53] At the hospital, she is trapped in silence, "a voice dying,"[54] as she listens to the screams of a traumatized woman who has been forced to kill her husband. Nonceba associates herself with the lament of women in similar situations as she tries to elicit language to express her own pain. She struggles with capturing the pain in a way her readers can hear: "Unable to shape words into language, she will have to find the sources of sound inside her. . . . Words will flow, then language. Only then will she discover a world in contrast to her predicament."[55] Julia Kristeva notes the victim's inability to verbalize traumatic events.[56] She describes such traumatic states using the image of the black sun and the black hole to symbolize the void felt by the person experiencing trauma and loss of cultural memory. Kristeva labels this void "the Thing." For those who experience trauma, "the Thing, like the self, is a downfall that carries them along into the invisible and unnameable."[57]

Nonceba's struggle to verbally express her traumatic experience resonates with Vera's difficult task, as she faces challenges in telling her story to a Zimbabwean audience. Writing about the genocide against the people of

Matabeleland, Vera uses the government's control of her freedom of speech as an opportunity for women like herself to speak out against oppression and as a catalyst for change. Through her dialogic narrative, she wants to ensure that the voices of women are heard during the period of healing and reconstruction after the war. The question of reconstruction would entail not only the liberation of women but also the reconstitution of male identity.

In her book *Precarious Life*, Judith Butler engages with post-9/11 politics, reflects on "the powers of mourning and violence," and considers "what, politically, might be made of grief besides a cry for war."[58] She further argues that the experience of mourning and grief can pave the way for "another normative aspiration within the field of politics."[59] Butler's book aims to develop ethics in response to the human experience of vulnerability to political violence and consider the possibility of reimagining a community in ways that transcend loss.[60] Just as Butler tries to reconfigure a way of building a new international community in the aftermath of September 11th, Vera attempts to re-imagine ways for men and women to live together in the aftermath of the violence that took place in Matabeleland.

Vera's rewriting of gender relationships is vital for men and women living together after the violence. In the novel, men both inflict the violence and provide healing from the resulting pain. It is a man, Cephas, who creates a home for the female subject of political and sexual violence. When Cephas arrives in Kezi upon reading about what has happened to Nonceba and her sister in a newspaper clipping, Nonceba suspects that he might be an army dissident or a member of the Fifth Brigade. Cephas informs her that he lives in Bulawayo where he files documents for an archive. Cephas is eventually able to convince Nonceba to travel with him to Bulawayo, where she embarks on a journey of healing through her redemptive relationship with him. They slowly develop feelings for each other, though their relationship remains platonic. Theirs is a relationship that bears witness to an equitable, nonhierarchical relationship between men and women.

Vera's hopeful scenario, in which Cephas eases Nonceba's suffering, enables the reader to imagine men in roles other than that of perpetrators of violence. The novel creates a scenario of male kindness and generosity toward the female Other, which takes up the question of men's responsibility toward female victims of patriarchal violence. If men like Sibaso emerge as monsters in the aftermath of the war of liberation, Vera attempts to humanize the image of men through the character of Cephas, as she believes that it fell upon good men like him to create a home for traumatized women who have ever been subjected to violence. Her representation of Cephas has significant implications for feminist politics in that she imagines a future for the female subjects of rape and violence. By emphasizing his position as benefactor for Nonceba, Vera does not put Cephas in a traditional male role. The greatest evidence of Vera's optimism about male/female relations in Zimbabwe lies in Cephas' ability to love Nonceba enough to let her follow her own path, even if it means her leaving him: "Nonceba has grown on him. . . . He wants her not to doubt her own freedom."[61] As Nonceba embarks on the road of recovery and self-transformation, Cephas thinks about "the beehive hut, to be installed at Lobengula's ancient kraal, kwobulawayo."[62] The beehive huts are one of the valuable assets of Zimbabwe's cultural heritage to be preserved and reconstructed for the future. Vera assigns Cephas the task of restoring this relic from the past, performing an imaginative act parallel to the author's narrative organization of the novel. The parallel is revealing in the way it shows both the author's and Cephas' ability to transcend the boundaries of time and space and explore the past, the present, and the future. By having Cephas restore this relic from the past, Vera is also succinctly appealing for a sincere acknowledgment of the human rights violations of the past. In the introduction to their book *Trauma, Resistance, Reconstruction in Post-1994 South African Writing*, Jaspal Kaur Singh and Rajendra Chetty argue that while new South African writings are informed by the past, they are also underpinned by a new ethic urging reconciliation and inclusiveness.[63]

Unfortunately, a precarious human rights situation continues unabated in Zimbabwe, a decade after the publication of Vera's novel. Even today, the story of masculinity in Zimbabwe is still a defensive narrative. According to Human Rights Watch, violence has increased since the emergence of the Movement for Democratic Change in 1999. Those perceived as supporters of the party were targets of violence during the country's elections in 2000, 2002, and 2005.[64] Ultimately, the ending of this dictatorship is not only an issue of moral responsibility, but also a necessity for advancing the collective interests of all Zimbabweans.

NOTES

1. Yvonne Vera, *The Stone Virgins* (New York: Farrar, Sraus and Giroux, 2002).
2. Dobrota Pucherova, *The Ethics of Dissident Desire in Southern African Writing* (Trier, Germany: Wissenschaftlicher Verlag Trier, 2011), 95.
3. After completing her master's and doctorate degrees in literature in Canada, Vera returned to Bulawayo to direct the National Gallery of Zimbabwe. She won prestigious African and international prizes, including the 1997 Commonwealth Writers Prize for her novel *Under the Tongue*. Vera's early death in 2005 from complications caused by AIDS was deeply lamented by critics as the loss of a great writer. See Helon Habila, "Obituary: Yvonne Vera," *The Guardian*, April 27, 2005, http://books.guardian.co.uk/news/articles/0,6109,1471087,00.html (accessed October, 8, 2007).
4. Arlene Elder, *Narrative Shape-Shifting: Myth, Humor & History in the Fiction of Ben Okri, B. Kojo Laing and Yvonne Vera* (Rochester, NY: James Currey, 2009), 131.
5. Brian Raftopoulos and Tyrone Savage, *Zimbabwe: Injustice and Political Reconciliation* (Harare, Zimbabwe: Weaver Press, 2005), 150.
6. Ibid., 185.

7. Terence Ranger, "History has its Ceiling: The Pressures of the Past in the *Stone Virgins*," in *Sign and Taboo: Perspectives on the Poetic Fiction of Yvonne Vera,* eds. Robert Muponde and Mandi Taruvinga (Harare, Zimbabwe: Weaver Press, 2002), 209.

8. Ibid., 206.

9. Shoshana Felman and Dori Laub, *Testimony: Crisis of Witnessing in Literature, Psychoanalysis, and History* (New York: Routledge, 1992).

10. Maurice Blanchot, Elizabeth Rottenberg and Jacques Derrida, *The Instant of My Death* (Stanford, CA: Stanford University Press, 2000), 30.

11. Lene Bull-Christiansen, *Tales of the Nation: Feminist Nationalism or Patriotic History: Defining National History and Identity in Zimbabwe* (Uppsala, Sweden: Nordiska Afrikainstitutet, 2004), 203. "Zanu(PF)" refers to the ZANU-PF, the Zimbabwe African National Union–Patriotic Front.

12. Linda Hutcheon, *A Poetics of Postmodernism: History, Theory, Fiction* (New York: Routledge, 1988).

13. Joan Wallach Scott, *Gender and the Politics of History* (New York: Columbia University Press, 1999).

14. Yvonne Vera, *Nehanda* (Harare: Baobab Books, 1993).

15. In Zimbabwean society, some women achieved social prestige by becoming a healer, a midwife, or a spirit medium, positions practiced only by postmenopausal women. See Katrin Berndt, *Female Identity in Contemporary Zimbabwean Fiction* (Bayreuth: Eckhard Breitlinger, Bayreuth University, 2005), 15.

16. Yvonne Vera, *Stone Virgins*, 51.

17. Ibid., 54.

18. Ibid., 120.

19. Ibid., 56.

20. Ibid., 55.

21. Jane Parpart, "Masculinities, Race and Violence in the Making of Zimbabwe," in *Manning the Nation: Father Figures in Zimbabwean Literature and Society*, eds. Kizito Muchemwa and Robert Muponde (Harare, Zimbabwe: Weaver Press 2007), 103.

22. Frantz Fanon, *The Wretched of the Earth*, trans. Constance Farrington (New York: Grove Press, 1968), 37.

23. Grace Musila, "'A Man Can Try': Negotiating Manhoods in Colonial Urban Spaces in Dambudzo Marechera's *The House of Hunger* and Yvonne Vera's *Butterfly Burning*," in *Manning the Nation: Father Figures in Zimbabwean Literature and Society*, eds. Kizito Muchemwa and Robert Muponde (Harare, Zimbabwe: Weaver Press, 2007), 143.

24. Praise Zenenga, "'Boys': Performing Manhood in Zimbabwean Drama," in *Manning the Nation: Father Figures in Zimbabwean Literature and Society*, eds. Kizito Muchemwa and Robert Muponde (Harare, Zimbabwe: Weaver Press, 2007), 131.

25. Ibid.

26. Yvonne Vera, *Stone Virgins*, 5.

27. Ibid., 70.

28. Ibid., 12.

29. Ibid. 18.

30. bell hooks, "The Imperialism of Patriarchy," in *Ain't I a Woman* (Boston: South End Press, 1981), 117.

31. Ibid., 107.

32. Tanya Lyons, *Guns and Guerilla Girls: Women in the Zimbabwean National Liberation Struggle* (Trenton, NJ: World Africa Press, 2004), 208.

33. Josephine Nhongo-Simbanegavi, *For Better or Worse? Women and ZANLA in Zimbabwe's Liberation Struggle* (Harare, Zimbabwe: Weaver Press, 2000).

34. Tanya Lyons, *Guns*, 229.

35. Ibid., 230.

36. Dobrota Pucherova, *Ethics*, 94.

37. Jane Parpart, "Masculinities, Race and Violence in the Making of Zimbabwe," 113.

38. Elaine Showalter, "Male Hysteria: W.H.R. Rivers and the Lessons of Shell Shock," in *The Female Malady: Women, Madness and English Culture 1830-1980* (London: Virago, 1987), 169.
39. YvonneVera, *Stone Virgins*, 82.
40. Ibid., 84.
41. Terence Ranger, "History has its Ceiling," 206.
42. Yvonne Vera, *Stone Virgins*, 110.
43. Ibid., 141.
44. Ibid., 82.
45. Ibid.
46. Ibid., 72.
47. Ibid., 69.
48. Ibid., 71.
49. Ibid.
50. Ibid., 103–104.
51. Maurice T. Vambe, "Problems of Representing the Zimbabwean War of Liberation in Mutasa's *The Contact*, Samupindi's *Pawns* & Vera's *The Stone Virgins*," in *War in African Literature Today*, ed. Ernest N. Emenyonu (New York: James Currey, 2008).
52. Judith Herman, *Trauma and Recovery* (New York: Basic Books, 1992), 181.
53. YvonneVera, *Stone Virgins*, 139.
54. Ibid., 90.
55. Ibid.
56. Julia Kristeva, *Black Sun: Depression and Melancolia* (New York: Columbia University Press, 1989), 57.
57. Ibid., 15.
58. Judith Butler, *Precarious Life: The Powers of Violence and Mourning* (New York: Verso, 2006), ii.
59. Ibid., 26.
60. Ibid., 20.
61. Yvonne Vera, *Stone Virgins*, 178.
62. Ibid., 184.
63. Jaspal K. Singh and Rajemdra Chetty, *Trauma, Resistance, Reconstruction in Post-1994 South African Writing* (New York: Peter Lang, 2010), 7.
64. Tiseke Kasambala and Georgette Gagnon, *Zimbabwe: "Bullets for Each One of You": State-Sponsored Violence Since March 29 Elections* (New York: Human Rights Watch, 2008).

Chapter Six

Political Satire in Tess Onwueme's Play *No Vacancy*

Tess Onwueme is one of Nigeria's leading women writers. Like Yvonne Vera, Onwueme has become well-known nationally and internationally for her poignant characters and explosive narratives that address a number of politically charged issues. Onwueme and Vera belong to the same generation of African women writers. Both authors write against a repressive government that has exploited and impoverished its people. Their Anglophone countries of origin, Nigeria and Zimbabwe, respectively, possessed extraordinary potential at the time of their independence, but both squandered their wealth as a result of rampant corruption and unchecked exploitation of resources. Nigeria had the opportunity to create a sustainable economy built on oil, but this has not materialized. In 1980, at the time of its own independence from the former British colony of Rhodesia, Zimbabwe possessed rich agricultural lands and an intelligentsia, but was hurled back into poverty by President Robert Mugabe. Dictatorships and other political and economic circumstances in both countries have been the same, provoking similar responses from intellectuals and writers.

A prolific writer, Onwueme is the recipient of many national awards, including the Association of Nigerian Authors Drama Prize for her plays *The Desert Encroaches* (1985), *Tell It To Women* (1995), *Shakara: Dance-Hall Queen* (2001), and *Then She Said It* (2003). She has also won prestigious international awards such as the Fonlon-Nichols award (2009), the Phyllis Wheatley/Nwapa award for outstanding black writers (2008), the Martin Luther King, Jr./Caesar Chavez Distinguished Writers Award (1989/90), and the Distinguished Authors Award (1988). Her plays, which explore questions of gender and national and global politics, have been lauded by critics and identified with literature for social justice. As Chris Dunton points out, "few

Nigerian dramatists have written about social injustice with such bite and energy. . . . Her output as a whole shows a restless search for appropriate form, from the early group of realist plays on oppressive social norms, to the fable plays."[1]

Onwueme's writing has been influenced by a broad range of ideas, in particular the socialist ideology and revolutionary tradition in which drama is considered a weapon for social change. In her interview with Iniobong Uko, she stresses the influences of Ngugi's and Sembene's representations of women and the masses, as well as the Brechtian methodology of revolt, upon her work:

> [M]y sensibilities were influenced to some extent by the ideological impetus of Ngugi Wa Thiong'o, Sembene Ousmane and maybe Femi Osofisan. Beyond these, one writer whose dramatic aesthetics and ideology had such significant impact on me was Bertolt Brecht. . . . More and more, since the last decade, the masses and the dispossessed tend to gain more prominence in my works.[2]

Likewise, Onwueme is influenced by the African oral tradition because she derives her literary idioms from rituals, folkloric tradition, and mythology that have also defined the works of Wole Soyinka and other Nigerian writers and dramatists. Thus, her plays have to be read within the contexts of both African tradition and Nigerian theater,[3] each of which played an important part in shaping her themes. She states: "[My] dramatic impulse was born in the village, even as there was no theater. These experiences texturized into the inner fabric of my mind and shaped my sensibility. . . . Most evenings, our uncles, aunts, told us stories from which we learnt the folktales, histories, norms and values of our people."[4] Onwueme's testimony, with reference to her literary influences, is an indication that African drama is not exclusively literary in origin. Drawing on Frantz Fanon's prescriptions for literary engagement, as outlined in his book *The Wretched of the Earth*, Nelson O. Fashina classifies African dramatic literature into three phases. The first phase involves the generic evolution from oral to written literature. The second phase is the postcolonial, revolutionary phase. The third phase involves the emergence of a new form of world literature, a hybrid of African and Western linguistic and cultural traditions.[5] Onwueme's work fits within this third phase; however, it also embodies elements from the first and second phase given that it is grounded in the oral tradition as well as the postcolonial African dramatic tradition.

PROLETARIAN THEATER

A salient work on the effects of capitalism and globalization on the unemployed, Onwueme's *No Vacancy* (2005) stresses the theme of revolutionary struggle and resistance against oppression. The play had its world premiere in Nigeria in 1986 under the initial title of *In Search of a Theme: All of US*. It was staged as the Vice-Chancellor's Command Performance at the Federal University of Technology, Owerri (FUTO) by the FUTO Theatre Troupe, which Onwueme directed at the time. The play was codirected by Steve Daniel, who now teaches at Ahmadu Bello University, Zaria.[6] The play, which focuses on frustrated unemployed youths in a time of extreme change and transition, opens up a dialogue on unemployment and other global issues, and offers young people a voice for articulating their frustrations. The play extends the theme of the proletarian theater of Onwueme's previous plays, *The Desert Encroaches* and *Ban Empty Ban*, which "explore the dominance of a capitalist social order erected upon the systematic exploitation of the productive sector of society (the proletariat and the peasantry)."[7]

SATIRIC ALLEGORY

Above all, the play functions as political satire of a global political climate that promotes unemployment and the social marginalization of young people. Onwueme relies on ideological abstractions to present a utopian narrative and political desire for change by the unemployed. She explains that she employs allegory as a metaphoric and satiric medium to critique national and global politics: "For more than anything, the privileges of allegory liberate me from particularities into identifiable universal tropes and contexts."[8] The play is most easily read as an allegorical representation of the unemployed's desire for justice, freedom, and equality. Using satire, the author personifies critical ideas to convey her criticism of political problems. Onwueme maintains her use of allegory by assigning to the characters names such as "LIBERTY," "FREEDOM," and "JUSTICE," allowing the reader to interpret them as ideas. As performance, the play calls for a different response from its audience, as only then can it come to life as a dramatization of people's lives.

The title of the play appears to be an allusion to Jean Paul Sartre's play *No Exit*, an allegorical play of resistance. Its central message is that hell is other people; it is not torture chambers or fire, but what humans experience in relationship to one another on a daily basis. From this hell, there is no exit. Sartre insinuates that resistance is the stage upon which a person's freedom is made meaningful, and the Other is the enemy of one's freedom. One of the recurring themes in *No Exit* is the idea of personal freedom. Man is endowed with freedom; however, with freedom comes responsibility. Inside each one of us is an empty space, termed *neant* (nothingness) by Sartre, and that space is freedom. The principle actors in *No Exit* (Garcin, Ines, and Estelle) are confined to hell and have to come to terms with the concept of freedom. Some embrace it, but others lapse into what Sartre terms *mauvaise foi* (bad faith). He introduces the concept by alluding to the way people escape the freedom they already have by denying the extent of human freedom. He also examines the idea of "people's justice" and contrasts it with "class justice." Resistance is fundamental to achieving social justice, for "in order to deserve the right to influence people who are struggling, one must first of all take part in their struggle, one must first of all accept many things if one wants to try to change some of them."[9]

Onuweme names her main characters LIBERTY, FREEDOM, JUSTICE, FAITH, and EQUALITY, drawing on concepts at the core of Sartre's philosophy. The ideals of freedom, equality, and justice are all but an illusion, and the play immediately directs our attention to the reality of the "New World Order of Big Business Oil Club."[10] Irony is evident in the striking disparity between the fictive names of JUSTICE, LIBERTY, FAITH, FREEDOM, and EQUALITY, and the extreme injustice and oppression present in the real world of the unemployed, a disparity that readily lends itself to the double-voiced discourse of allegory. The play, which lifts these symbolic references beyond the Nigerian context, makes no reference to particular dates or locations. The lack of a Nigerian context emphasizes that the unemployed are alike everywhere. Use of generic terms might also allow the playwright to avoid censorship. Nevertheless, it is important to situate the play within the context of Nigerian history and politics. Since "Independence" in 1960, dictatorships have existed in Nigeria:

> The military administration of General Ibrahim (1985-1993) established in Nigeria intricate forms of corrupt practices. . . . That trend was worsened by the economic repression resulting from an unprecedented fall in crude oil prices globally . . . and a general social disaster as well.[11]

Other major recessions followed as the country fell further into debt. It has yet to begin the process of recovery. Unemployment reached a peak rate of 25 percent in 2003, and with an estimated 40 million Nigerians without work, it is one of the country's most pressing problems. During the period of military dictatorship, Nigerian intellectuals and activists who overtly wrote about controversial topics experienced censorship, which often entailed risking one's life. "It is for articulating such opposition," states Maureen Eke, "that writer activist Ken Saro-Wiwa lost his life. On November 10, 1995, he was executed by the Nigerian military government for his opposition to the illegal appropriation and environmental destruction of Ogoni farmland by multinational oil corporations."[12] Onwueme hints at the role of multinational corporations in exploiting the Nigerian masses for profit, often in active partnership with the Nigerian government. However, in order to avoid persecution or censorship, she immediately directs the reader's attention to the theater of globalization, instead of focusing specifically on Nigeria. The play presents a rich satire of Nigerian politics as well as post-9/11 America, which at its extreme presents a disturbing picture of its constitutional ideals. *No Vacancy* is very much a play reflective of the times it was originally performed. At the time it was written, the United States was in the midst of a recession in the aftermath of 9/11, and unemployment all over the world was on the rise. Onwueme criticizes the resulting isolationist policy of the United States when the country, traumatized by the loss of life in the 9/11 attacks, decided to wage a war against terrorism.

The setting of the play is an improvised Youth Camp wherein the characters plan to stage a revolution against the larger political/capitalist system at the heart of the unemployment problem. At the center of the camp is a flag banner and a sign reading "Nation of the Unemployed." A large mural representing the image of "Big Brother" is prominently featured in the camp. The mural, symbolizing the Nigerian head of state, is psychologically reinforced in the viewer's mind by images of armed guards[13] that accompany it. Proletarian theater has a history, and Big Brother is found in many guises. The term was coined by George Orwell who was born in Bengal, then part of the British colonial empire. In Orwell's novel *1984*, Big Brother is a fictional character who stands for the dictator of Oceania, a totalitarian state in which the dominant elite oppress the natives. The people are continually reminded that "Big Brother is watching them," and they are under constant surveillance by agents of the totalitarian state.[14] Similarly, allegory in Onwueme's play stages the production of domination and totalitarianism in scenes depicting the absolute, invasive control of people living in a police state. In one scene, the police use harsh, undifferentiated repression to control the unemployed protestors. One of the job seekers attempts to cross the fence to meet with EQUALITY, who is so overcome by emotion that she failed to notice him or the other job seekers.[15] EQUALITY confronts police repression with a speech revealing her deep anger at the system: "And that is precisely why the police guns burrow into the head of youths. . . . /The/brain is a dangerous weapon."[16] Parallels between Big Brother and US President George W. Bush are not lost on the reader. The play also portrays the Bush doctrine, preemptive post-9/11 foreign invasions in the name of justice and liberty, and construction of the prison camp at Guantanamo Bay. Through obvious satirical characterization, Onwueme exposes what is presented as the clandestine agenda of the US leader. Amiri Baraka has stated that "revolutionary theater should force change, it should be change. . . . The revolutionary theater must expose. . . . It must accuse and attack because it is a theater of Victims."[17] Employing revolutionary theater, Onwueme uses the character FREEDOM to mimic and satirize a speech delivered by George W. Bush: "Fellow citizens. . . . Our economy is blowing . . . pardon . . . blooming. . . . Million jobs are/Being catered. . . . I mean created by my own government. I'm blessed to deafen. . . . I mean defend this nation."[18] The speech uncovers the masquerading words of a president who does not want to be caught lying. The author is able to underscore an alternative message of Bush's speech that most American audiences may not easily recognize. Through allegory and satire, not only is the playwright able to escape the potential consequences of directly criticizing those in power, but she also chooses a structure that forces her audience to recognize the magnitude of the president's distorted speech.

Onwueme aims to suggest a contemporary political parallel between Bush's politics and the corrupt politics of the Nigerian head of state. The characters' diatribes against those who abuse power are best understood as a reference to the Nigerian dictatorships, and to policies and methods of the Bush administration: "Their Patriot Act you heard it. . . . And you too dare not. Or. . . . Locked up without charges. . . . In God we trust! . . . The New World Order."[19] At the national level, the play is a satire of local Nigerian politicians whose corruption has led to the unemployment problem. At the global level, it is a critique of world politics that have allowed such corruption to take place. Thus, the play draws parallels between two countries that have poured millions of dollars into expanding their military rather than providing social services and creating jobs. The play also calls attention to the urgent need to treat unemployment as the most prescient national security issue.[20] Onwueme highlights the economic and emotional turmoil that results from war. She describes how the global economy of the past few decades has depleted the wealth of local communities, effectively moving the wealth of nations to multinational corporations. In the scene where FAITH plays the role of trader, advertising clothing for sale, the author points to the problem of job outsourcing. Jobs are being exported elsewhere because of cheap labor costs.[21] The playwright's message is subtle: globalization of markets and industries that have been moved overseas and sold to foreign owners has exacerbated the economic problem of unemployment.

THE PLAY WITHIN THE PLAY

Consisting of a series of interrelated acts, *No Vacancy* is framed by the meeting of unemployed university graduates who are planning a revolution against the system. The play is activist and future-oriented because the characters do not merely want to grouse, but hope to seek justice. They use the stage as rehearsal space for acting in the world. Reminiscent of classical Greek tragedy, the audience is a vital part of the play, demonstrating a rare and complete convergence with the characters, cheering and sharing in the actors' lines. The shared social background between the characters and intended audience, themselves young job seekers, shows that the playwright is focusing on the youth of Nigeria. Hence, using different techniques to engage them, the play appeals directly and immediately to the young audience. It uses entanglements of roles and activisms, multiple levels of diction, role-playing, and episodes of a play within the play. The author employs idiomatic expressions, slang, local Nigerian dialects, and contemporary jargon derived from youth culture to invite young audiences to identify with the characters onstage. This is evident in an exchange in which FREEDOM has to remind her fellow characters that they need to forget about their ideological conflicts and focus on the audience instead.[22]

In the manner of Shakespearean drama, *No Vacancy* stages the juxtaposition between illusion and reality: the illusion of freedom, justice, and equality, and the reality of social injustice and political oppression. The play also dramatizes conflicts encountered by those unemployed who cannot face reality and who choose a world of theatrical illusion instead. In the manner that Shakespeare raises questions about art, power, and reality in his play *A Midsummer Night's Dream*, Onwueme draws on her characters' artistic and creative instincts to support their dreams and aspirations for a better life. She admits in her interview with Iniobong Uko that Shakespeare has "influenced her dramatic and artistic impulse."[23] Certain features of *No Vacancy* are also modeled after Bertolt Brecht's play *Caucasian Chalk Circle*, a work that transcends the specifics of origin and addresses American audiences. In his antirealist style, Brecht uses the play-within-a-play device to undermine theatrical illusion, employing characters who constantly remind the audience that they are watching a play and a director who repeatedly interrupts the play to address the audience.

In a manner characteristic of Shakespearean and Brechtian drama, Onwueme uses the play within a play to highlight reality versus illusion in dreams held by the unemployed. The characters of the outer play act out events of the inner play, and the fiction in which the characters believe ("their dream for change and a better life") is set within another fiction of the play within the play. In doing so, the play functions in analogy to a dream-within-a-dream, because the characters' dream for a better life is played out in the inner play. The play within the play, therefore, belongs to the imagination rather than problematic reality, which draws attention to the constructed nature of art. The psychological structure of the play within the play corresponds to a wishful dream, with the characters and their audience as the dreamers. The actors are divided between those who want to "hold onto the dream" (FREEDOM and EQUALITY) and those, like FAITH and LIBERTY, who are awakened to the harsh reality that the majority of people are faced with the challenge of finding food, housing, health care, and jobs.[24] JUSTICE proclaims, in a poem, that "never have our dreams/Been so dead drowned/In a thirsty sea/In a land/Where oil ceases to anoint."[25] The pessimism of the poem prompts the audience of unemployed youth to urge the actors to "Stretch/their/dream!"[26]

In trying to reinforce the ideals of her revolutionary protagonists, Onwueme uses art to draw attention to an oppressive capitalist society. FAITH, who had adamantly refused to believe in dreaming, plays the role of the oppressive officer who wields force against the protesters. There are also hints in the play that the playwright considers play-acting and dreaming to be related activities. While imploring his fellow actors to "hold on to their dream,"[27] FREEDOM praises their acting: "I never knew I had such wonderful actors and actresses in this camp. (*Turning to FAITH.*) . . . /H/ow come you're such a skilled actor?"[28] FAITH then lapses into a meta-theatrical discourse about acting versus reality: "I never did . . . acting in school. But I have come to see *living as acting*. . . . What then is my reality?"[29] In short, FAITH must deconstruct his acting in order to stress his reality. His view, that living is acting, also mirrors the interplay between art and reality. In this way, the dream in the play within the play is a dramatic rehearsal of real life.

The technique of the play within a play immerses the audience in the meta-dramatic experience, forcing them to reconsider the fictional conditions as well as actual reality. The breaking of boundaries between the two plays eventually causes the audience to realize that the events that take place in the inner play are not only part of a fictional story, but also a reflection of their own lives. In his play *Hopes of the Living Dead*, in the act titled "A Charge to the Actors," Ola Rotimi notes that African audiences "naturally possess acting skills" and collaborate with the actors on stage.[30] Onwueme's play underscores this point. The technique of the play within a play draws the audience to the performance. Having characters discuss the play brings the discourse closer to the audience. In the first encounter, the "voice offstage," who identifies itself as the mouthpiece of the actors, talks about life as a rehearsal and welcomes the audience to "the world of the unemployed." It also states that we human beings are all actors on the world stage.[31] This scene, which initiates the play within the play, involves the audience as members of the world of the unemployed. JUSTICE, the director of the play-within-the play, declares to the audience: "We forbid unemployment. That is what our play is about."[32] He appeals to them to count on him because he is going to lead them to justice. Representations in the play of the desire for justice are intended to incite the audience, who readily shares such desire with the characters. In his book *Theater and Postcolonial Desires*, Amkpa Awam uses the notion of "postcolonial desire" to define theater as the act of interpreting a utopian social reality that is based on social justice and democracy.[33] Because the characters in Onwueme's play desire the freedom of human action in a world divorced from such action, they become the actors enacting their own desires. Their desire is thus a dynamic force and a motivator for social change.

National and global politics are satirized throughout this play within a play. At the very outset, JUSTICE laments the nation that is "lost" and "drifting," and proclaims he is from the state of the abandoned.[34] LIBERTY agrees that theirs is "a country without a nation."[35] For the unemployed, the new world of globalization to which the nation has sold out has created new forms of exclusion and disappointment. In *Wasted Lives*, a study of the side effects of globalization on human lives, Zygmunt Bauman writes:

> What we all seem to fear is abandonment, exclusion, being rejected, black-balled, disowned, dropped, stripped of what we are, being refused what we wish to be. We fear being left alone, helpless and hapless. . . . We fear to be dumped—our term to be scrapyard. What we miss most badly is the certainty that all that won't happen—not to us.[36]

Bauman further points out that the unemployed are the redundant in society: "Where the prefix 'un' in unemployment is used to suggest a departure from the norm as in 'unhealthy' and 'unwell'—there is no such suggestion in the notion of 'redundancy.' No inkling of abnormality, anomaly, spell of ill-health or a momentary slip. 'Redundancy' whispers permanence and hints at the ordinariness of the condition."[37] The fear of being abandoned, of becoming waste, and of exclusion, is the emotional backdrop of Onwueme's theater of the unemployed. Free-floating, ambient anxiety is evident in the characters' dialogue and action, and their concerns for themselves are related to their current conditions, as well as to the dire potential consequences they imagine they might suffer if they do not find jobs. Indeed, the play delves into the psychology and emotional climate of the unemployed, who have "'gone crazy' from years of unsuccessful job hunting."[38]

FAITH, the first character to enter the stage, informs the audience that beyond the broken fence there is "sheer madness." The capitalist elite have sold out the nation, and powerless, marginalized citizens are staging revolts against the system.[39] FAITH questions such a revolution and dismisses his friends' dream of overthrowing "the rich capitalist rulers with their corporate allies"[40] as sheer madness. He admits that he too was crazy as he believed he could change the system. Here, FAITH confronts the meaning of resistance when one must rely on agents of power for mere existence. How can he survive as a human being in any meaningful way when his "youth is gone. Taken. Smoldered. Burnt. Burnt away?"[41] The ensuing dialogue between LIBERTY and FAITH reveals that the two have decided to change their identities. They are doing this because they now realize it is futile to fight the system. LIBERTY now sees that money and power are all that matters in today's world.[42] She confides to the audience that she has given up the struggle. She has decided to assume a new sexual identity, thus shifting the terms of her identification and activism. She decides to use her body to make money, instead of waiting for the government to create jobs for her.[43]

Act Two opens with LIBERTY and FREEDOM alone on stage. LIBERTY is flirting with the audience. Entering the stage from the opposite direction, and announcing to the audience that he has a story to tell, JUSTICE is shocked by LIBERTY's actions. He chastises her for chasing after men.[44] Dialogue between the two characters is fraught with tension. In her play, Onwueme presents gender relations as an important source of tension in society, especially in the global age. In the Western mindset, liberty is often depicted as female, as exemplified in the American Statue of Liberty, or Marianne, the national emblem of the French Revolution. The representation of liberty as female works on a paradoxical premise; Onwueme presents the ideal of liberty as female because women are kept far from political and social liberty in Nigerian patriarchal society. JUSTICE is represented as male because Nigerian men, on a societal level, are unjust to women.

JUSTICE asks LIBERTY and FAITH to act out their drama. LIBERTY, who announces to the audience her new role of real-life sex worker, refuses to play her part. When JUSTICE threatens to dismiss her from the play, she assures him that "it's only a temporary condition."[45] Thus, even her newly assumed sexual identity is not stable as she does not view her sexual performances as permanent in the sense that, as an actor in the inner play, she might not assume the identity of the character she is playing in the outer world. In reaction to LIBERTY's refusal to play the role he assigned to her, JUSTICE leaps onstage and asks if someone from the audience can play LIBERTY's part.[46] In reaching out to the audience, the director invites the unemployed youth viewing the performance to become an active part of the play. Consequently, the boundary between what is perceived as reality and the fictive play disappears. In response, hordes of young audience members "jump from their seats to grab the costumes." Their eager reaction to the director's call brings attention to their real-life hunger for jobs. JUSTICE declares to the audience: "The drama can proceed. . . . You join. . . . The drama is *you*. . . . It's all about you. . . . us. . . . In search of life" (author's emphasis).[47]

In the third Encounter, entitled "Brain, Butter or Bullets," FAITH and JUSTICE are "scheming and creeping towards the status of Big Brother." JUSTICE declares one truth to be that "cowards survive."[48] This act also introduces DJ FREEDOM, dancing and celebrating his existence. But the gaiety is abruptly checked when DJ FREEDOM and JUSTICE are confronted with guns and other weapons wielded by EQUALITY and LIBERTY, who threaten them with military force. As a representation, DJs are an important feature of popular youth culture. Therefore, it is significant that the playwright includes a DJ in her narrative. She uses the character to voice a strong commentary about African youth being destroyed by the repressive power of the military: "The military . . . draining all . . . creative human investments."[49] And while DJ FREEDOM dances, JUSTICE is seen cowering helplessly on the sidelines until a job leaflet falls from the sky. This is a plot device that moves the story into the next scene: the job interview.

The scene of the job interview shows job seekers shoving each other aside in a frantic attempt to gain the attention of the chairman. For JUSTICE, an interview with the chairman is an occasion to vent his anger over national politics that have led to his unemployment. He reduces the nation to a nonentity when he claims that he is "a bona fide citizen in this country. . . . From the Zero State."[50] When asked about his vision and goals for the job, JUSTICE replies that the country is "sick . . . polluted," and that his patriotism will be the only way to "purge" the system and remedy the "ailing motherland."[51] Tension rises in the dialogue between JUSTICE and the chairman, who mocks the candidate's rants against the government. Ironically, the only job the chairman (played by FREEDOM) can offer JUSTICE, that he thinks matches the latter's vision and goals, is that of a secret service security guard in the army. When asked whether he accepts the job offer, JUSTICE responds sarcastically: "Sure, of course! Haven't I been told that I'm being offered the most noble job in the world? You will be hearing from me."[52] JUSTICE might seem "insolent" and disrespectful to the chairman during the job interview, but his use of sarcasm allows him to establish control and agency in a painful situation wherein familiar roles have been reversed. Sarcasm disarms his opponent. Interestingly, the play illustrates that the youth are able to assert power and demonstrate intelligence through subversive use of sarcasm. It is then ironic that JUSTICE will emerge as a spy for the very government he criticizes.

A verbal exchange between the chairman/FREEDOM and his secretary/LIBERTY also reveals the commodification of women in the job market. Forgetting about the long line of job candidates waiting eagerly outside his door, the chairman carries on flirting shamelessly with his secretary. In response, the secretary/LIBERTY defiantly retorts, "I'm just being a good product. Yours!"[53] She then censures EQUALITY, the first woman to come in for a job interview, for using her sexuality to stand out from all the other applicants, in effect calling attention to the role women are forced to play in struggling economic times. When asked about her vision for the job, EQUALITY replies, "I'll serve at the pleasure and design of the president. . . . So long as I have the job."[54] The scene highlights the impact of the global economy on marginalized groups in society, and this is especially true of women. Amkpa Awam points out that gender roles and gender relationships form an important facet of Onwueme's social commentary: "From her location as a woman in an inter-modernist landscape, Onwueme injects the social significance of her sex into discourses of postcolonial desire by highlighting an intra-modernist crisis over gender roles and expectations in post-imperial Nigeria."[55] This is clearly addressed through Onwueme's exploration of the ways in which the new economy has affected the process of identity construction in Nigerian women. This particular scene from *No Vacancy* suggests that the commodification of women in the workplace is critical to the understanding of sexual politics in patriarchal society, thus affirming the author's view. Such a conception resonates with Western feminists who have theorized that women are powerless victims exchanged between men. In her essay "Women on the Market," Luce Irigaray notes: "All the systems of exchange that organize patriarchal societies . . . are men's business. The production of women, signs and commodities is always referred back to men, and they always pass from one man to another. . . . The workforce is thus always assumed to be masculine."[56] This idea is also espoused in Marxist ideology, which argues that women are products of exchange in the masculine and patriarchal economy of capitalism.[57] In Onwueme's play, however, women are not defenseless victims, but strong-willed resisters who are engaged in a revolution to change the system.

The last two acts of the play stage the fierce resistance of the unemployed in their attempt to overthrow Big Brother. Their protests are met with a harsh crackdown by FAITH, the army officer who opens fire on them, then handcuffs and denounces them as terrorists. In the last encounter, the actors are all shocked by JUSTICE's change of identity and betrayal when he joins FAITH in shooting at the protesters. JUSTICE apologizes to his fellow activists, with whom he plots to ambush Big Brother and oust him from power. In the end, JUSTICE dies in the ambush. His fellow activists, by now armed, topple Big Brother and take over "strategic positions."[58] In a sense, his death signals the fact that he has redeemed himself.

What is most interesting about the play is the author's assertion that, in the end, ideas triumph despite the despotism of nation-state leaders and their henchmen. Here, EQUALITY mocks the agents of totalitarianism, who are incapable of killing "ideas": "Eternal fools. You lock us up. Kill. And kill . . . me . . . us. . . . But do you think you can stop . . . kill an idea? And lock it up? Come. . . . Arrest my Mind. But know this, what you seek to arrest is a potent seed. Winged seed."[59] Clearly, giving characters in the play broad, ideological names emphasizes this point. The characters insist on "Life for Life."[60] For Onwueme, ideas live on through history, while art serves the masses in their struggle to overcome their oppressors. Ultimately, it is art and the imagination that prevail over despotic power. Thus, art and acting become crucial components of revolution.

NOTES

1. Chris Dunton, *Make Man Talk True: Nigerian Drama in English since 1970* (London: Hans Zell Publishers, 1992), 95.

2. Iniobong Uko, *Gender and Identity in the Work of Osonye Tess Onwueme* (Trenton, NJ: African World Press, 2004), 240.

3. In his essay "Drama and Theater in Nigeria after Soyinka: Trend, Focus and Development," Stephen Inegbe leads off with "In Nigeria, theatre is a reflection of life." He then concentrates on the years after Soyinka: "Wole Soyinka, no doubt, is a master of his art. . . . Since Soyinka, major playwrights and theatre practitioners whose work cannot just be wished away, have emerged." Stephen Inegbe, "Drama and Theater in Nigeria after Soyinka: Trend, Focus and Development," *Africa e Mediterrano* 4, no. 3 (2007): 46, http://www.africaemediterraneo.it/articoli/art_enegbe_4_03.doc (accessed December 15, 2009).

4. Iniobong Uko, *Gender and Identity*, 221.

5. Nelson Fashina, "Alienation and Revolutionary Vision in East African Postcolonial Dramatic Literature," *Ufahamu: A Journal of African Studies* 35, no. 2 (2009): 3–4, http://escholarship.org/uc/item/63k8d46k (accessed December 1, 2009).

6. Information regarding the production of *No Vacancy* was provided to me by Tess Onwueme in email correspondence, May 11, 2010.

7. Olu Obafemi, "Towards Feminist Aesthetics in Nigerian Drama: The Plays of Tess Onwueme," in *Critical Theory & African Literature Today*, eds. Eldred Durosimi Jones, Eustace Palmer, and Marjorie Jones (Trenton, NJ: Africa World Press, 1994), 88.

8. Iniobong Uko, *Gender and Identity*, 237.

9. Jean Paul Sarte, *No Exit and Three Other Plays*, trans. Abel Lionel (New York: Vintage International, 1989), 334. See also *Huis clos, suivi de les mouches* (French Edition).

10. Tess Onwueme, *No Vacancy* (Trenton, NJ: Africa World Press, 2005), 32.

11. Iniobong Uko, *Gender and Identity*, 61.

12. Maureen Eke, "Introduction," in *What Mama Said* (Detroit: Wayne State University Press, 2003), 10.

13. Tess Onwueme, *No Vacancy*, 6.

14. For more information about Orwell's use of Big Brother in *1984*, refer to http://en.wikipedia.org/wiki/Big_Brother_(1984).

15. Tess Onwueme, *No Vacancy*, 61.

16. Ibid.

17. Amiri Baraka, "Black Revolutionary Theater," in *The Norton Anthology of African-American Literature*, ed. Henry Louis Gates, Jr. and Nellie Y. McKay (New York: Norton, 1997), 1899.

18. Tess Onwueme, *No Vacancy*, 68–69.

19. Ibid., 24.

20. Ibid., 29.

21. Ibid., 35.

22. Ibid., 68.

23. Iniobong Uko, *Gender and Identity*, 240.

24. Tess Onwueme, *No Vacancy*, 67.

25. Ibid., 63.

26. Ibid.

27. Ibid., 64.

28. Ibid., 67.

29. Ibid.

30. Ola Rotimi, *Hopes of the Living Dead: A Drama of Struggle* (Ibadan, Nigeria: Spectrum Books, 1988), ix.

31. Tess Onwueme, *No Vacancy*, 7.

32. Ibid., 23.

33. Amkpa Awam, *Theater and Postcolonial Desires* (London: Routledge, 2004), 10.

34. Tess Onwueme, *No Vacancy*, 52.

35. Ibid., 18–19.

36. Zygmunt Bauman, *Wasted Lives: Modernity and Its Outcasts* (Oxford: Blackwell Publishing LTD, 2004), 128.
37. Ibid., 11.
38. Tess Onwueme, *No Vacancy*, 18.
39. Ibid., 10.
40. Ibid.
41. Ibid.
42. Ibid.
43. Ibid., 11.
44. Ibid., 15.
45. Ibid., 17.
46. Ibid.
47. Ibid., 22.
48. Ibid., 27.
49. Ibid., 29.
50. Ibid., 52.
51. Ibid., 56–57.
52. Ibid., 57.
53. Ibid., 58.
54. Ibid., 49–50.
55. Amkpa Awam, *Theater and Postcolonial Desires*, 63.
56. Luce Irigaray, "Women on the Market," in *This Sex Which is Not One*, trans. Catherine Porter (Ithaca, NY: Cornell University Press, 1985), 177.
57. Using materialist analysis, Marxist feminists such as Heidi Hartmann and Christine Dephy have explored the connection between capitalism and patriarchy in the structuring of labor markets. Christine Delphy, *Close to Home: A Materialist Analysis of Women's Oppression* (London: Hutchinson, 1984); and Heidi Hartmann, "Capitalism, Patriarchy and Job Segregation by Sex," in *Signs*, 1, no. 3 (1976): 137–168.
58. Tess Onwueme, *No Vacancy*, 92.
59. Ibid., 88.
60. Ibid.

III

Reflections on Islam, Identity, and Gender

Chapter Seven

Islam, Gender, and Identity in Leila Abouzeid's *The Last Chapter*

A Postcolonial Critique

Leila Abouzeid is one of the most prominent Moroccan novelists to emerge in the postindependence period. Chronologically, she is situated between Assia Djebar and Malika Oufkir. Both Abouzeid and Oufkir are known outside Morocco, and their work has been translated into English and other languages. Compared to Oufkir, whose long imprisonment turned her into an activist for human rights, Leila Abouzeid, though very critical of the corruption rampant in Moroccan society, remained largely silent on delicate topics such as the Moroccan monarchy. Her more modest class also kept her virtually unknown in elite circles. Abouzeid's work was introduced to American audiences thanks to feminist scholar Elizabeth Fernea (University of Texas, Austin), who had Abouzeid's novels translated and did a great deal to promote her work. Abouzeid's much-acclaimed novel *Year of the Elephant* would not have been known in the West if Fernea had not helped get it translated it into English.

Increasingly, thanks to Abouzeid's lead, Moroccan women have presented their versions of Morocco to the world in literature and cinema. Abouzeid's novels are available in English, Arabic, and twenty other languages. Born in Rabat in 1950, she benefited from the politics promoted by male nationalists who called for women's emancipation in terms of education and job opportunities. In tracing the history of Moroccan feminism, Fatima Sadiqi points out that Abouzeid is among "the first liberal feminists who embraced modern ideas and practices without rejecting their local specificities, including being Muslim."[1] The writings of these feminists appeared in journalism, sociology, and various literary genres. Among emerging Moroccan postcolonial writers, Leila Abouzeid is distinctive, not only because of her gender but also for her political positions. While in her works she offers the same critique of colonialism and nationalism expressed by other writers of her generation, such as Khnata Bennouna, Driss Chraibi, Ahmed Sefroui, and Tahar Ben Jelloun, she nuances her reading of Moroccan culture as she reflects on the complexity of her identity as both a woman and a Moroccan. Like other Moroccan women, Abouzeid too faces challenges, for while she is obliged to rebel, she also wants to retain ties to her Arab Muslim heritage.

Within postcolonial criticism and cultural studies, understanding Moroccan literature sensitively requires attention to history and context. In her novel *The Last Chapter*, Leila Abouzeid positions herself within the context of Islam, modernity, and Morocco's postcolonial politics. The novel, which draws attention to the intersections of gender, nationality, religion, and language, centers on a middle-aged, unmarried Moroccan Muslim woman named Aicha, who, through a series of flashbacks and anecdotes, relates her failed relationships with Moroccan men. These men play different roles in her life—as national leaders, employers, suitors, or lovers. After a string of failed relationships and broken promises, Aicha realizes that she has had enough and decides to retreat from society. In assessing her identity and re-evaluating her own life, the protagonist stresses her self-determination and need to establish her independence without compromising her sense of cultural identity. Through Aicha's story, Abouzeid illustrates the difficult lives of Moroccan women in postindependence Morocco. She also characterizes and contrasts educated and religious men and their fragmented and inauthentic identities. The story of gender relationships unfolds, not insignificantly, within the context of both secularism and Islam in present-day Morocco. Scenes resonate with bitter ironies from the background presence of educated and religious men who lack coherent identity and authenticity; there are various overtones and undertones of superstition grounded in the neuroses of victimized women. In a further twist, both men and women credit witchcraft with either fostering or severing love relationships. The novel also establishes a hierarchy of narrative voices that challenge the prevailing patriarchal ideology and problematize individual and political identities. Abouzeid's allegory exposes the failure of postindependence Morocco to emancipate women and to establish national independence. This postindependent patriarchal ideology, touted as authentic national and religious identity, can also be considered as a misrepresentation. The novel, a narrative based on the struggles of women, men's crisis of identity, and Morocco's sociopolitical and religious upheaval during the year following independence, suggests alternative views.

THE POLITICS OF LANGUAGE

The novel draws attention to the question of language choices for Moroccan writing, actively engaging in the hotly disputed topic of the language of the postcolonial writer. Unlike those of her generation who write in French, the predominant Western language of choice since independence, Abouzeid chooses to write in Arabic and English instead. In the Afterword of her novel *The Last Chapter*, she explains:

> I was in a private school in Rabat where Arabic and French were the languages of instruction. I loathed reading in French and developed an aversion to using it outside the classroom. . . . My intense aversion toward French may explain why I turned to English as my means of communication with the West.[2]

Abouzeid criticizes other Maghrebian writers for writing in French, the language of the former colonizer. In an interview, she asserts: "When a Moroccan writes in French, he writes for France and he must comply with what it understands and what pleases it. He must maintain its preconceived images about Moroccans."[3] However, Abouzeid's claim does not apply to today's writers in Morocco, who use French to write for Moroccans, publish books, and reside in Morocco. Valerie Orlando's work on emerging Francophone women writers backs this claim.[4] While some critics might view Abouzeid's embrace of English and rejection of French as an anomaly, there is no contradiction in what she says about languages. She turns away from French because in Morocco it was the language of domination, one synonymous with colonialism and in which that colonial experience remains embedded. French colonial education, initially established to serve the colonial bureaucracy, contributes to a sense of crisis in Abouzeid's novels. The author suggests that colonial education has led to fragmentation and a sense of alienation at both personal and national levels. The younger generations of Moroccan writers would totally contradict this idea because such schizophrenia for them is merely polyglotism. While Abouzeid displays an indifference toward French, other Moroccan writers like Abdelkébir Khatibi drew inspiration from the very resistance offered by the French language. In his book *Maghreb Pluriel*, Khatibi negates the mythical image of a French colonial Maghreb by foregrounding the cultural plurality of the region, where identity has no essence and thus cannot be homogeneously represented.[5] Khatibi views bilingual writing in the Maghreb as an act of translation, what he characterizes as "speaking in tongues" as the mother tongue is ever-present in the French language.[6]

Abouzeid, on the other hand, believes that Moroccan languages, and the French colonial language, are two separate entities: "Morocco existed before 1956 as a nation, with all that entails, including literature—both in oral and written form in the languages of the people: Tamazight and Arabic."[7] For her, the fact that her Arabic novel *Year of the Elephant* has been translated into twenty-two languages shows that Moroccan writers no longer need to write in French with the purpose of reaching out to a wider audience.[8] In the same interview, Abouzeid commends Khnata Bennouna for being the first Moroccan woman writer to write in Arabic in the 1960s.[9]

The Last Chapter was originally written in Arabic and then translated into English. This form of presentation has enabled the author to distance herself from the alleged Eurocentrism of the pioneering Francophone generation of educated Moroccans. English too was a language of empire, but not of the empire that imposed itself on the culture where Abouzeid was born and raised. Ian Munro rightly points out that Abouzeid's "use of English is the product not of foreign mentorship, but of an autonomous choice of a global language in contest with a dominant Francophone literary tradition that is in decline."[10] For her own expression, Abouzeid uses Arabic, a language she venerates and claims as part of her Arab heritage. She also turned to English, as she insists, as her means of communicating with the West, and she found congenial translators with whom to collaborate and upon whom she could rely. She thereby enhanced her understanding of how her work would be received by English readers worldwide, whom she would in effect be instructing.

FEMINIST POLITICS

During the 1970s, when Abouzeid began her career as a writer, promises of women's liberation were not delivered, despite King Mohammed V's earlier gesture to urban women, allowing them to relinquish the veil and work outside their homes. His notable act in 1954, liberating women when he unveiled his daughter Lala Aicha in public, was soon lost with the increased power of the Ulema under the leadership of Hassan II, who enacted oppressive family laws in the 1960s. In the first decade following Morocco's independence from the French in 1956, the nationalists encouraged women's emancipation, and their efforts to educate them radically changed the status of women. Despite women's accomplishments during this period, the family law drafted by the Ulema reflected the autocratic monarchy's rule and set women back almost fifty years.

Leila Abouzeid confronts such "masculinist politics" in postindependence Morocco as well as the secular practices that misread Islam in the name of modernity. While her novel steers clear of contemporary Moroccan women's campaigning for gender rights and justice, it clearly hints at how masculinist politics, which are reinforced by secular and religious practices, impinge on the lives of women. In her essay "Feminism, Islam and the Modern Moroccan Woman in the Works of Leila Abouzeid," Eva Hunter argues that unlike Fatima Mernissi and Nawal Saadawi, Abouzeid does not outright denounce the patriarchal politics of postindependence Morocco.[11] Hunter attributes Abouzeid's muted critique to her strategic alliance with Muslims against American imperialism.[12] Nevertheless, the fact that Abouzeid does not discuss Islamic fundamentalism and current global events like terrorism, and the fact that she defines herself as a nonfeminist, does not necessarily imply anti-Americanism on her part. At the beginning of her career, when she chose to write under a male name, Abouzeid did not begin by denouncing her country's overbearing patriarchal politics. Professing not to be a feminist, the author fashioned her own strategies for accomplishing her aims.

During my interview with Abouzeid at the African Literature Association conference in 1999, she insisted that she is not a feminist in the Western sense because of her conviction that Islam embodies equal gender rights and freedom for women.[13] To avoid being pigeonholed, or linked with a particular movement, she stresses her overlapping memberships and her integrationist approach, especially to pressures that divide and stratify. She insists on her specific identities and may rightly prefer not to be fitted into compartments. Abouzeid positions herself as a "modern Moroccan woman," and at the same time rejects secularism as foreign to her culture.[14] As a modern Muslim woman, within the contexts of Islam, feminism, modernity, and postcolonial politics, she may prefer not to be identified with particular "leaders" of a "movement," nor have her views compromised by what a movement's membership calls for.[15]

ABOUZEID'S VIEWPOINT ON ISLAM AND SECULARISM

In *The Last Chapter*, Leila Abouzeid critiques the distorted version of Islam practiced in Moroccan society. She believes that change in Morocco requires a corresponding transformation in religious thought to make Islam more relevant to society. Critical of Muslim tradition that is enmeshed in backward superstition and patriarchy, she laments that some Moroccans have lost touch with their authentic Muslim heritage. In fact, she sees relationships between Moroccans—both men and women—as sometimes being held together only by eccentricities like witchcraft. The author uses her character Um Hani to curse religious men for their dishonesty:

> This is what they do then, toying with people's lives. And when God strikes them with drought they pull on their djellabas and throng through the streets, calling: "O God, provide your servants . . . with rain!" . . . May He provide you with a rain of locusts, you hypocrites! You men who are not men at all![16]

Here, the author derides the masculine model of traditional Islam as being based on duplicity. For her, the major problem in Morocco is a decaying Muslim civilization. Inherited religious and cultural customs must give way to more rational attitudes, but the narrator sees little hope for positive change: "We're Muslims by birth, nothing more. . . . When Musa Ibn Nussair . . . . presented Islam to the people, they said, 'we'll think about it.'"[17]

The author also discovers in colonialism the roots of the corruption and symbolic violence that characterizes life in today's Morocco. Upon her visit to Granada, Spain, a study of history enables Aicha, the narrator-protagonist, to understand that despite official declarations of goodwill toward the colonized, colonization undeniably means the exploitation of people's lands and resources, as well as the imposition of another language and culture in the name of education.[18] Worse, political independence does not initiate a new era; rather, it marks the start of corruption and violence. Abouzeid sees the sham religious and political systems as leading to the disintegration of Moroccan society. Her views regarding the sociopolitical climate of her homeland may seem very pessimistic, but they are relevant to the attitudes of other African writers such as Chinua Achebe, Wole Soyinka, Ama Ata Aidoo, and others who likewise address the problem of corruption in newly independent African countries. But while the views of these writers are at least sympathetic, Abouzeid's views are full of contempt and hopelessness.

The author also condemns the Moroccan secular tradition that equates modernity and notions of human freedom and progress with the West and being Western. While the novel does not refer to specific dates, it alludes to the colonial years as well as the years following independence, when there was still a strong French presence in the country. That the novel includes a speech by a nationalist leader who bears an unmistakable resemblance to the secularist Istiqlal party leader, Allal El Fassi (1910–1974), further confirms the timeframe. The author sees that universalist and secularist ideologies that the nationalists absorbed from their French colonial education are in fact complicit in the production of the exclusions and divisions in today's Morocco. Being that there has never really been a "secular" time period in Morocco, Abouzeid's reference here points to the French secular influence on Moroccans. Her novel was published in the post-9/11 era when terms such as secularism, Islam, and postcolonialism acquired new meanings. In the wake of September 11, Abouzeid feels the urge to problematize the secular tradition as inherited from Europe. Along the same lines, postcolonial critics such as Homi Bhabha have cautioned: "[The] trouble with concepts like . . . secularism is that we think we understand them too well. These are ideas that are increasingly complicit with a self-reflective claim to a culture of modernity whether it is held by the elites of the East and West, or the North and South."[19] Bhabha argues that concepts like secularism are "immediately and accurately recognizable as belonging to the European enlightenment."[20]

Therefore, it seems important "to consider them in relation to the colonial and imperial enterprise which was an integral part of that same enlightenment."[21] Similarly, Leila Abouzeid believes that such Western values and ideals are embedded in the colonial genealogy of secularism that has produced divisions between the different groups in Moroccan society.

The novel points not only to gender divisions but also to the racist assumption during the colonial period that there is an irreducible difference between the French and Moroccans. In this sense, the colonizer's values of modernization become synonymous with an entrenching sense of ethnocentrism and Eurocentrism. In reminiscing about her early school years, Aicha recalls the French teacher Mademoiselle Doze who assumes an attitude of superiority toward her Moroccan students and insults anyone who does not conform to her Eurocentric view of civilization.[22] Thus, through Aicha's teacher, the author implies that the colonizer's values include an assumed monopoly on "civilization." Colonialism, for Abouzeid, intensified racial divisions not only between the French and Moroccans, but also between Arabs and Berbers. Through the character of Salim, Aicha's former classmate who insists on identifying himself as Berber, the novel also hints at these internal divisions and the "divide and rule" colonial policy which fostered such divisions. In his book *Morocco since 1830*, C. R. Pennell points out that the French "divided Arabs from Berbers and assigned to each a series of characteristics that were apparently based on scientific principles but which were really little more than prejudices that justified colonial methods and created a hierarchy of local populations."[23] Berbers became targets of the colonizer's assimilation policy on the basis of their difference from Arabs. For Abouzeid, the secularism Salim inherited from his French education is to blame for his self-identification as Berber. Her position toward colonial secularism is very clear in her critique of educated Moroccans' overwhelming readiness to use the French language she views as having been thrust upon them by a colonial educational system. Aicha, the narrator-protagonist, questions the identity of educated, secular men she encounters in postcolonial Moroccan society, and she challenges the trade-offs they are making.

ABOUZEID'S PORTRAITS OF MOROCCAN MEN

Aicha, the female protagonist, gains agency as she redefines male identity. As she applies her feminist viewpoint to the construction of male characters, she represents them as given to escape and denial, inadequate in themselves and disappointing to narrator-protagonist Aicha. The first scene in the novel is set in a Moroccan classroom in the early 1960s, a space depicted as a contact zone for both males and females.[24] Most notable here is the lack of gender segregation that Moroccan society demands. Aicha feels overpowered by the dominant number of male colleagues in the same room, at a time when education was exclusively for men. She is introduced as a bitter character, haunted by the persistent segregation that benefits patriarchal institutions: "This is where partition has brought us; to the point where we are two distinct species."[25]

Male characters become allegorical because the author uses them to represent, as well as interrogate, aspects of Morocco as a postcolonial (patriarchal) nation-state. The novel maps out the various ways in which Aicha finds men lacking, distorted, inadequate, and false. Upon reuniting with her high school friends, al-Raddad and Salim, Aicha finds their identities deficient because of their rootlessness. Al-Raddad worries about whether his French "r's" are pronounced correctly, while he makes every effort to comply with the French teacher's "colonialist notions of civilization."[26] He exemplifies the emptiness that postcolonial Moroccan men experience in their quest for identity. After the failure of his American dream, he turns to Islam. His Arabic, however, has "a slight foreign accent."[27] Al-Raddad is characterized as uprooted, refusing to establish a connection to his present situation even when he recounts the sense of abandonment and homelessness he felt in America. Nevertheless, he discovers that the racism that caused his alienation in America ironically exists in Moroccan society too. The novel relates al-Raddad's transformation into a religious Muslim as a form of escape and as a means of evading an authentic identity. Fundamentalist Islam becomes an alternative to his feelings of marginalization. Aicha is shocked by al-Raddad's sudden change: "What a transformation! Could this really be the same sallow wretch who had once planted lies against me?"[28] Al-Raddad is thus bent on finding a reality that is situated elsewhere, as neither America nor Morocco is real to him. His assumed security in fundamentalist Islam accords with a general pattern of escape among some Moroccan youth. While in America, he dreams of his Moroccan past, but when faced with Morocco's reality of corruption and racism, he feels betrayed and disillusioned: "My mother used to say, 'Corruption and adultery aside, Moroccans are highly virtuous.' Meaning of course that we're nothing of the sort."[29] Aligning himself with a "pure" version of Islam nevertheless does nothing to dispel his inner hollowness. To Aicha, al-Raddad's radical change from a secular Muslim to a fundamentalist one is neither genuine nor authentic, but merely an escape into the past in order to deny the present.

Aicha's male friends all indulge in some form of escape or denial, as is also clear in the narrator's story about Salim, with whom she was once involved in a romantic relationship. She depicts Salim as insecure, unstable, and inauthentic, an exact copy of the nationalist leader. Salim mimics every gesture the leader makes, thus losing his sense of authenticity.[30] The author ridicules not only Salim, but also the nationalist leader for his poor Arabic during a speech, wherein he condemns the superstitions that have replaced the religious heritage.[31] Abouzeid does not see such alienation from one's own culture and language as a sign of unity and nationalism. Salim and his nationalist leader perceive progress and education as the type of development that would solve all of Moroccan society's problems. But Salim and the leader, the narrator suggests, are deluded and confused about their own identity. They speak better French than Arabic; when Aicha criticizes Salim for not knowing the Arabic poet Al-Mutanabbi, he replies that Arabic is not his native language, after all, as he is Berber.[32] To the narrator, that Salim identifies himself as Berber, against his Arab Muslim identity, speaks of the lack of social unity that is often the case in postcolonial Morocco. Men like Salim have no fixed values from which they may define their identity, and they have no sense of belonging to their society. This is what explains the failure of Aicha's love relationship with Salim.[33]

Aicha's relationship with another man, Karim, develops later on in the novel. Karim is a Touareg from the Western Sahara who was introduced to Aicha by Isabelle, a European woman who works for an international organization. He too represents the fragmented and displaced personality. Upon meeting him, Aicha tells him that he has been misled by the Polisario and that he should embrace his Moroccan identity.[34] In her interview with Ian Munro, Abouzeid describes Karim as a "Touareg [who] is blue; he has African roots and Spanish roots as well. He represents the relation of Morocco to Africa, its roots, which are African, but we do not realize it?"[35] The narrator represents Karim as a victim of historical and political accidents; thus, he is unable to create an identity for himself. His fragmented personality epitomizes the fragmented reality and disunited structure of Morocco itself. The narrator shows Karim to be paradoxical in his values and ideals. He denounces the disrespectability of Moroccan girls he encounters at the beach and questions whether Morocco is really a true Muslim country. At the same time, he is worried that Aicha is too moral and religious to engage with him in a free sexual relationship. Karim's confusion about religion shows his lack of serious meaning. His contradictory attitudes attest to his inauthenticity and lack of identity. Like the other male characters, Karim indulges in pretenses as a means of escape. He fantasizes about Aicha, makes her fall in love with him, and lures her into visiting him in Spain. She later finds out that he is married to a Spanish woman.

Abouzeid sees these men's inauthenticity, corruption, and lack of identity as arising out of the lack of shared ideals, preventing improvement and development, and thereby stunting growth. While at the Ministry of Interior Affairs, Aicha describes her colleague Benabdellah as the epitome of corruption in today's Morocco. At the center of Aicha's relationship with Benabdellah is the dialectic between sincerity and duplicity. It is in such terms that the conflict between the two must be understood. Aicha is appalled and disappointed by Benabdellah's professional incompetence and lack of integrity. He represents the type of Moroccan who only wants to exploit rather than help build the country. While working as the head of supplies, Benabdellah would steal soap and brooms, and use the office phone for personal calls. To justify his theft, he blames bad administration for robbing ordinary Moroccans and depriving them of their rights.[36]

The narrator observes that Moroccan individualists like Benabdellah work individually for personal gains rather than collectively for societal benefits. Such self-seeking fosters isolation and impedes the growth of a unified society. Benabdellah finds some sort of identity through denial of the present situation, as is clear from his fantasy that Morocco is making progress and that it is no longer in the Third World.[37] His fantasy about development nonetheless remains illusory. The concept of "Third World" itself indicates that he has accepted the racist definition of himself given him by the former colonizers. To Aicha, real progress is feasible only by removing corrupt and incompetent men who occupy many positions of responsibility.[38] Whereas the agents of colonialism were European men, contemporaneously the practitioners of neocolonialist patriarchal ideology are Moroccan men who preclude women's full participation despite their education and qualifications. Benabdellah forces Aicha to resign from her job, proof of his own incompetence and disempowerment.

THE PATHS OF FEMALE CHARACTERS

The novel interrelates men's corruption, problematic self-conceptions, secularism, and Islam with the difficult lives of Moroccan women. At the very outset, a female classmate is represented as a source of anxiety and fear for the protagonist: "I am not suggesting that male society is evil and female society is good . . . if woman has an enemy it is other women."[39] The reader's sympathies here are confused, and the ironies are rich and subversive. Certainly, the novel does not reveal a simplistic dichotomy that pits women against men as it also delves into the nature of conflicts and divisions that exist between women in postindependence Morocco. Female characters in the novel are also conflicted in themselves. Abouzeid's critique is accomplished through her protagonist Aicha, who attributes the failure of her romantic relationships to jealous women who use witchcraft as their only "trump card." Her series of failed relationships with young, educated men lead her to wonder whether fulfillment is at all possible for single women. Aspiring to "have it all," like privileged women worldwide, she expresses disappointment in an unsupportive and corrupt culture where men and women betray each other and where images of true love are very rare.

The author introduces female characters from different social backgrounds such as Aicha, the intellectual single woman, Um Hani, the married woman who is a former schoolmate of Aisha's, and a bourgeois elite woman named Latifa. Following the trajectory of each one of these female characters makes us presume that Abouzeid is trying to illustrate the extreme difficulty, maybe even the impossibility, of women's independence in Morocco. To show these characters as happy and fulfilled would not be in tune with Abouzeid's goal: revealing painful truths about her female characters. While Abouzeid herself is a politically engaged writer striving to promote emancipation and liberation of Moroccan women, her female characters engage in simultaneous rebellion and submission to men and patriarchy.

The narrator's patriarchal figures illustrate the repressive and oppressive structure of patriarchal Moroccan society, which makes life hard for women. Through Latifa's story, the novel gives precedence to the father-daughter configuration in which the father is violent and abusive. Latifa, one of Aicha's female classmates, belongs to a rich, bourgeois Fassi family. Fassis, the original inhabitants of Fez, represent wealth and prestige in Moroccan society. They receive favors and occupy elite positions in business and politics.[40] Latifa is introduced as a rebellious young woman who smoked cigarettes and wore provocative clothes.[41] She also undermined the patriarchal Moroccan standard through her romantic marriage to a Frenchman, thus opting for freely chosen love over the constraints of aristocratic patriarchal marriage. Her father, a corrupt feudalist, whose socialist opponents accused him of exploiting small landowners,[42] will later disown her for marrying a Frenchman. Latifa challenged her father and dared take him to court, but she lost the case. The narrator charts Latifa's tragic story and ultimate destitution following her divorce from the Frenchman. Although her initial freedom of choice may be construed as signaling her resistance to the pressure to conform to societal expectations, her choice to become a belly dancer implicates her in the very patriarchal ideology she appears to be resisting. While Latifa's story offers an alternative to marriage, it fails to account for women who, although free to choose, are no more socioeconomically free than the women constrained by contracted marriages. In her interview with Ian Munro, Abouzeid explains that the reason she ends Latifa's story in *The Last Chapter* with a quote from the *Arabian Nights* is to establish "a link with the past, between modern Arabic literature and ancient Arabic literature, to say that not much has been changed for women, to say that this story could have been a part of the *Arabian Nights*."[43]

Aicha revisits her own experience with parental authority during her interview with Susan, who was conducting research on Moroccan marriages. The father imposes his will on Aicha when he forces her to reject the proposal from a civil servant, because he wants her to marry someone from his village. Aicha, the intellectual, has long severed her ties with patriarchy, but has not managed yet to disengage herself from her own father's authority. Her sense of duty to him forces her to obey his orders: "My supposed freedom from illiteracy . . . the veil was . . . an illusion. I still had a chain around my neck."[44] Aicha describes her father as a secular intellectual who does not fit in the normative behavior of an intellectual; he is depicted as the antithesis of what an intellectual is imagined to be. Our male intellectuals, she says, love to express their liberal views in public forums and discussions, while in the private sphere of their homes they are nothing more than dictators and tyrants.[45] Her father's pretence does not live up to the intellectuals' ideals of democracy and freedom of choice. Aicha excuses her deference to him by telling Susan that "compliance is a little different than submission."[46] Aicha's mother remains complaisant even as her daughter seeks her support: "She couldn't stand up to him. He did what he liked."[47] Apart from her father's overbearing image, the narrator also dwells on his weak and duplicitous nature when she refers to his polygamous marriage to another woman in Marrakech.

Toward the end of the novel, the author introduces Um Hani, who contrasts with Aicha and represents a crucially important aspect of the novel. Um Hani is a Moroccan alter-ego of Aicha. The author/narrator here recreates herself as an oppressed Moroccan woman victimized through marriage to a Faqih. This doubling process in *The Last Chapter* occurs twice, first as a metamorphosis of author Leila Abouzeid into Aicha, and then of Aicha into Um Hani. Thus, the narrator-protagonist, as metamorphosed into Um Hani, is now in identity crisis, oppressed as a common Moroccan woman: "I got married to a faqih and I traded in my modern wardrobe for a djellaba."[48] Significant here is also the intimacy of the first-person narrative, whereby Um Hani traces her emotions and psychological traumas with detailed precision. Abouzeid clarifies the relationship between Aicha and Um Hani when she explains that both were in the same school. But while Um Hani knew Aicha and admired her for her intelligence from a distance, Aicha did not get to know Um Hani. Abouzeid further explains that she used Um Hani's story as a counterpoint to Aicha's. Here Um Hani's traditional life does not mark the author's generation of educated women who have broken away from tradition itself.[49] Nevertheless, Um Hani has vision enough to see into her predicament. She reproaches herself for marrying the Faqih, who she thought to be "someone with a special knowledge of God's Book . . . but [she] discovered otherwise."[50]

Um Hani also realizes that her husband resorts to witchcraft and has cast spells on pictures that belong to Aicha. The Faqih worked for both a man named Muhammed, who never wanted Aicha to marry, and for another client named Slimane, who wanted Aicha to love him. Commenting on the Faqih's immoral and duplicitous behavior, Abouzeid states: "[The Faqih] is using people's lives to earn money, like eating bread that is dipped in blood. The sorcerer is supposed to be a Muslim—but . . . people have gotten away from religion."[51] In fact, the author does not put forth any positive views of religious men. It would seem then that she does not really hold any hope for men at all—secular, religious, or agnostic. The narrator's disappointment with men leads her to reject marriage altogether. Abouzeid's novel thus betrays a negative view of marriage, depicting it as oppressive and constraining. This becomes clear from Aicha's brief encounter with an old Moroccan woman at the airport:

> An older woman sat next to me in the airport. . . . She was observing an old couple. The man was holding his wife's arm and carrying her coat. They were foreigners, most likely Europeans. "Look at that," sighed my companion, "they could be friends. . . . Have you ever seen a Moroccan couple their age looking like that?"[52]

As she confronts issues of marriage, Aicha toys with ideas of the liberated West, traditional Morocco, and dishonest Moroccan men: "Husbands in our country are born with an instinct for betrayal. . . . Meanwhile, we jump to ostracize a woman guilty of the slightest transgression."[53] By pointing to the harmonious foreign couple, Aicha is tempted to look at marriage in cultures different from her own. Is she rejecting Moroccan men as objects of ideal relationships? Is she advocating turning to Western men instead? If she is, then how can she do that without colluding with Western ethnocentrism? Third World feminists like Chandra Mohanty have pointed out that one postcolonial feminist task is to critique universalizing Western models of women's liberation that are dependent on modernist assumptions about individualism and progress.[54] What follows then, is the question of whether non-Western women are obliged to appropriate Western modernity (secularism) to critique tradition and patriarchy. This is a tempting but unsatisfactory prospect in light of Moroccan history, demographics, and possibilities.

In the final chapters of the book, Aicha, an intelligent and educated woman, resists being a victim of either the patriarchy of Islam or a secular colonial tradition that treats women as second-class citizens and renders them economically and politically powerless. Highlighting the difficult lives of Moroccan women, the narrator discloses to the reader why she has refused marriage thus far. She seeks fulfillment beyond the role of homebound wife and therefore inevitably enmeshes herself within the larger identity politics of modernity. Here, Abouzeid joins other Moroccan intellectuals like Abdullah El Aroui and Mohammed El Jabri, who argue that Islam is compatible with a modern style of life. Mohammed El Jabri insists that concepts like democracy and human rights are not linked to the Western tradition alone. They are rather a product of modernity, the same modernity in which the Muslim world participates.[55] She also joins Moroccan feminists like Fatima

Mernissi who have resorted to *Ijtihad* and the reinterpretation of Muslim law to show that Islam in its original message guarantees gender equal rights.[56] Like Mernissi, Abouzeid, in her novel *The Last Chapter*, protests the archaic traditions that have corrupted and distorted the basic principles of Islam and its core of liberal, universalist beliefs. Hers and her protagonist's dilemmas will only be resolved in a more authentic Islam wedded to a modern, more fully realized Morocco. This resolution can serve as a model in other contemporary Arab societies. In sum, the novel advocates for an authentic, original Islam for a modern Morocco. Abouzeid's double critique is very insightful for the understanding it provides, not only for Morocco but also for postcolonial Arab societies in general. In English and other languages, it exhibits alternatives useful elsewhere in the world.

NOTES

1. Fatima Sadiqi, "Feminization of Public Space: Women's Activism, the Family Law and Social Change in Morocco," *Journal of Middle East Women's Studies* 2 no. 2 (2006): 15.
2. Leila Abouzeid, "Afterword," *The Last Chapter*, trans. John Liechety (Cairo: American University Press, 2003), 154.
3. Michael Hall, "Leila Abouzeid's *Year of the Elephant*: A Postcolonial Reading," *Women: A Cultural Review* 6, no. 1 (1995): 70.
4. In her rejection of French, Abouzeid does not connect with any of the younger writers writing in French, like Houria Boussejra and Siham Benchekroun, who do not care about France or colonialism but have nevertheless chosen to write in French simply because they like the language. For a list of names of these young authors, and to get an idea of who they are, refer to Valérie Orlando, *Francophone Voices of the New Morocco in Film and Print: (Re)presentations of a Society in Transition* (New York: Palgrave Macmillan, 2009).
5. Abdelkébir Khatibi, "Double Criticism: The Decolonization of Arab Sociology," in *Contemporary North Africa: Issues of Development and Integration*, ed. Halim Barakat (Washington, DC: Center for Contemporary Arab Studies, 1985), 9–19.
6. Ibid., 186.
7. Leila Abouzeid, "Interview with Leila Abouzeid for the Revised Edition," in *Year of the Elephant: A Moroccan Woman's Journey toward Independence*, trans. Barbara Parmenter (Austin: University of Texas Press, 2009), 124.
8. Ibid.
9. Ibid., 123.
10. Ian Munro, "Interview with Leila Abouzeid, Moroccan Writer," *Journal of Commonwealth and Postcolonial Studies* 10, no. 2 (2004): 3.
11. Eva Hunter, "Feminism, Islam and the Modern Moroccan Woman in the Works of Leila Abouzeid," *African Studies* 65, no. 2 (2006): 139–155.
12. Ibid., 139.
13. Disputing the common claim that feminism is a Western phenomenon and that Islam and feminism are incompatible, Abouzeid notes that "Muslim women do not have to look to the Western tradition to promote gender justice. Women's rights have always been an integral part of Arab and Muslim discourses." Touria Khannous and Soraya Mekerta, Interview with Leila Abouzeid, African Literature Association Conference, Fes, Morocco, May 1999. Unpublished.
14. Eva Hunter, "Feminism," 141.
15. Critics of Abouzeid have wondered why Muslim women who are outstandingly successful in a world dominated by men take such a position, and how their views relate to the religion in which they were reared and to which they remain attached. Abouzeid knows a great deal about the history of Islam and does not wish to be the target of assumptions made by those not

well informed about the extent of her knowledge. Furthermore, "her" Islam may not be the Islam of today's front pages in Al-Jazeera, *Le Monde*, or the *New York Times*. Abouzeid explains that it is historical conditions that have limited the possibility of actualizing women's liberation in Muslim societies. Touria Khannous and Soraya Mekerta, "Interview."

16. Leila Abouzeid, *The Last Chapter*, trans. John Liechety (Cairo: American University Press, 2003), 151.
17. Ibid., 19.
18. Ibid., 121.
19. Homi K. Bhabha, "On Subaltern Secularism," *Journal* 6 (1995): 5–7, http://waf.gn.apc.org/journal6p5.html (accessed October 20, 2008).
20. Ibid., 7.
21. Ibid.
22. Leila Abouzeid, *Last Chapter*, 6.
23. C. R. Pennell, *Morocco since 1830* (New York: New York University Press, 2000), 159.
24. "Contact zone" is a term coined by Mary Louise Pratt in her book *Imperial Eyes: Travel Writing and Transculturation*. The concept of contact zone suggests "copresence and interaction" even from "within radically asymmetrical relations of power." See Mary Louise Pratt, *Imperial Eyes: Travel Writing and Transculturation* (New York: Routledge, 2008[1992]), 8.
25. Leila Abouzeid, *Last Chapter*, 2.
26. Ibid., 6.
27. Ibid., 20.
28. Ibid.
29. Ibid., 19–20.
30. Ibid., 31.
31. Ibid., 33.
32. Ibid., 24.
33. Ibid., 27.
34. Ibid., 89.
35. Ian Munro, "Interview," 13.
36. Leila Abouzeid, *Last Chapter*, 79.
37. Ibid., 80.
38. Ibid.
39. Ibid., 3.
40. Rachel Newcomb, *Women of Fes: Ambiguities of Urban Life in Morocco* (Philadelphia: University of Pennsylvania Press, 2009), 18.
41. Ibid., 9.
42. Ibid., 7.
43. Ian Munro, "Interview," 11.
44. Leila Abouzeid, *Last Chapter*, 51.
45. Ibid.
46. Ibid., 53.
47. Ibid., 52.
48. Leila Abouzeid, *Last Chapter*, 131.
49. Ian Munro, "Interview," 13.
50. Leila Abouzeid, *Last Chapter*, 131.
51. Ian Munro, "Interview," 14.
52. Leila Abouzeid, *Last Chapter*, 28.
53. Ibid.
54. Chandra T. Mohanty, "Under Western Eyes: Feminist Scholarship and Colonial Discourses," in *Third World Women and the Politics of Feminism*, ed. Chandra Mohanty, Ann Russo and Lourde Torres (Bloomington: Indiana University Press, 1991).
55. Abed Mohammed Al Jabri, *Democracy, Human Rights and Law in Islamic Thought* (New York: L. B. Tauris Publishers, 2008).
56. Fatima Mernissi, *The Veil and the Male Elite: A Feminist Interpretation of Women's Rights in Islam*, trans. Mary Jo Lakeland (Reading, MA: Addison-Wesley, 1991).

Chapter Eight

Strategies of Representation and Post/colonial Identity in Farida Benlyazid's *Door to the Sky* and Moufida Tlatli's *Silences of the Palace*

North African women filmmakers like Assia Djebar (Algeria), Moufida Tlatli (Tunisia), and Farida Benlyazid (Morocco) have been involved in independent filmmaking over the last forty years. Their groundbreaking work has influenced more recent women filmmakers, among them Leila Merrakchi. However, no matter the generation, these women still have to function in a very male-dominated cinematic arena, and as a result, their work has often been ignored and poorly distributed. My aim in this chapter is to highlight another aspect of postcolonial North African cinema by offering an analysis of two films: *Samt Al Kusur* (*Silences of the Palace*) (1994) by Tunisian director Moufida Tlatli and *Bab Sma Maftouh* (*Door to the Sky*) (1988) by Moroccan director Farida Benlyazid. In their films, Tlatli and Benlyazid provide audiences with their own representations of women in colonial and postcolonial culture in North Africa. Their films offer perspectives on North African history and women's agency different from those evident in Assia Djebar's *La Nouba*. Unlike *La Nouba*, which foregrounds Algerian women's voices and the active role they played during the Franco-Algerian revolution, Tlatli's film emphasizes women's strategies of resistance against silences surrounding their experience in the Beys' palace and draws attention to the way both patriarchy and colonialism intensified the immobility of Tunisian women, reinforcing their seclusion from the public sphere where national discourse is being founded. Benlyazid's film, on the other hand, locates female agency and solidarity in an all-female, potentially liberating space, where women have the freedom to play roles that may not be available to them in a rigid patriarchal society.

Tlatli's and Benlyazid's films differ from films by the younger generation of filmmakers, represented in this book by Leila Merrakshi (see chapter 9), in the sense that they are more authentic in reflecting a traditional local culture still insulated from European modernity. While Merrakshi's film *Marock* (2005) is positioned as the transnational film revealing the influence of globalization on Moroccan youth's consumerist practices, Tlatli's and Benlyazid's films are rooted in local history and culture. Nevertheless, what unites these two generations of filmmakers, with their diverse interests and styles of filming, is their focus on gender identity and social change. In response to Laura Mulvey's question, "What part does the theme of women and their liberation play in [North African] cinema?" Tunisian filmmaker Moufida Tlatli states that the condition of women and their liberation is a central theme in her film:

> I've worked with several male and two female directors and I've noticed that they share a common interest in the condition of Arab women. I often wondered why it was that male directors should be so preoccupied with the question of women, until I realized that, for them, woman was the symbol of freedom of expression, and of all kinds of liberation. . . . I think that each country in the Maghreb tends to take up particular themes and their theme of women's liberation is the one that has been special to Tunisia. [1]

Tunisian Abdellatif Ben Ammar, who directed *Aziza* (1982), points out that "women are the alternative. Victims yesterday, and still sometimes so today, tomorrow they will be pushing forward a genuine renewal."[2] Farida Benlyazid, one of the pioneer female directors of Morocco, on the other hand, underscores the fact that, although male directors are preoccupied with the condition of women, they do not really give a fair representation of women in their films. Speaking specifically of Moroccan director Mohammed Abderrahman Tazi and his representation of women in his film *Badis* (1989), Benlyazid states: "I'm happy he's talking about women . . . still, it is a more subtle, nuanced truth than that. . . . Women have more strength than he shows us having."[3]

Benlyazid's statements raise issues of representation that are so important to feminist Maghrebi cinema. Films by North African women show a concern with the ways in which representation reinforces power relationships and becomes, as well, a site for subverting oppressive relationships. The narrative strategies their films deploy to decolonize the gaze and locate women in spatial terms show that North African women filmmakers are very aware of the significance of representation in light of postcolonial politics. Tlatli's and Benlyazid's representations of the female gaze and female space demonstrate the way they experiment with different techniques to subvert dominant discourses of power. The camera is a challenge to colonial and patriarchal representations, and it epitomizes for them a defiance of the dominating gaze. Both films deploy the female gaze as an opposition to the male gaze and as a form of the female collective. The question is how do these women filmmakers use the camera differently from men? And does the audience respond differently when it is a woman who is behind the lens? Both Tlatli's and Benlyazid's films differ from the way Arab male filmmakers direct their films, as they pay more attention to details that are shaped by female agency (or lack thereof) and perceptions. The female protagonists deal with men who are shaped only by how they are perceived by these women filmmakers. In both films, men are marginalized and their speech is kept to a minimum. The films also, for the most part, take place in predominately female spaces (rooms, *hammams*, gardens with gates, etc.), spaces often neglected or underrepresented in North African films made by men. The privileging of space in these films becomes understandable if we take into consideration women's immobility in patriarchal and post/colonial spaces.

While *Silences of the Palace* highlights the agency of the female protagonist Alia, who questions Tunisian Beys' silencing of women during anticolonial struggle, Farida Benlyazid is not generally concerned with a feminist critique of anticolonial nationalist discourse. Her film presents, within the context of Islam, the story of a woman's search for a new identity in postcolonial Morocco. Tlatli initiates her critical reflections through uncovering a history of marginalized, enslaved women within a patriarchal Muslim society, while Benlyazid resorts to a history of powerful Muslim women, a history that consists, in Ella Shohat's words, of "female spirituality, prophecy, poetry, and intellectual creativity as well as revolt, material power, and social and political leadership."[4] Each of their films testifies to the different approaches North African feminists adopt in their attempts to create alternative realities and provide blueprints for the future.

SILENCES OF THE PALACE

Moufida Tlatli's film *Silences of the Palace* presents striking parallels between women's silences and Tunisia's colonialism. The film begins by establishing the unstable political situation in Tunisia on the eve of its independence from France. Tlatli highlights the background of political events in the film in a very realistic way, using the medium of radio coverage. The Tunisian political situation forms the background for women's increasing silences, which coincide with the rising anticolonial protests outside the palace. The connection between the silenced women servants in the palace and the colonized nation is established through an obvious parallel the filmmaker makes in one scene between the women servants fighting inside the kitchen and the anticolonial struggle happening outside the palace. Houssin, the son of the senior woman servant, pleads with the women to stop fighting and listen to the demonstrations against the colonizer that are taking place outside. The identification of the women servants with the anticolonial struggle is clear from one woman's words: "I don't belong to myself. I want to go out in the street, naked, barefoot, to run without being stopped, to scream and shout out loud. Only their bullets can shut me up."[5] When she hears the radio announce the curfew that the French have imposed on the Tunisian natives, one woman declares: "Our lives are like curfews." Not only female slaves, but also privileged women in the palace are silenced and have no political power. Women's silence at this crucial revolutionary moment in Tunisia's history underlines Tlatli's pessimism regarding women's liberation, even in the aftermath of Tunisia's independence. There have been a lot of debates recently on women's silence and enfranchisement in contemporary Tunisia with respect to the Arab Spring. It is interesting to note that in current debates in Tunisia, women's place and roles as active agents in society are being challenged once again by hardline Islamist parties that seek to silence them.

Like Assia Djebar's *La Nouba*, *Silences of the Palace* and *Door to the Sky* are, therefore, good examples of what Ella Shohat characterizes as feminist "cinematic counter-telling,"[6] which characterizes contemporary films produced by women directors in developing countries. Shohat further argues that what characterizes these films is their experimentation with new narrative forms and techniques by way of subverting mainstream cinema. It would be limiting, however, to focus on these films' modern techniques and aesthetic aspects while ignoring their political and feminist overtones. Both *Silences of the Palace* and *Door to the Sky* have clearly been made with conscious feminist and political agendas, which is evident in the alternatives they offer to both colonialism and patriarchy.

Set in Tunisia, during and after French colonialism in the 1950s, Tlatli's film centers on Alia and her mother, Khedija, who live like slaves in the Beys' palace. The film reveals the lives of the silenced in North African cinema, as it focuses on poor women slaves who are subjected to labor as well as sexual slavery to the Beys in colonial Tunisia.[7] Tlatli's courageous probing of the representation of slaves in Tunisian society opens a new debate in readings of precolonial Muslim societies. In his book *Islam's Black Slaves*, Ronald Segal points out that slavery in the Arab world began eight centuries earlier than the Atlantic slave trade and that it had dissimilar manifestations. He argues that the difference between the two slave trades lies in their different systems. The slave trade in the Arab world "was conducted on a different scale and with a different impact. . . . The social and cultural importance of slavery itself was greater than its economic one."[8] While slaves served as a source of labor and a means of economic production in the

Americas, the Arab elite, Segal argues, used slaves as guards and soldiers, as concubines, as cooks, and as musicians "with slavery itself primarily a form of consumption rather than a factor of production."[9] Feminists from North Africa have also analyzed the history of the Arab Muslim world in an attempt to identify its dominant discourses of power. In *The Veil and the Male Elite*, Moroccan sociologist Fatima Mernissi hints at the issue of slavery and argues that certain sociopolitical factors in North Africa justified the enslavement of poor women. She explains how domestic female servants were not protected, as protection would hinder the male elite's right to sexually exploit them.[10] Mernissi further points out that "minorities, women, and slaves are the groups that have historically constituted a challenge and a limitation to Islam's claim to universality and equality."[11] It is exactly such a claim to universality that Tlatli's film challenges when it chooses to shed light on Tunisia's margins.

Tlatli's film unveils Tunisian women's history in colonial and postcolonial Tunisia by presenting the lives of poor women slaves in the Beys' palace. Here, the powerful Beys play a dominant role, relegating women and servants to marginal roles. Tlatli's purpose is to probe the correlation between gender/class oppression both within the contexts of colonialism and patriarchal Tunisia. Her explorations of marginal gendered positions in the film lead to a strategy of "seeing/filming from below," which has liberating consequences.[12] Feminist theorists like Nancy Hartsock and Donna Haraway deploy the liberating strategies of "seeing from below" and prefer "the standpoints of the subjugated" in an attempt to subvert power relationships.[13] In response to "the men who were a little bit shocked that a woman who comes from the most liberated country in the Arab world would make a film about women's conditions," Tlatli replies that "it is because we are the most liberated country in the Arab world that I made such a film."[14] Her response reflects her own personal paradox: The emancipation of women in her country offers her the freedom and distance to probe patriarchy and class oppression in Tunisian society as power dynamics. Tlatli achieves such distance in her film through Alia's journey into Tunisia's past, which takes the audience back in time to when Tunisia was on the verge of independence in the 1950s. Alia takes two key journeys in the film: one physical journey to the Beys' palace upon learning about the death of Sidi Ali and one journey dramatized through her consciousness and memories. Her physical and mental journeys provide a narrative strategy in the film for reflecting on the Tunisian woman/nation and its history.

In the first sequence of the film, we learn that Lotfi, the revolutionary hero, who had assured Alia that her family background would not pose a problem to their relationship in independent Tunisia, refuses now to marry her. The film here makes an obvious critique of the male nationalists who have failed to keep their promises to bring about gender and class equality in postcolonial Tunisia. The later scenes, which depict Alia's silent revolt while in the palace, highlight her desire for expression in her secret attraction to Lotfi, who acts as her ideal. In one of Alia's flashbacks, Lotfi predicts that Alia "will be a great singer" and that "[her] voice will enchant everyone."[15] Lotfi's equation of Alia's voice with the birth of the nation, in the same scene, is typical of the male nationalists who often deploy women's bodies as emblems or symbols of the nation, but once independence is won, they reinforce the same patriarchal structure that determined their preindependent nations. Drawing upon the postcolonial theory that often equates colonialism with patriarchy, Dorit Naaman comments that "the newly-emerged nation-state goes through a metaphorical 'sex-change' shortly after independence and literally engages in asserting its newly acquired patriarchal power to suppress those who were oppressed all along, women."[16]

Alia is shown to still be suffering in the postcolonial present as she confesses in front of her mother's grave, in a voice-over: "I thought Lotfi would save me. I have not been saved. Like you, I've lived in sin. My life has been a series of abortions. I could never express myself. My songs were stillborn. And even the child in me, Lotfi wants me to abort it."[17] The film shows that the political and sexual relationship of the Tunisian woman with her colonized man is a problematic one. Lotfi, a formerly colonized man, becomes the colonizer of Alia in a specific sense. In one of her interviews, Tlatli points out that

> Tunisian women are the colonized of the colonized," and goes on to insist that "the Tunisian man, as the colonized person, has his revenge by colonizing the underclass which are the women. They in turn put their frustrations into their daughters. In the Arab world, the woman does pay. At an unconscious level, she is responsible for keeping the status quo as regards her own position. I wanted to show how she can break from the past.[18]

Here, the film presents parallels between Alia's abortions and postcolonial Tunisia, and thus equates the painful stage of the independent nation in transition to the condition of women in postcolonial Tunisian society. This is what Ben Mehdi, the leader of the National Liberation Front, implies when speaking to the young revolutionary Ali Lapointe in Pontecorvo's film *The Battle of Algiers*: "It is difficult to start a revolution. . . . More difficult to sustain it, . . . and still more difficult to win it. But it's later when we've won that the real difficulties begin. There is still a great deal to do."[19] That Tlatli deploys flashbacks as a narrative mode in *Silences of the Palace* shows that she is interested in subverting the narrative chronological method, which was previously used in Maghrebi cinema. In this film, the protagonist is portrayed mainly through the filmmaker's exploration of the different locations where the main events take place. These places include Alia's memory, which is associated with geographical places within the palace: the hallways, the upstairs and the downstairs, the kitchen, the gate, and so on. Alia's flashbacks and memories are triggered by her return to the palace after she learns about the death of the Bey Sidi Ali, who could be her father. Alia, now an adult, enters the palace, forcing herself to surrender to the dreaded act of remembering. It is as if the rule of silence, which was necessary at first in the palace in order to make life bearable, has to be broken eventually. Through her memories and flashbacks, Alia tries to come to terms with her mother's history as an enslaved and colonized woman, and with her own personal history. Access to the buried memories of her childhood and to "the past [she] thought she buried with [her] mother" is necessary for her psychological freedom.

Through Alia's flashbacks, Tlatli enunciates the painful memory of the Beys' violations of women's rights of ownership over their own bodies and their lack of voice in the palace. Alia reflects back on how her mother was sexually exploited by the Beys and did not have the power to break the silence. In one scene, she is shown urging her mother, Khedija, to escape the palace and resist the Beys: "You are worried about them. Don't [be]! Others can serve them, dance for them. . . . To see you say 'no' for once! 'No, I won't serve.' 'No, I don't belong to you.'"[20] In another later scene in the film, Alia runs around in circles in a moment that captures her inner pain and confusion. Her subsequent witnessing of her mother's rape by Sidi Bashir, Sidi Ali's brother, results in her being sick and confined to bed for weeks. As the camera pans across the bodies of mother and daughter, it also reveals the scars of rape as it revisits the pain of the mother's preparation for abortion. Khedija's resistance takes the form of self-inflicted violence. Her decision to end the pregnancy that resulted from her rape stems from her acquired sense of the shame and privacy she feels about her body.

Tlatli experiments with different narrative strategies of using predominately female voice, gaze, and space in the film by way of representing women's resistance to silence and subordination. She explains that women's silences in her film stem from her own personal experience, as she felt obliged to make this film after attending to her sick mother who refused to speak during the last five years of her life: "Five years before my mother died she stopped speaking. I think that her decision to remain silent came out of an accumulation over the years of all those little silences. It became a form of protection while at the same time it was a signal that she did not want to prolong the fruitless dialogue."[21] Here, Tlatli obviously admits to a certain kind of identification with her protagonist Alia, who struggles to come to terms with her mother's pain and silences in the film. Silence in the film surrounds the mother's illicit sexual relationship with Sidi Ali and the identity of her daughter's father. In the sequence that portrays Alia's birth, Hadda, the senior servant, censors a woman servant who inquires about the name of Alia's father. Women in the palace have opted for silence out of fear of the Beys, and thus their oppositional speech is not disclosed.

Against such silences, and as an alternative to women's representations within Tunisian patriarchy and colonialism, the film presents a compelling feminist quest for voice and self-discovery in the person of Alia. The act of filming itself becomes for Tlatli an immediate form of representation and constitutes a kind of delegation of voice with political overtones. Tlatli's attempt to give voice to her protagonist is expressed through Alia's creativity as a singer and through metaphors and symbols in the film that connote creativity—the lute, for instance. Through Alia's keen interest in music, Tlatli shows how the representational act and the ability to speak can be nurtured and realized through music. Khedija has bought Alia the lute against the Beys' unspoken rule that servants are not supposed to learn and play music. She hopes that by learning music, her daughter might escape her mother's fate in the palace. Alia's singing, however, only stirs the Beys' sexual interest in her. Her singing is exploited as another kind of slavery in the palace because she is now expected to sing for and entertain the Beys.

The possibility of resisting power without allowing that resistance to be sabotaged by the Beys is, therefore, a persistent struggle in the film. In her efforts to explore Alia's voice, Tlatli is aware of the power of the Beys that neither Alia, nor her mother, can ever overcome, which inevitably influences their actions. She demonstrates how Alia subversively exploits existing discursive realms in the palace. The film shows that only the elite are allowed to own and use the lute. By playing a musical instrument that is forbidden to servants, Alia is forging her own voice against the voices of the elite. Tlatli's film celebrates music and singing as resistance to power and defiance against women's harsh realities in post/colonial Tunisia. The scene that portrays Khedija's screams from her fatal abortion coincides in the film with Alia singing the Tunisian anthem in her first performance as a singer in the palace. Alia's song becomes reflective of the country's rise against colonialism and contrasts sharply with the narrow backward world represented by the patriarchal Beys. This scene also stresses Alia's identification with the upheavals of the nation.

In addition to voice, Tlatli's representation of the gaze in the film demonstrates the way she questions the power dynamics that constitute the ideologies of the Beys' palace. On the surface, women are objects of the Beys' erotic looking, but Tlatli's manipulation of the gaze is more complex. Despite the presence of the male gaze, the controlling gaze in the film is the female gaze. Tlatli has explained in her interview with Laura Mulvey that she feels compelled to make up for women's silences in the film by granting them instead the power of looking:

> If the mouth is closed then the eyes speak. I wanted to make their eyes speak—and say a great deal. All the women are within the tradition of taboo, of silence, but the power of their look is extraordinary. They have had to get used to expressing themselves through their eyes. So Alia's attempt to find out her mother's actual role in the palace has to become an investigation. She looks through keyholes, through a crack in the door. Her look is searching for things that she shouldn't see.[22]

Unlike the male gaze, which is associated with sexual desire in the film, the female gaze primarily exists as a knowing, inquisitive gaze. In her essay "Historical Trauma and Male Subjectivity," Kaja Silverman draws a distinction between the knowing, protective gaze, on the one hand, and the traumatic, painful gaze, on the other hand.[23] The female gaze in Tlatli's film is not as objectifying and controlling as the male gaze, as it mainly reinforces the female characters' perceptive power. It needs to be pointed out, however, that the film does not present a unitary female perspective, as not all women are unified in how they gaze. Women in the film seem divided against each other by jealousy, class, or relationships to men. The wife of Sidi Ali, for instance, who cannot bear children, demonstrates insightful perception in the film in that she is able to guess the extent of Sidi Ali's fondness for Alia and the sexual affair between him and Khedija. Though she suffers in her watching, it is hard to characterize her gazing as controlling because she is shown to be silent and waiting passively throughout the film.

Alia also demonstrates such power of perception in the film because she is shown to be inquisitively searching for the male gazes that follow her mother. Tlatli has commented that as a child, Alia exhibits an innocent, "voyeuristic" look, but as a young woman, she becomes the object of the Beys' voyeuristic gazes herself.[24] The controlling male gaze is subverted in Tlatli's film through the absence of scenes showing requited gazing between the Beys and their women servants. Tlatli also identifies Alia's powerful gazes as a key stage in her protagonist's struggle against hegemonic discourses and toward psychological freedom. The film foregrounds Alia's powerful self-gazes as when she looks at the mirror, and the influence of her female, observational gaze—as when she gazes at her mother, her unacknowledged father, Sidi Ali, and the other women in the film. In gazing back at the men who make sexual advances to her, like Sidi Bashir, Sidi Ali's brother, Alia liberates herself from the patriarchal male gaze. Her gazes, however, are also a source of pain and inner torment in the film. In one scene, watching her mother's rape by Sidi Bashir results in Alia's nervous breakdown. This type of look, according to Tlatli, "bears witness to her feelings, to her fear and her panic. Her contact with other people is reduced to the tiny nuances of a half look."[25] Tlatli's experimentation with the different types of gazes in her film testifies to her quest for narrative aesthetics that are capable of expressing the reality of Alia and the other women servants in the palace.

The filmmaker's representation of space also aims to shed light on patterns of domination in the palace. Through her structuring of place, Tlatli represents Alia's mother, whose subject positions "downstairs" are defined by poverty, slavery, and gendered subordination. It is this legacy of multiple Othering that Alia is shown to be inheriting in the film. The "upstairs" space is where the princes and their wives and children live. It symbolizes wealth and the upper class. The "downstairs," on the other hand, is the world of the servants. As the child of an illicit sexual union between a woman servant and the Bey Sidi Ali, Alia's existence is relegated to the in-between, an identity that reinforces the marginality of occupying a space in limbo between the downstairs world of her mother and the upstairs world of her unacknowledged father. In her interview with Laura Mulvey, Tlatli points to the ambiguous position of Alia who is caught between the two opposing worlds of the Beys and the servants: "For Alia, the attic is an intermediate space that she's made for herself, between the world of the servants and the world of the princes. She is uncomfortable in both worlds. . . . The attic is upstairs, but it's also poor."[26] Tlatli locates the freedom and desires of Alia in the attic as a peripheral but potentially liberating space. Alia's claiming of a separate physical place also signifies a space that has psychologically therapeutic and creative implications. It is in the attic that Alia plays with her lute, sings, and dreams.

In associating the life of women servants within the Beys' palace with French colonialism and national independence, Moufida Tlatli has made of the woman question a historical issue that is rooted in the colonial and the postcolonial phases of Tunisia's history. Thus, Tlatli has put the problem of the Arab Muslim woman in general, and of the Tunisian woman in particular, within its general, true framework, taking into account the fact that the problem of the Arab Muslim woman is an objective result of certain historical factors. Echoing the past and dealing with the present, Tlatli's film constitutes an effort to represent women who have previously been marginalized and silenced.

DOOR TO THE SKY

Produced in 1988, *Door to the Sky* centers on a young woman who journeys from France to Morocco to attend her father's funeral. Nadia, the protagonist, seeks an alternative to the secular/exile of France in Moroccan Muslim culture and decides to turn the family house she inherited from her father into a *zawiya* (shelter) for poor women seeking charity. In her comments on this film, Ella Shohat argues that "*A Door to the Sky* envisions an aesthetic that affirms Islamic culture, while inscribing it with a feminist consciousness, offering an alternative to both the Western imaginary and Islamic fundamentalist representation of Muslim women."[27] The film enacts its double critique of Islamic fundamentalism, as well as women's liberation, within a Western feminist context, through its recourse to spiritual, liberal Islam.

In its images, Benlyazid's film dramatizes the divide between the "modern" and the "traditional" that characterizes Morocco's contemporary social formations. Sabry Hafez argues that "One of the recurring themes in [Maghrebi] cinema is the conflict between modernity and tradition, which is often treated in terms of its relevance to the quest for identity."[28] The contradictions and opposing images that characterize this film, such as images of Westernized women in a modern city and traditional women in the old Medina, are indicative of the paradoxes within Morocco's social formations. Like Djebar's film *La Nouba*, Benlyazid's film, in its images, enacts the double alienation that Moroccan writer Abdelkébir Khatibi refers to when he asks the people of the developing world to "follow a third way . . . a subversion that is in a way double."[29] Khatibi may be considered as perhaps the most outstanding proponent of North African postcolonial theory. Khatibi opens his *Maghreb Pluriel* (*The Plural Maghreb*) (1983) with a similar approach to Frantz Fanon's own proposed solution to European colonialism when he urges the formerly colonized to make new discoveries and seek answers to their problems elsewhere than in Europe.[30] Khatibi's own proposed solution to European imperialism is his theory of "double critique," by means of which he aims to critique both European imperialism and Arab Muslim social formations.

Dedicated to Fatima El Fehriya, a Muslim Tunisian woman who founded Al Karawiyin University in Fez in the tenth century, Benlyazid explores spiritual, traditional Islam as a "third way," offering an alternative for Moroccan women beyond the discourses of Westernization and Islamic fundamentalism. Other Moroccan women writers have also probed women's negotiation of tradition and modernity in the aftermath of Morocco's independence from the French. As noted in chapter 8 in her novella *Year of the Elephant*, Moroccan writer Leila Abouzeid exposes the postcolonial Moroccan elite to harsh criticism. She recounts the story of Zahra, a woman who fought for independence alongside her husband, a national revolutionary, who abandoned her for a Westernized woman in the aftermath of independence. Abouzeid makes her protagonist embrace Islam and Moroccan tradition in repudiation of the ideology of the modernized elite, like Zahra's husband, who failed to keep the promises of the national revolution.

Both Benlyazid's film and Abouzeid's novel enact a clear decentering of Western feminism in their potential positioning of a "Moroccan feminism" that is conceptualized around a notion of female identity rooted in Muslim culture. Benlyazid's film makes use of an all-female space to affirm such a female collective. This point is made by the camera's repeated privileging of space over action in the film. Often, the camera focuses on women's spaces in their rooms and the kitchen, and all action stops. The all-female spaces represented in the film, and women's free agency in the huge family mansion, challenge the Western feminist assumption that all Muslim women are confined to oppressive domestic spaces. In her autobiography, *Dreams of Trespass*, Fatima Mernissi draws a clear distinction between the "imperial harems" of imperial Muslim society, in which polygamy was universally practiced, and domestic harems where "extended families . . . with often monogamous couples . . . carried on the tradition of women's seclusion."[31] Mernissi defines the *hudud* of the harem as the sacred frontier of the Islamic tradition: "To be a Muslim is to respect the hudud [and] to respect the hudud was to obey."[32] Frontiers are also defined as signifiers of power: "The frontier indicates the line of power because whenever there is a frontier, there are two kinds of creatures walking on Allah's earth, the powerful on one side, and the powerless on the other."[33] Benlyazid's film highlights an alternative model of the gendered organization of space to that delineated in Mernissi's novel. Unlike the harem spaces in Mernissi's novel and Tlatli's film, the family mansion becomes, in Benlyazid's film, a vehicle of empowerment for its women.

A Door to the Sky is set in the city of Fez, whose old medina abounds in such spacious family mansions. In her comments on the setting of the film, Sandra Gayle argues that "Fez as the location is symbolic of the cultural depth of Moroccan society, the persistence of tradition in the face of the modern. . . . What more perfect setting for the intricate memory, tradition, modernity, faith, rationality, disenchantment, idealism and personal discovery?"[34] Fez, one might add, is also the city whose historical landmarks, such as Al Karawiyin University, testify to women's rich intellectual history and cultural contributions within the context of Islam. The setting of the film also has historic reverberations in Morocco's colonial relation to France. Like *Silences of the Palace*, the central narrative in *Door to the Sky* is organized as a journey. Nadia takes different journeys in the film; such journeys bring forth her bilingualism. While she communicates to the women in the zawiya in Arabic, Nadia uses only French to address her female lawyer Touria, her French ex-boyfriend Jean Philippe, and her educated Moroccan boyfriend Abdelkrim. The first journey revealed in the film is Nadia's trip from France to Fez. Nadia arrives at the airport dressed in jeans and a leather jacket. There she meets her sister Laila who immediately disapproves of her way of dress and reminds her that she is now in traditional Fez. The film opens with the question over how to reconcile between Westernization and traditional Muslim culture. The alienation caused by French colonial education creates hybrids like Nadia whose double culture—European and Muslim—drives them into cultural confusion.

Charting Nadia's struggle to come to terms with her dual allegiances to France and Morocco, Benlyazid introduces another sequence in which Nadia resists her sister's plea to wear a Moroccan dress and join the mourners in her father's funeral. The scene dramatizes Nadia's revolt and confusion as she drowns her sense of despair in alcohol. In the same scene, Nadia's voice-over declares in the letter she writes to her French boyfriend: "I feel a stranger. . . . Everything is so absurd. I am confused and I feel guilty. Why? And for what?"[35] In a subsequent scene that portrays her encounter with her French boyfriend in the Merinid hotel in Fez, Nadia is shown to be experiencing an inner conflict between her love for him and the ties by which she is bound to her family and religion.

As she makes contact with the Moroccan female collective, Nadia will later embark on a spiritual journey through which she rediscovers spiritual Islam with the help of Karina, an old family relative. On the other hand, Nadia's brother, who has also journeyed from France to Fez to attend his father's funeral, has decided to cut his ties to Morocco. In a scene where the family is having dinner, the brother declares that Nadia and he have chosen France over Morocco, a claim immediately dismissed by Nadia who responds "I am both." Through Nadia's brother, the film points to the Westernized Moroccan elite, who are a product of European colonialism and who often disassociate themselves from the Moroccan masses. Cutting Nadia's brother from subsequent scenes, the film turns its focus to Nadia, through whom Benlyazid advocates a type of decolonization that deploys spiritual Islam as an alternative to both European imperialism and Islamic fundamentalism.

On the day of her father's funeral, Nadia wears white mourning clothes according to Moroccan custom; as she listens to the *Qur'an*, she is enthralled by the rhythms of Muslim chants. Kirana's recitation of the *Qur'an* on the day of the funeral incurs a transformation in Nadia, who now begins to gradually become interested in spiritual Islam and decides to break up with her French boyfriend Jean Philippe. In the letter she writes to him, Nadia cites racism and capitalism as the major reasons behind her decision to leave France forever:

> I often dreamt that we are in our place in Paris, and Mr. Le Pen appeared suddenly, insulted me and threw me out. I would wake up humiliated, guilty and I hated you . . . the hordes of starving children throughout the world, the bombs, and the bloodshed. . . . My lack of power tortures me and comfort makes me sick. I don't need to witness the guilty Western conscience at mealtimes. . . . I belong here, not elsewhere.[36]

To appease her conscience, Nadia decides to turn the old family mansion house into a zawiya for poor women and battered wives out of *khayriya* (charity). While the film reinforces a positive image of Islam as a force of social justice and liberation, it is also critical of discriminatory patriarchal Islamic laws, such as the law that favors the male in inheritance. In order for Nadia to be able to open the zawiya, she has first to engage in a legal battle against her brother, who now resides in France and who is entitled to half of the inheritance according to Islamic law. In the following conversation with her lawyer, Touria, Nadia questions narrow male interpretations of Islam that have often subordinated Muslim women:

> Touria: You want to create a women's lib in Fez?
>
> Nadia: No, it always existed in our country. The problem is that we are losing the best aspects of our culture. You know in Islam, women have always used their wealth freely and have financed shelters for deprived and unhappy women.
>
> Touria: Yes, but in our case the law favors your brother.
>
> Nadia: I am ready to fight to the end. This house must become a shelter.[37]

Ultimately, Nadia wins the case and secures the rights to the house. Upon opening the shelter, Nadia begins to explore the spiritual heritage of Islam. She comes to discover such Muslim philosophers and mystics as Imam Ghazali and El Halaj, who have endorsed Islam's message of equality, love, and tolerance. Sufism, the mystical tradition of Islam, plays a role in Nadia's spiritual initiation and has undoubtedly influenced Benlyazid's images.[38] Farida Benlyazid grew up in Fez, Morocco's spiritual capital, where the Sufi tradition is very prevalent. As Nadia is initiated into Sufism, she is focused on achieving unity with God through prayer and charitable work. Like Sufis, she also uses dance and music to achieve such an ecstatic state. As she visits shrines of Moroccan saints like Moulay Abdesellam, Nadia begins to experience visionary dreams and assume the task of a healer. One of the people she eventually heals is Abdelkrim, an artist, who suffers from depression. The two fall in love and quickly get married against the rising protests of women who would prefer to keep the zawiya segregated along gender lines. Through the women's fierce protests against Abdelkrim and Bahiya, a Westernized young woman who the women insist be removed from the zawiya, Benlyazid subtly criticizes Islamic fundamentalism. In one scene, Nadia, in conversation with Kirana, protests the narrow interpretations of Islam and evokes Ibn Arabi, a Sufi who often equated Islam with love: "Why do people see Islam through the narrowest door? Islam is love. [Do] you read Ibn Arabi?"[39] Here, Benlyazid suggests that a spiritual Islam, which is based on tolerance, social justice, and charity, must be sought as a viable alternative to Islamic fundamentalism.

Door to the Sky also illustrates the limitations involved in understanding feminism in purely Eurocentric terms. Some audiences have criticized the film's emphasis on Islam as a solution for Moroccan women; they regard the denouement, in which the protagonist turns to Islam and to marriage as an alternative to feminist struggle, as unconvincing. Against the common argument about the incompatibility between Islam and feminism, Miriam Cooke argues in her book *Women Claim Islam* that "Islamic feminism is not a coherent identity, but rather a contingent, contextually determined strategic self-positioning. . . . This label is not rigid. It does not describe an identity, but rather an attitude and intention to seek justice and citizenship for Muslim women."[40] Through Nadia's questioning of the Islamic *Shari'a* that favors her brother in terms of inheritance, Benlyazid condemns male interpretations of Islam that have allowed women's subjugation to exist in Muslim countries. Muslim feminists have proposed different interpretations of Islamic law. Leila Ahmed, for one, argues that equality is inherent in Islam: "The ethical voice of Islam [explains why] Muslim women frequently insist, often inexplicably to non-Muslims, that Islam is not sexist. They hear and read in its sacred text . . . a different message from that heard by the makers and enforcers of orthodox, androcentric Islam."[41] Winifred Woodhull notes that by engaging religious law and Islamic tradition, feminists like Leila Ahmed and Fatima Mernissi aim "to beat the traditionalists at their own game, perhaps at the price of compromising the secularist, cosmopolitan stance they had adopted in the past."[42]

Women filmmakers like Benlyazid and Tlatli have successfully intervened into male-dominated film culture to highlight women's agency and to demand change in the sociopolitical factors that constrict women's freedom. They give the reader insight into a decadent Arab, Muslim society that has lost its direction, while hinting at the urgency for reform. They thus suggest that social change for women is contingent upon urgent critiques of archaic Muslim practices such as slavery, as well as Islamic fundamentalist discourses. Their experimentation with modern techniques and film aesthetics testifies to their awareness of the specificity of the postcolonial condition and the situation of women.

NOTES

1. Laura Mulvey, "'Moving Bodies,' Interview with Moufida Tlatli," *Sight and Sound* 5.3 (1995), 18.
2. Quoted in Lynn Teo-Simarski, "North African Cinema: Through North African Eyes," *Saudi Aramco World* (February 1992): 30–35, http://www.saudiaramcoworld.com/issue/199201/through.north.african.eyes.htm (accessed January 20, 2000).
3. Ibid.
4. Ella Shohat and Robert Stam, *Unthinking Eurocentrism: Multiculturalism and the Media* (New York: Routledge, 1994), 165.

5. Moufida Tlatli, *Samt Al Kusur (Silences of the Palace)*. Film. Directed by Moufida Tlatli, Tunisia, 1994.

6. Ella Shohat, "Post-Third-Worldist Culture: Gender, Nation, and the Cinema," in *Feminist Genealogies, Colonial Legacies, Democratic Futures*, eds. M. Jacqui Alexander and Chandra Mohanty (New York: Routledge, 1997), 183.

7. See Mohammed Ennaji, *Serving the Master: Slavery and Society in Nineteenth-Century Morocco*, trans. Seth Graebner (New York: St. Martin's Press, 1999).

8. Ronald Segal, *Islam's Black Slaves: The Other Black Diaspora* (New York: Farrar Straus and Giroux, 2001), 3–4.

9. Ibid., 4.

10. Fatima Mernissi, *The Veil and the Male Elite: A Feminist Interpretation of Women's Rights in Islam*, trans. Mary Jo Lakeland (Reading, MA: Addison-Wesley, 1991), 186–187.

11. Fatima Mernissi, "Arab Women's Rights and the Muslim State in the Twenty-First Century: Reflections on Islam as Religion and State," in *Faith and Freedom: Women's Human Rights in the Muslim World*, ed. Mahnaz Afkhami (Syracuse, NY: Syracuse University Press, 44).

12. Nancy Hartsock, "The Feminist Standpoint: Developing the Ground for a Specifically Feminist Historical Materialism," in *Discovering Reality: Feminist Perspectives on Epistemology, Metaphysics, Methodology, and Philosophy of Science*, eds. Sandra Harding and Merill B. Hintikka (Netherlands: Kluwer Academic Publishers, 2003), 283.

13. Donna Haraway, "Situated Knowledges: The Science Question in Feminism and the Privilege of Partial Perspective," *Feminist Studies* 14, no. 3 (Fall 1998): 589.

14. Judy Stone, "'Silences of the Palace' Has Everybody Talking: Director Moufida Tlatli Honored at S.F. Festival," *San Francisco Chronicle*, April 23, 1995, 31, http://www.sfgate.com/cgi bin/article.cgi?f=/c/a/1995/04/23/PK45698.DTL&ao=2 (accessed February 20, 2000).

15. Moufida Tlatli, *Samt Al Kusur (Silences of the Palace)*.

16. Dorit Naaman, "Woman/Nation: A Postcolonial Look at Female Subjectivity," *Quarterly Review of Film and Video* 17, no. 4 (2000): 333.

17. Moufida Tlatli, *Samt Al Kusur (Silences of the Palace)*.

18. Lizzie Francke, "Revolution on the Quiet," *The Guardian*, March 1995, 213.

19. Gillo Pontecorvo and Franco Solinas, *The Battle of Algiers*. Film. Directed by Gillo Pontecorvo. Co-Produced by Igor Film and Casbah Film. Algeria: 1966.

20. Moufida Tlatli, *Samt Al Kusur (Silences of the Palace)*.

21. Lizzie Francke, "Revolution," 213.

22. Laura Mulvey, "'Moving Bodies,'" 20.

23. Kaja Silverman, "Historical Trauma and Male Subjectivity," in *Psychoanalysis & Cinema*, ed. Ann E. Kaplan (London: Routledge, 1990), 110–127.

24. Laura Mulvey, "'Moving Bodies,'" 20.

25. Ibid.

26. Ibid., 19.

27. Ella Shohat and Robert Stam, *Unthinking Eurocentrism,* 165.

28. Sabry Hafez, "Shifting Identities in Maghrebi Cinema: The Algerian Paradigm," *Alif: Journal of Comparative Poetics* 15 (1995), 43.

29. Abdelkébir Khatibi, "Double Criticism: The Decolonization of Arab Sociology," in *Contemporary North Africa: Issues of Development and Integration*, ed. Halim Barakat (Washington, DC: Center for Contemporary Arab Studies, 1985), 11.

30. Fanon, *Wretched*, 315.

31. Fatima Mernissi, *Dreams of Trespass: Tales of a Harem Girlhood* (Reading, MA: Addison-Wesley, 1994), 34.

32. Ibid., 3.

33. Ibid., 242.

34. Sandra Gayle Carter, "Farida Benlyazid's Moroccan Women," *Quarterly Review of Film and Video* 17, no. 4 (2000), 357.

35. Farida Benlyazid, *Bab Sma Maftouh (A Door to the Sky)*. Film. Morocco: France Media, Centre Cinématographique Marocain, SATPEC, 1988.

36. Ibid.

37. Ibid.

38. Florence Martin, *Screens and Veils: Maghrebi Women's Cinema* (Bloomington: Indiana University Press, 2011), 38.

39. Benlyazid, *Bab Sma Maftouh (A Door to the Sky)*.

40. Miriam Cooke, *Women Claim Islam: Creating Islamic Feminism through Literature* (New York: Routledge, 2001), 61.

41. Leila Ahmed, *Women and Gender in Islam: Historical Roots of a Modern Debate* (New Haven, CT: Yale University Press, 1992), 88.

42. Winifred Woodhull, "Feminism and Islamic Tradition," *Studies in Twentieth Century Literature* 17, no. 1 (Winter 1993), 34.

Chapter Nine

Islam, Youth, and the Global

Leila Merrakshi's Controversial Film, Marock

Farida Benlyazid, Leila Abouzeid, and Leila Merrakshi are at opposite poles of Moroccan consciousness. Merrakshi lives in exile, while Abouzeid resides in Morocco. These women authors differ from each other not only because they belong to different generations of writers and filmmakers, but also because of the identity or voice they choose to reflect through their language choices. While Abouzeid retains a strong sense of her Arab Muslim heritage and writes exclusively in Arabic, Merrakshi primarily uses French. Merrakshi represents the very class of Westernized Moroccan intellectuals that Abouzeid loathes. Abouzeid and Benlyazid reject the Western models of female liberation in an attempt to indigenize the Moroccan women's feminist struggle and create a feminism in tune with national and religious identity. Merrakshi, on the other hand, frames the emancipation of Moroccan women from patriarchal and familial control in terms of Western feminist notions of the liberation of female sexuality or Western notions of romantic love. This dichotomy illustrates how women writers and filmmakers are not always in solidarity and may approach feminism in different ways.

Merrakshi represents a new generation of filmmakers that began to emerge in the early 2000s. As part of the Moroccan diaspora, she has a unique vantage point as a commentator from both inside and outside her society.[1] Her personal narrative of her own diaspora enables her to create an art of defiance where identity does not have to be fixed and coherent. While Merrakshi's conservative critics assume that Moroccan identity is a fixed signifier and that society appropriates and regulates identity, the points of convergence between different cultures in her film *Marock* (2005)[2] challenge hegemonic definitions of identity as coherent and integrated. As Morocco transitions to modernity, female directors like Merrakshi are now being scrutinized for their daring films that push the envelope with respect to themes and messages, and that broach controversial issues such as sex, religion, prostitution, and so on. Being the center of others' scrutiny presents these women with a predicament peculiar to feminism and women's liberation struggles.

The early 2000s saw a turning point for cinema in Morocco, as the government guaranteed more freedom of expression for young artists and filmmakers. Such democratic openings have led to the breaking of taboos through film and media, opening up possibilities for the presence of women in most aspects of Moroccan cinema. Furthermore, there has been an increase in the number of women filmmakers, whose films demonstrate that women in Moroccan society are not silent recipients of dominant discourses, but are rather active in their opposition and in expressing their voices. This is reflected in films that have shown well at international film festivals, as they present a postcolonial society undergoing rapid and controversial changes. Films such as Farida Benlyazid's *Casablanca* (2002), Nourredine Lakhamari's *Casanegra* (2008), and Lasri's *L'os de fer* (*The Iron Bone*) (2007) frame for audiences the new sociopolitical changes in the country and reveal the modernization of the family structure where men continue to be favored, but women are increasingly beginning to represent themselves.

Emerging women filmmakers like Leila Merrakshi, Zakia Tahiri, Narjis Najjar, and Yasmine Kassari, among others, document the changes happening in Moroccan society and freely reflect societal transitions in ways those who once controlled the images never could. In her book *Screening Morocco: Contemporary Depictions in Film of a Changing Society* (2011), Valerie Orlando notes that Morocco's emerging women filmmakers "demonstrate an 'écriture feminine' on the screen that virtually depicts the voice of Moroccan women, a voice that is diverse and, at the same time, unified in its expression of feminine *being* in contemporary times."[3] More importantly, these women's films are increasingly becoming the site in which sociopolitical and cultural changes with respect to women are reflected. Such changes will mean that a single, uncontested discourse and set of images about gender will probably never exert the influence that was the reality a generation ago.

Testing the limits of new democratic structures and freedom of expression in the new Morocco, *Marock* (2005) can be classified in the same emerging category of "shocking" films along with Narjis Najjar's *Les yeux secs* (*Dry Eyes*) (2003), which deals with the rites of prostitution as practiced by women in a small Berber village in the middle Atlas Mountains. Merrakshi's film influenced more recent and definitely more shocking films, such as that of Aziz Salmy's *Les amours voilées* (*Veiled Loves*) (2008), which deals with the issue of premarital sex in Morocco, and *Les ailes de l'amour* (*The Wings of Love*) (2011). *Marock*, which tells the story of an atypical love relationship between a Muslim girl and a Jewish boy, resonates with the personal experience of its director. A Moroccan woman who is married to a Jewish film director, the film can be read as a retelling and justification of Merrakshi's own youthful rebellion and choices. Merrakshi's marriage is illegal under the Moroccan version of Muslim law. However, the situation of women has evolved since 2005 when the film was released. The ascension of Mohammed VI to the throne in 1999 marked a new moment for the women's movement. Changes in Moroccan law under King Mohammed VI have not only extended women's rights but proved the compatibility of Islam and modernity with regard to the emancipation of women. With respect to the new Constitution declared by King Mohammed VI in the aftermath of the Arab Spring,[4] Islam is being "toned down" and openings are occurring for other religious possibilities, one of which is the possibility to sanction women's marriages outside the faith.

Merrakshi made her film at a time of great transition in Morocco. The transition to democracy and liberalization has involved a breaking away from taboos of the past, the easing of arbitrary controls on individuals, the increasing cultivation and awareness of human rights, and the gradual reduction or even removal of censorship. In her book *Through a Local Prism*, Loubna Skalli adds a new perspective to the debates on Morocco's liberalization policies by exploring the ways in which local Moroccan culture has been influenced by global culture and how such global connections have impacted gender roles. She argues that women have consequently come to inhabit a cultural context marked by schizophrenia and the disjunction between the modern and premodern.[5] Indeed, such complex interplay of the modern and the traditional operates on all levels in Moroccan society. In Merrakshi's film, both the secular and the Islamist exist within Casablanca's urban bourgeoisie. According to Moroccan scholar Abdellah Laroui, the bourgeoisie in Arab states such as Morocco embraces both modernization and traditionalism at the same time: "On the one hand, it profits from modern culture" in order to consolidate its power; on the other hand, "it profits from its fidelity to traditional culture by legitimizing an exclusive authority."[6] King Mohammed VI's liberalization of society, however, has strengthened the secular, modernist faction of Morocco's elite that benefited from globalization. This shift reveals how Moroccan national identity has become, in recent years, more and more bound to the global economy and a Western consumerist culture.

MAROCK, THE FILM

Marock is unique as a Moroccan film in that it is directed by a woman and has a modern female character at its center. The film thus subverts traditional notions of gender and women's experience. Because it draws on the genre conventions of romance and the female bildungsroman, *Marock* can be interpreted as a film about female development and rebellion. The film's point of view is feminine; the director uses the camera mostly to show Rita's point of view and to reinforce the female gaze. Daring in its theme—the film traces the love relationship between a Moroccan Muslim girl and a Moroccan Jewish boy—it thus challenges traditions and creates controversy. The film is set in Casablanca, which is represented as a global space and "contact zone" that not only allows religious and gender minorities to express their identity but also enables free sexual encounters. Mary Louise Pratt uses the notion of "contact zone" to refer to "the space of imperial encounters"[7] during the colonial past; this notion can also be a relevant concept in discussing Casablanca as a globalized contact zone between different identities in the film. Through the character of Yuri, a Moroccan Jew, the film emphasizes the presence of various minorities in Morocco, while indirectly hinting at the larger issues of Jewish diaspora. In one scene, a teacher is lecturing about Spinoza, an excommunicated, secular Jew. Yuri's Jewish family lives in Morocco but is never at home. His parents are always traveling, which alludes to the fact that Jews do not feel welcome in contemporary Morocco. This becomes particularly obvious when Yuri states "my parents are always scared, particularly since the first Gulf War."

Fast narratives situated in the upscale Anfa district on the outskirts of Casablanca characterize the film, wherein the female protagonist engages in a romantic relationship with Yuri. The love story becomes an allegory of gender, national, local, and global interactions in a rapidly changing Morocco. Rita and Yuri, who fall in love just before their baccalaureate exams, are introduced as students attending the French-speaking Lycée Lyautay. They are the children of the elite class of Casablanca, which holds the reins of power and privilege. The use of montage highlights multilayered spaces and shows the director doing something avant-garde with the narrative. Montage in the film constructs a new space and an imaginary reality for the two lovers. The camera pans the sea and sky, and the viewer is directed to gaze on the two lovers bathing in the waves. Here, Merrakshi is deliberately trying to step outside of the narrative and construct an imaginary space. The music in the scenes and the long camera shots suggest a utopian space for the two lovers, who are shown conversing about leaving or staying in Morocco. Rita suggests they travel to Paris where they would not have to hide their relationship and could even live together: "Je voudrais tellement que tu viennes à Paris, toi aussi. . . . On n'aurait pas besoin de se cacher. . . . On pourrait se voir tous les jours. On pourrait même habiter ensemble." [I would really like you to come to Paris. . . . There we would not need to hide. . . . We could see each other every day. We could even live together.] Yuri is worried that Rita's parents will be upset about their departure. Ultimately, Yuri dies in a car accident, an ending that typifies the tragic side of development in the female version of the bildungsroman. Rita's quest for real autonomy is replaced by her reconciliation to a life of diminished scope because of the sudden and unexpected ending of her romance.

THE CONTROVERSY OVER THE FILM

The release of this glitzy, Hollywood-like film into a Moroccan society still considered "traditional," and trying gradually to modernize, created a scandal that resulted in calls from the religious right to have the film banned. While it was largely applauded on the left for showing the new schizophrenic Morocco, *Marock* was harshly criticized by traditional political parties, in part because of the way it handled issues of female sexuality, disregarded "family values," and promoted a sense of entitlement among the elite. The censorship efforts against Merrakshi's film reflect the mindset of Moroccan conservatives, who have a vested and clearly articulated stake in preserving the patriarchal and religious foundations of the country. The push to ban *Marock* was led by conservative politicians and Islamists who, for the most part, did not see the film. For the Islamists, it is more than a little shocking when a woman director makes a movie that deals with an interreligious romantic relationship. According to Abdelilah Benkirane, a member of Parliament for the Islamist Justice and Development Party, the film "shocked the entire population. . . . It doesn't deserve to be seen and shouldn't be authorized in a Muslim country."[8] The Secretary General of the Moroccan Theatre Syndicate, Mohammed Hassan El Joundi, observes that "this kind of production must not be screened in a country which respects its traditions."[9] El Joundi adds: "This communiqué is not addressed to *Marock* only, but to all artistic creations having the intention of blemishing the reputation of our country. Everything has a limit, including freedom."[10] The Moroccan film director Nabil Lahlou condemned Merrakshi's *Marock*, saying "the film has nothing to do with Morocco because it serves all kinds of cultural colonialism."[11] *Le Journal L'Hebdomadaire* published a very well-received article on the "polémiques de Marock" (controversy over *Marock*) entitled "Ce que pensent les politiques du film 'Marock'" (What the politicians think of the film *Marock*). According to the article: "La relation entre Youri Juif et Rita La Musulmane est au coeur du debat." [12] [The relation between Youri, who is Jewish, and Rita, who is Muslim, is at the heart of the debate.] The controversy surrounding the film raised many questions about Merrakshi's own Moroccan identity: In what sense is the film director Moroccan? Does she mean to attack Morocco, or defend its modernity? The criticisms also raised questions about Merrakshi's representation of female sexuality in her film: Does this film represent a threat to traditional notions of womanhood? Why should a woman filmmaker's exploration of alternative sexualities elicit a call for censorship? Can there ever be democracy in a country whose leading politicians want to ban a film for its mere representation of a relationship between a Jew and a Muslim? Merrakshi is viewed by her Moroccan critics as the modern film director who has overstepped societal norms. What was also made evident during the controversy was the struggle for recognition of a female director in the midst of what constitutes a growing trend of commercialized consumption of the female as object. Because it runs counterpoint to the taboos of the old days, the film has also ironically become readily marketable.

A GLOBAL FILM

The film not only contains global themes in its narrative, but is also a global production that necessitated the cooperation and coordination of the director and foreign producers. Merrakshi made the film in collaboration with a French production company while residing in France. The film, which has a worldwide audience and is made of a soundtrack with three languages, was hugely popular upon its release and achieved box office success for the most tickets sold. Merrakshi was also awarded the prize "Un Certain Regard" at the 2005 Cannes Film Festival for directing the film. The title, *Marock*, is a play on the French country name, "Maroc," and "rock." Merrakshi explains the choice of the title thus: "J'ai justement choisi le titre Marock . . . pour rendre compte des paradoxes d'une jeunesse partagée entre la tradition du Maroc ancien et certaines aspirations plus rock 'n' roll."[13] [I have precisely chosen this title to account for the paradoxes of a youth culture that is divided between the traditions of an ancient Morocco and aspirations that are more rock 'n'' roll.] The film's popular reception directly illustrates how Moroccan youth are fascinated by imported mass culture, and thus aspire to a global culture.

Marock represents one of the most significant manifestations of global consumerist culture in Moroccan cinema. In his reading of the film, Brian Edwards approaches it from a global perspective and traces its global cultural meaning.[14] Edwards draws on Benjamin Lee and Edward LiPuma's meditation on "cultures of circulation" to discuss Merrakshi's cultural choices. The circulation of American cultural products in the film promotes a Hollywood-like product that becomes the dominant narrative. Edwards describes *Marock* as a Hollywood teen flick and definitively disassociates it from other genres such as French *cinéma vérité* or Bollywood. Because American movies have been influential and innovative for so many decades, they are seen, discussed, and imitated the world over. The Hollywood pattern has become generic and is copied globally.

The film, which reveals new Moroccan consumerist practices and the role of the protagonists as ultimate consumers, focuses on a variety of spaces—diners, cars, public pools, discos, and bars—associated with and signifying a youth consumerist subculture. *Marock* takes the viewer to a number of other spaces as well, such as the estate belonging to Rita's parents and its surrounding neighborhood, the roads that lead to it, the nearby ocean, the school Rita attends, the ball court, and area nightclubs. What is important here is not what space is presented, but how Merrakshi has worked with her chosen space(s) in order to emphasize the motif of consumerism.[15] Just as there is a divide in the film between the rich and the poor servants who tend to cooking and cleaning, there is also a divide between adults and youth. While the adult generation desires prosperity associated with a Western model of modern living, they reject the imported codes of youth culture and rebellion. The consumption of rock 'n' roll music articulates a symbolic resistance for the youth who flout their families' values. They do this on a symbolic level by also wearing denim jeans and black leather jackets, riding motorcycles, driving BMWs, and listening to rock 'n' roll. Youth in the film represent increasing purchasing power in Morocco's globalized marketplace, a sanctuary of modern consumer culture for those coming of age.

Most interesting in this respect is the representation of American pop culture and its supposedly bad influence on Moroccan teenagers. The t-shirts youth in the film wear are emblazoned with the logos of multinational corporations and universities in other countries. The film further makes mention of pop icons like "Trump," touting a Western-specific brand, and fashionable "textiles and exports" that can be found in virtually any market around the world. In different scenes we see these logos and how they remain out of sync with the reality of the majority of Moroccan culture. Merrakshi shows them because she is an outsider. However, such logos are less prevalent in films made by filmmakers who reside in Morocco. Hicham Lasri, who directed *L'os de fer* (*The Iron Bone*) (2007), is of the same generation as Merrakshi. Although *L'os de fer* also focuses on youth, international logos are nowhere to be found in this film.

The relationship of the female protagonist to youth culture and consumerism is a structuring theme throughout *Marock*. In one scene, Rita and her girlfriends are talking at the disco while playing with their cellphones. In another scene, they are sitting on the roof flipping through teen fashion magazines. According to film critic Teresa Delauretis, feminist cinema subverts the social construction of gender and resists dominant representations. Delauretis uses the term "space off" to designate a space inhabited by woman outside what can be seen within the frame, or male-centered representations of woman.[16] In Merrakshi's film, Rita and her girlfriends occupy the "space off," the "elsewhere" of dominant Moroccan discourses. But this elsewhere in which they are inserted is the space of consumerist culture. The film implies that despite their different ethnic and religious affiliations, Rita and Yuri can bond (along with their friends) in the secular sensuality of affluent consumer culture. Yuri is never seen practicing Judaism, and except for the Star of David he wears on a chain, the viewer would never guess he is a Jew.

The film eroticizes Rita and Yuri's movements within the city, making evident a connection between their romance and consumption. In pursuit of Rita, Yuri rides through the city in his racy black BMW, which he decorates and fetishizes. The car is accessorized so as to convey an aura of supermasculinity. The car is not simply a means of transportation, or for thrills and speed, racing, and conquest; it is a private space in which their romantic relationship develops and unfolds. Their ideas about romance are also imported along with other commodities from the West. In his book *Mensonge romantique et vérité romanesque*, Réné Girard argues that love is based on a triangular relationship between subject, object, and model.[17] According to Girard, desire is awakened not by the object of desire but by the revered Other. Mimetic desire lies neither in the subject nor in the object but in a model imitated by the subject. Girard's concept of the triangular relationship is relevant to Rita and Yuri's Western ideas about love. Through their relationship, the film posits the question: What possibilities does romance open up for practical formulations of contact between cultural groups in Morocco? From Chela Sandoval's theories of romance as the impetus of tactical coalition,[18] to Kaja Silverman's use of romance as a new model for identification based on difference,[19] there is a shared attempt among Western feminists to envision new ethical models of coalition in the face of the divisive forces of globalism. However, in placing romance in the foreground as a model of contact, the film does not disconnect itself from consumer culture.

Commercial culture has an empowering impact on the female protagonist who is allowed to move freely in the public sphere of the rich. We never see Rita anywhere else, which means that she would have a different sort of agency in the shanty town of Sidi Moumen or other poor areas in Casablanca. Her independence challenges the authority of the male-dominated public space. Rita first enters the scene with a Westernized appearance. Her lifestyle is defined by the trappings of Western consumer culture. Being from the upper class in Casablanca, she lives the life of material abundance and upward mobility. Her purchasing power, however, is dependent upon the affluence of her parents. In this vein, the film also exposes the vulgarity of Rita's pseudo-autonomy, as her taste for luxury and trendy clothing goes beyond the consumer attitude of the average Moroccan teenage girl. In the opening scenes, Rita conveys only her desire for cigarettes, nightclubs, and sex. She defies the authority of the police, the servants, her family, and religion. In one sequence of the film, Rita, dressed in a bikini, is looking at herself in the mirror. Her relation to her own reflection in the mirror explains her inability to accept the ideal image traditional society expects of Moroccan women.

When her brother Mao claims authority over her, on religious grounds, their first conflict arises. Compared to Rita's modern consumerist identity, her brother Mao is portrayed as traditional and religious. Rita refuses to accept Mao's religious authority. Her recorded music with English lyrics is one way she demonstrates her rebelliousness. The conflict is followed by a shot of Rita in front of the stove, her face showing her disgust. She defiantly proclaims, "je n'ai pas besoin de la religion pour dormir tranquille." [I do not need religion in order to sleep peacefully.] In one scene, she stands in a bikini top and shorts mocking her brother who is prostrated in prayer. In another scene, she is shown eating and smoking during Ramadan. According to Mohammed Hirschi's reading of the film, Merrakshi deploys the characters of Mao and Rita to make evident the cultural pluralism in Moroccan society: "Both characters represent a microcosm that can only be understood within the framework of a society struggling to reconcile religiosity and secularism."[20]

A FEMINIST FILM?

From my analysis of *Marock*, it becomes clear that the perspective offered by the film suggests not a reaction against feminism but a continuation of what some critics have called "neo-feminism," a doctrine that focuses on the autonomy of the female body (free sexuality, etc.) and that has been advocated by, among others, Helen Gurley Brown and Naomi Wolf. In her book *Neo-Feminist Cinema: Girly Films, Chick Flicks and Consumer Culture*, Hilary Radner argues that neo-feminist films share a number of traits that include "an emphasis on fashion and consumer culture; the disappearance of chastity as 'a feminine virtue'; romance as a significant theme (if not necessarily the primary plot)."[21] The film foregrounds Rita's persona as an expression of a certain strand of contemporary Moroccan feminism and its relation to the neo-feminist paradigm.

Merrakshi's feminist enterprise is problematic, however. While the film foregrounds female sexuality to a public that had previously repressed it, it also reinforces stereotyped notions of female sexuality in a consumer society. The film relies on notions borrowed from a global-level consumer culture that positions the woman as spectacle. In addition to appealing to the Moroccan public's consumption of sexuality, it adopts a more widespread and mundane view of sexuality, one associated with Western consumer markets positing the Hollywood love story as the dominant narrative for blockbuster films. Merrakshi tries to break old taboos, but she paradoxically reinforces the very same essentialized notions of female sexuality that her critics uphold, and thus deprives women of the chance to construct an identity free from stereotypical notions of womanhood. Public consumption of female sexuality is witnessed first-hand in the stir the film caused. Part of the controversy that lies behind Merrakshi's *Marock* is how the film, more than those of other Moroccan female directors, is about exposure.[22] The film reveals how the young female protagonist thinks and how she is moved by her desires and frustrations. Such exposure coincides with the commercialization of images of women. The mise-en-scènes of Rita and Yuri's sexual encounters, and the sexually provocative covers of magazines like *Telquel*,[23] revealing images of Rita's half-naked body, cater to the hungry gaze of the public, thus rendering Rita an object of voyeurism.

Just as much as Merrakshi pushes the limits of socially acceptable norms, she is complicit with the commercial forces that objectify women. The uncontrolled female sexuality that stirs the controversy surrounding the female director is fueled by consumer culture. American cultural critic Susan Douglas calls the phenomenon at work here "enlightened sexism,"[24] which celebrates a woman's free agency over her own body and her sexuality, touting "girl power" as a new version of feminism. But the downside of such enlightened sexism is exploitive commercialism. Enlightened sexism underscores the media's commercialization of female sexuality. While Merrakshi's neo-feminism challenges Morocco's traditional politics, it remains complicit with the hegemony of globalization. The film's ironies arise from the conundrum of using film as a form of rebellion against traditional values to promote female agency, when the production of cinema imposes its own forms of hegemony through globalization, sometimes in the form of a "Hollywood aesthetic."

NOTES

1. Hamid Naficy has stressed the importance of the "exile, émigré, refugee, and expatriate" in the production of the transnational film. According to him, films made by postcolonial filmmakers living in the diaspora are "accented." Their different accent stems from their different modes of production, as well as their stylistic and cultural variation. In Naficy's terms, Merrakshi has the profile of an "accented filmmaker." Naficy argues that accented filmmakers, "however marginalized they are within the center, their ability to access the means of production may prove as empowering to the marginalia of the post-industrial era as the capturing of the means of production would have been to the subalterns of the industrial era." Merrakshi's displacement is a voluntary one because, within the center, she would not be marginalized in as much as she is part of a small elite who is able to make any films at all. Hamid Naficy, *An Accented Cinema: Exilic and Diasporic Filmmaking* (Princeton: Princeton University Press, 2001), 11.

2. Leila Merrakshi, *Marock*, (France and Morocco: Pan Européenne Distribution, 2005), film, 105 minutes.

3. Valérie Orlando, *Screening Morocco: Contemporary Depictions in Film of a Changing Society* (Athens, OH: Ohio University Press, 2011), 125.

4. The Arab Spring has resulted in a new constitution in Morocco that was instituted in July 2011. Under the new constitution, the prime minister becomes the head of the executive branch. The new constitution has also given more power to the parliament and judiciary. The constitution grants more rights to women and to the Amazigh Berber population. Refer to

Kenneth M. Pollack, Daniel L. Byman, Akram Al-Turk, et al., *The Arab Awakening: America and the Transformation of the Middle East* (Washington, DC: Brookings Institution Press, 2011).

5. Loubna H. Skalli, *Through a Local Prism: Gender, Globalization, and Identity in Moroccan Women's Magazines* (Lanham, MD: Lexington Books, 2006), 62.

6. Abdellah Laroui, *The Crisis of the Arab Intellectual: Traditionalism or Historicism?* (Berkeley: University of California Press, 1976), 165–166.

7. Mary Louise Pratt, *Imperial Eyes: Travel Writing and Transculturation.* (New York: Routledge, 2008[1992]), 8.

8. "The Marock Debate." March 2006. http://riadzany.blogspot.com/2006/01/marock debate. html (accessed September 1, 2008).

9. Ibid.

10. Ibid.

11. Ibid.

12. Hicham Houdaifa and Fedoua Tounassi, "Marock: Le vrai debat," *Le Journal L'Hebdomadaire* (May 27–June 2, 2006), 24.

13. Karim Boukhari, "*Marock*: Le film de tous les tabous," *Telquel* 223 (May 2005), http://www.telquel-online.com/223/couverture_223_1.shtml (accessed January 5, 2009).

14. Brian Edwards, "*Marock* in Morocco: Reading Moroccan Films in the Age of Circulation," *Journal of North African Studies* 12 (2007): 287–307.

15. A good article on the issue of space in the film is Safoi Babana-Hampton's work published in *The Journal of North African Studies*. Refer to Safoi Babana-Hampton, "Bringing into Focus Narrative Text and Subtext in Moroccan Film: *Marock*'s Hors-Champ," in *The Journal of North African Studies*, 15, no. 3 (September 2010): 289–303.

16. Teresa de Lauretis, *Technologies of Gender : Essays on Theory, Film and Fiction* (Bloomington: Indiana University Press, 1987), 25–26.

17. Réné Girard, *Mensonge romantique et vérité romanesque* (Paris: Grasset, 1961).

18. Chela Sandoval, *Methodology of the Oppressed* (Minneapolis: University of Minnesota Press, 2000).

19. Kaja Silverman, *The Threshold of the Visible World* (New York: Routledge, 1996).

20. Mohammed Hirschi, "The Ethics and Politics of Laila Marrakchi's *Marock*," *South Central Review*, 28, no. 1 (Spring 2008): 93.

21. Hilary Radner, *Neo-Feminist Cinema: Girly Films, Chick Flicks and Consumer Culture* (New York: Routledge, 2011).

22. The notion of exposure both as object and as a mode of representation has been explored in a collection of essays: Kathryn Banks and Joseph Harris, eds., *Exposure: Revealing Bodies, Unveiling Representations* (Oxford: Peter Lang Publishing, Inc., 2004).

23. Leila Boukhari, "Marock." In its 223rd issue that appeared in 2005, a few weeks after *Marock* was released, the magazine *Telquel* dedicated its headline story to the film. The front cover of the magazine featured Rita in a bikini looking down at her brother who was prostrating in Muslim prayer.

24. Susan J. Douglas, *The Rise of Enlightened Sexism: How Pop Culture Took Us from Girl Power to Girls Gone Wild* (New York: St. Martin's Press, 2010), 11.

IV

Internet Discourse and Women as Agents of Change

Chapter Ten

Debating Islam, Gender, and the Arab Spring

Moroccan and Tunisian Women's Cyberspace

Like literature, testimonial writing, and film, social media has played a significant role in promoting social and political change. Authors and filmmakers are no longer the only cultural producers fostering change. Women contributing to social media have amply shown that they can act as agents of change in their own societies. Just as importantly, access to online social networks now heralds the emergence of a new generation of young, politicized, activist feminists who utilize the new technologies of the Internet to agitate for reform. As a consequence of this new medium and the web of connections it offers, a number of questions arise: Why is social media more effective than literature, testimony, or film in promoting women's causes? How do "literary forms" connect to "Internet forms" of resistance? How would authors like Bessie Head have used blogging, Twitter, and Facebook to advance their cause? Would Head's writing have been different? And how, for example, would the Internet have helped to stop apartheid if it had been in existence then? Literature, film, and testimony inform and have long been informed by media forms. The Internet has been approached by some critics as a form of literature and as an emerging linguistic medium with its own language codes and dialects. Moreover, while books and films reach a certain number of people at a given time, cyberspace offers endless potential for attracting new audiences, advancing activist discourses, and effecting real change.

Feminist activists from Africa are increasingly affirming their identities to the world via the Internet. They are using blogs, Facebook, and other social networking sites to communicate their views about women's rights and political reform to a wider public. Social media allows them to communicate in a direct and uncensored way, and situate themselves on the international stage. The context of their Internet activism is global, highly political, and important worldwide, especially in light of recent uprisings sweeping North Africa and the Middle East. Facebook use and blogging are timely, and international responses take on more importance than the blogs themselves. Feminist activists from Morocco and Tunisia have deployed Facebook and blogging in recent years as a tool for networking with other feminists and forming various groups. This chapter looks at how they converse online on issues of gender, Islam, and the Arab Spring in the present globalized context. Tunisian women contributed to the 2011 Jasmine Revolution by sharing information through the Internet at the grassroots level. Similarly, Moroccan women's Internet activism was a contributing factor in passage of the new family code or *Moudawana* of 2004. Facebook and blogging, which allow these women to speak freely to one another and encourage them to organize, are platforms that are not only useful for coalescing around key social and political issues pertaining to women, but also for initiating change on social and political levels. Data from postings on Facebook and blogs in English, French, and Arabic show what women want to communicate with each other. They desire reform of family law, greater freedom in public spaces, fuller participation in the economy, and stronger representation in their nations' politics. Questions that have emerged from my research, are: How can these women's cultural-political-religious discourse be used as a tool for change? What is the nature of responses to their online postings? Can the online community of feminist activists engage in debate more freely than in other venues? Are there discourse rules for this venue that differ from other forms of discourse?

A NEW EMERGING PUBLIC

Women's Internet discourses need to be placed within the overall context of what Dale Eickelman and Jon Anderson describe as a newly emerging public perception in Muslim societies. In their book *New Media in the Muslim World: The Emerging Public Sphere*, Eickelman and Anderson argue that "a new sense of public is emerging throughout Muslim-majority states and Muslim communities elsewhere. It is shaped by increasingly open contests over the authoritative use of the symbolic language of Islam. New and increasingly accessible modes of communication have made these contests increasingly global."[1] Social media has allowed the public in large numbers to contribute to civil society in a new space that is beyond the control of state institutions. In countries of the Arabian Peninsula, for instance, Internet communications, through videos, e-mail, CD-ROMs, and Facebook, have helped spread criticisms of Arab regimes. Eickelman and Anderson further explore the role of social media technology in activism for social and political change: "The proliferation of actors able to assert a public role leads to a fragmentation of authority, and it increases the numbers of persons involved in creating and sustaining a religious-civil public discourse."[2] Accordingly, the effect these media have had on Muslim countries has been revolutionary; the Internet and related technology have transformed notions of gender, justice, politics, as well as religious authority: "What distinguishes the present era from prior ones is the large number of believers engaged in the 'reconstruction' of religion, community, and society. . . . Today, the major impetus for religious and political change comes from below."[3]

However, the authors elide the relevance of gender to conducting civil society activism and to bringing about such religious and political change. In her essay "Curses and Blessings: Women and the Internet Revolution in the Arab World," Deborah Wheeler compares data pertaining to Internet use among women in five Muslim countries and concludes that women are using the Internet to empower themselves and negotiate both the public and private spheres. The Internet can also be used by women to negotiate the global community and participate in global culture. It can keep women informed about women's rights elsewhere as well as allow them to form coalitions and professional networks.[4] Along the same lines, Miriam Cooke argues that cyber-networking among individual women is very revolutionary as it allows them free movement and "virtual connections." The Internet is "de-territorialized and gender inclusive. . . . Unlike in the time of Ibn Khaldun . . . women today can travel, physically and imaginatively, forming their own networks."[5] Within the context of globalization, feminism in North Africa has been transformed due to an unprecedented number of social networks online. As Internet access increases among the low-income as well as the more privileged classes, and as cyber cafés have become prevalent outside major cities, the Internet has become a new conduit for communication among activists and a valuable tool in effecting change. Women activists are also using the Internet to cultivate their own feminism, despite the Internet censorship that strives at times to block content related to human rights issues and political reform.[6] Their calls for change in family laws and their countries' political systems have energized debate about women's issues across the region.

CONVERSING ON GENDER IN MOROCCO

Women in Morocco express their views online about the relationship between their religion and personal legal status. The category "Moroccan woman" is problematized in a way that sets the scene for the data presented as well as highlights the cross-cutting issues of class, education, and ethnicity that mark these women's identities. The "Moroccan woman" category raises the critical question of where the focus lies: users of the Internet or women of a particular class; conservative women, who have a different perception of religion, patriarchy, and sexuality, political reform, or the secular feminists? It follows that there are as many Moroccan female identities as there are Moroccan women. There are Moroccan women in the diaspora, Moroccan women youth, Islamists, seculars, nonbelievers, urban elites, and the rural poor, among others. This section traces the voices of Moroccan women that are not only Internet-active, but come from different cultural contexts and class backgrounds, and speak different languages. The authorship of these women is at times difficult to pinpoint due to the hidden identity of the bloggers and Facebook users, and some of the anonymous posts even turn out to belong to men. What unites these women, however, is their common access to social media and a desire to effect change.

Fractures in the country's political establishments regarding legal reforms affect women's personal status and must first be understood in order for these women's arguments to be more meaningful to readers of their online posts. In Morocco, early personal status laws were established during the colonial period, partly in imitation of pre-1975 French laws. Family laws based on "Islamic law," regulating such issues as marriage, divorce, and inheritance, were further codified in the postindependence period. Traditionally, Islamic law welcomes multiple interpretations and the diversity of opinions, but once codified, the set of family laws based on Islamic *Shari'a* became stultified and closed to debate or reinterpretation. The state regulated the relationship between men and women. Following independence from the French in 1956, a Moroccan civil law was codified in which women were viewed as equal to men. But under the 1957 *Moudawana* (the Family Code), which was based on Maliki jurisprudence, women were treated as legal minors. Male and female activists protested the existing *Moudawana*, and their efforts bore fruit when Mohammed IV introduced radical reforms in 2004, thus initiating a new era in women's rights. According to many feminist activists, however, such legal victories did not translate into any notable change in women's living conditions in Morocco. In a *New York Times* article, headlined "Family Law's Reach is Limited in Morocco," Steven Erlanger and Souad Mekhennet discuss the new *Moudawana*, which remains deeply controversial. Conservative religious figures object that many family judges, who impede successful implementation of the reforms, are susceptible to corruption, and a recent poll showed 49 percent of respondents opining that it "gave too many rights to women."[7]

A Netherlands-raised US-resident female anthropologist has commented on *The New York Times* review of the Moroccan *Moudawana* "from the field" (that is, from Morocco) in her blog, "bisahha: Adventures in Morocco." Among other comments, she states:

> The new law was passed by the parliament in Rabat. . . . But very little of it all penetrates the margins—by which I mean both those geographical areas far removed from the epicenter of government, as well as those communities far removed from any sense of power, through lack of money and lack of education. . . . Those women who stand to gain the most from these new laws—impoverished, uneducated, illiterate women in rural regions—are the least aware of their new rights, and continue their lives much as they used to.[8]

It is this lack of an outreach strategy, linked with conservatism and lack of education for women (about 38 percent of women nationwide are illiterate), that impel Moroccan feminist activists to raise the issue of women's rights through the Internet. They believe that the laws can change to suit women's social, economic, and political conditions. These feminists have considerable collective power, and they are using their global consciousness to exercise such power. They also understand that Islam is global, and they therefore need to make their lives within Islam fit in globally. More importantly, their activism has set the stage for changes in the legal codes of their predominantly Muslim nations.

In the Facebook groups they have created, Moroccan women express dissent, independence, and day-to-day reflections on their own lives in Morocco. "Moroccan Women's Rights" is one of the Facebook groups that explicitly challenge the role of women in Morocco. The group represents a variety of perspectives, from those who are secular and nonreligious to those who want to negotiate change from a religious position. The posts are written either in Arabic, French, or English. Members of the group share some common attributes. They all seem to be highly educated, articulate, socially active, and young. There is also a gender distribution of 70 percent female and 30 percent male among the participants. What first catches the attention of a visitor to this site are the photos of leading feminist activists Fatima El Mernissi, Houria El Naciri, Touria Jabrane, and other women at the forefront of the battle for women's rights in Morocco today. Some of the posts are obliquely referenced, as members of the group at times seem to be answering their opponents without quoting them. But some entries, like this one in which Nidal Chaouki states her views about women and inheritance laws in Islam, address at length a fundamental issue that dominates much of the discussion among Muslim feminists:

> It is mentioned in Surah An Nisa', that Inheritance must be shared between one another by dividing it into legitimate parts. . . . Thus, God gave to men 2/3 (the brother), and to women (the sister) 1/3. . . . The current issue nowadays, in the 21st century, is that . . . the Inheritance issue of the 14th century does not

> adapt itself anymore with the new social status of women nowadays. The solution should be that religious experts in *Shari'a* and Ulemma must develop the *Shari'a* to better meet the new woman's social role and requirements in the 21st century.[9]

Nidal's post raises the common argument that inheritance laws are sexist, where even when they inherit, women are forced to give up their rightful shares to their male relatives. The one clear message of these laws is that only men can be recognized as heads of households, responsible for supporting their families, and women do not need an income because they are being supported by their husbands or other male relatives. It should be noted that traditional inheritance laws have not undergone any changes under the new *Moudawana*. Nidal's post is an example of recent calls to bring changes to inheritance laws in order to protect the legal rights of Moroccan women.

The posts also raise important questions about the role of women in Moroccan society as it relates to the discourse of feminism. In one of her frequent posts, Nadya Chamor, drawing on Lesson 82 of the well-known Web site "Philosophie et spiritualité,"[10] writes: "The image of woman in postmodernity is but an image; it is not the essence of femininity"[11] Chamor laments the role of woman as an object of male desire in a postmodern, commodity-centered culture. While she denounces feminism in its traditional sense as an extreme form, which has made of woman the image of man, she also poses sophisticated questions about femininity. Another respondent, "Wiam," further argues that "feminism should not be looked at according to stereotypes: it is merely a way to correct a lot of misconceptions about women . . . redefine gender roles. . . . It is a constant trial to question some patriarchal (male-biased) norms that are still prevailing in our societies."[12] Yet another respondent poses the question as to whether Islam has defined femininity. Such reflections on feminism and femininity, from the perspectives of Moroccan women, are proof of emerging new viewpoints from women who are seeking to redefine feminism in a fashion that is suitable to their roles within their society. Their questions also show how they are trying to grapple with the contradictory claims of gender hierarchy and egalitarianism within Islam and elaborate an alternative set of interpretations that are friendly and inclusive of women. The issue of femininity as it relates to Islam is further debated in another discussion thread where the group considers the question of sexuality as constructed in a culture such as that of Morocco, which is pervaded by taboos, shame, and secrecy. The ensuing discussion explores various cultural constructions of gender and sexuality that shape Moroccan women's identities. Members of the group seem to agree that they need to not use religious arguments so that they do not judge others, and as populations are more and more mixed, laws should be rather secular, allowing for pluralism and diversity.

One of the groups' vibrant debates is the 2004 *Moudawana*, the groundbreaking reforms that have expanded women's legal rights in Morocco. In a posting entitled "F as Feminist!" Wahb begins the discussion by asking the question: "Could women and men be really equal? Are you satisfied with the new *Moudawana* regarding women's rights?"[13] Wahb uses the word "equal" as though it meant "same," and continues in a follow-up posting by seeming not to see beyond "wedding":

> Men and Women can never be equal because physically they are not. We complete and respect each other. The current *Moudawana* granted so many rights for women and now men are very scared from getting engaged or married!! The number of weddings has dropped dramatically in the last 3 years!! To get the exact statistics, you just need to call any wedding planner (*un traiteur*) and you'll hear him/her crying about the business they [have] lost!![14]

Wiam goes back to 1848, focusing on human rights and resistance to stereotypes: "People should correct first the misconceptions about feminism and [the] women's movement, [which] started universally in 1848 . . . and was asking for equality in terms of education, work, vote, etc. . . . generally speaking for female representation in male-dominated areas like business, politics, technology, education."[15] This posting encourages the reader to infer that feminism in Morocco is a middle-class movement, as it was in the United States. In Europe, feminism was more a movement of working-class women who participated in the labor movement, organizing in mills and factories. Wiam's most poignant allegation is that "those women who need [the *Moudawana*] the most have never heard of it." She states: "The problem is that the whole *Moudawana* is still a theoretical thing out of touch with miserable reality. . . . Those women who need it most have never heard of it . . . because it wasn't addressed to solve their problems."[16]

Adnane emphasizes that women do more than they get credit for, both in the marketplace and as their children's first teachers. He sees feminism as protecting and reinforcing the roles of wives and mothers.[17] He does not, however, address matters of equal pay for equal work, female inheritance, or financial protection for divorcees and widows. Wiam justifiably responds with reference to economic coercion and exploitation. In reducing all complaints to one issue that could be resolved if Moroccan men would treat Moroccan women with "respect," "Myriam" gives no clue as to why such respect is lacking. She vaguely claims, "There is something wrong with mentalities everywhere."[18] That does not explain what "challenging issues" Moroccan women are faced with, nor does it address specifically what they are organizing to change. Zineb, like Wahb, is not concerned with scaring men, but like Wiam, she wants legal protection for all members of society regardless of class or gender. She seems to see the goals of feminism in terms of human rights.[19]

The postings reveal how young people in Morocco who know English, French, and Arabic can approach the *Moudawana* from varying perspectives. What is noticeable is that members of the group choose to speak in French and English, especially when discussing taboo topics and very private matters, because it is often easier to discuss topics considered taboo in Arabic culture in a foreign language. When discussing the taboo topic of sexuality, most participants switched to English, a language that is furthest from their cultural context. In sum, the fact that young men and women are debating gender and Islam signals the beginning of a new feminist discourse in which both men and women are committed to democratic pluralism, human rights, and freedom of expression and ideas. The passion with which they debate the new changes happening in Morocco attests to their optimism about a new era where Islam is made compatible with women's rights, and not otherwise.

TUNISIA'S REVOLUTIONARY BLOGGERS

Since the institution of the 1956 Code of Personal Status, Tunisian women have been entitled to political, economic, and marital rights. The code proclaims equality between men and women, prohibits polygamy, legalizes abortion, and grants women rights in marriage and divorce. Even though women's causes received considerable support from both the governments and citizenry, feminist activists have contended that women have often been used as instruments by dictatorial leaders to justify their grip on power. Tunisian women, like their Arab counterparts, have not been fully integrated into civic society and politics and have been subject to censorship and repression. Under the rule of deposed dictator Zine Al Abedine Ben Ali, most intellectuals chose to remain silent. To evade censorship, young Tunisian women resorted to the Internet as a revolutionary and liberating form of communication. Blogging offers these women not only a means of communication but also a method to organize, act, and promote awareness. The press coverage that these blogs have received offers evidence of the significance of this new medium.[20] Tunisian women blog to share stories of injustices and to voice concerns about freedom of expression, political change, and the status of women in their country.

Under the Ben Ali regime, women were censored by the government for their Internet activism and, in some cases, subjected to intimidation and torture. One example is former blogger Amira Yahyaoui, who was exiled to Paris after posting her controversial opinions in a number of blogs. Notably, it was Web-savvy women like Yahyaoui who played a pivotal role in the Tunisian revolution of January 2011, when Tunisians revolted against the authoritarian regime of Ben Ali and forced him to flee the country. Blogger Lina Ben Mhenni was responsible for spreading the news of the events unfolding in Sidi Bouzid, the birthplace of the revolution, after Mohammed Bouazizi, an unemployed Tunisian, set himself on fire. Communiqués through her Facebook page and Twitter account served to spread the spark of revolution at the grassroots level. Mhenni was internationally recognized for her activism when she was nominated for the Nobel Peace Prize in 2011. She wrote in a blog, dated December 23, 2010: "While the fate of Mohamed Bouazizi, aged 26, from Sidi Bouzid remains unclear, Tunisian netizens used the incident to complain about the lack of jobs, corruption and deteriorating human rights conditions in their country."[21] She credits what she calls "citizen media" (e.g., blogs, Facebook, and Twitter) for covering a dire situation driving a number of Tunisian youth to suicide by self-immolation.[22] Bloggers like Lina Ben Mhenni started blogging because they want to express themselves in a state where traditional media outlets remain inaccessible to women who lack political representation. The need to express oneself publicly, coupled with the need to effect change, is reflected in their struggle for the cause of freedom of expression. In one blog, Mhenni expresses anger over government-appointed Internet police who hacked her blogs and Facebook account: "The act of hacking is an act of rape. . . . You can censor. You can hack. But you can't stop us from writing!"[23] Despite intimidation by the authorities, Mhenni continues to post entries and report political developments in Tunisia in her blog "A Tunisian Girl," which won the seventh annual Deutsche Welle International Blog Award.

Emna Ben Jemaa is another feminist activist who blogs over issues of justice and freedom of expression. In May 2010, she joined a demonstration on the steps of the Tunisian Ministry of Communication Technologies building in protest of Web censorship, for which she was later arrested and interrogated by the police. In a blog entry entitled "Je suis une citoyenne tunisienne qui a peur" [I am a Tunisian citizen who is scared], she expresses her perseverance in the face of fear: "Many people congratulate me on my courage. . . . Sharing a web link online has become an act of militancy. . . . I continue to express myself in a spontaneous and open manner. I resist fear."[24] In a different blog entry, Ben Jemaa expresses her outrage over the silence of authorities about what is happening during the revolution: "Tunisians are dying, killed by bullets, and what is horrible is that Tunisian TV is portraying the victims as delinquents. . . . I accuse all silent Tunisians of complicity."[25]

Women bloggers like Amira Yahyaoui, who was exiled by Ben Ali's regime for her involvement in the anticensure movement, have now returned to Tunisia to help rebuild the country: "Up until now, I have been active in the opposition in Tunisian politics. Now I want to propose and construct. I am at the head of the independent electoral list, Sawt Mostakel, with a real project which I am ready to go and defend in the constitutional assembly."[26] Women bloggers were apprehensive when the Islamist party, Ennahda, won the elections in October 2011. Yet, Amira Yahyaoui pins her hopes on the Ennahda party. According to her, women's rights were just cosmetic under Ben Ali's regime: "Just because you're wearing a bikini and drinking beer. . . . You are not free. I'd rather have the burqa and democracy. . . . And I am secular."[27] According to Mehrezia Labidi, a member of the Ennahda party, and the deputy speaker of the assembly, women are better represented in the new government than they were under the rule of the former dictator. Under his governance, only 20 percent of the labor force consisted of women, who were relegated to low-paying jobs, while rural women were kept poor and marginalized: "The former regime was selective in its enlightenment, choosing to favor only a tiny elite while portraying itself as the champion of women."[28] The Arab Spring, in her view, has created space for women's political representation and activism. Women now constitute 28 percent of the assembly and 48 percent of the Ennahda party. So far, the party has increased the number of women who are involved in the decision-making process and who are actively participating in the implementation of new policies for national development, thus empowering them to be agents of change. Women in the assembly are involved in the drafting of the new constitution to make sure that a legal framework, guaranteeing women's rights, is put into effect.[29]

Despite these gains in women's political representation, recent debates in the constituent assembly regarding the inclusion of *Shari'a* (Islamic law) in Tunisia's constitution have worried liberal parties and secular feminists who fear a backlash against women. Meriem Zeghidi, a human rights activist and a member of the Tunisian Association of Democratic Women, states that while women's rights have not yet been affected by the Islamists, recent references to *Shari'a* law, polygamy, Islamic marriages, and the veil, by some party leaders, are cause for concern.[30] On March 8, 2012, in commemoration of International Women's Day, feminist activists like Amel Ben Attia wore traditional garb to protest the foreign clothing styles adopted by Islamists and to show "all those who stole the revolution and who want to impose customs that are not ours that the niqab [the Saudi-style, all-concealing Islamic garb] does not represent Tunisian women."[31] The protests have compelled Prime Minister Rashed Ghannouchi to assure the public that *Shari'a* law will not be applied in the new constitution. In a blog entry entitled "Ennahda et la Chariaa" [Ennahda and Shari'a], Emna Ben Jemaa states that the Ennahda party has announced that it will keep Article 1 of the 1959 Tunisian constitution, which stipulates that Tunisia is a free state, independent and sovereign: Islam is its religion, Arabic its language, and the republic is its regime.[32] Ben Jemaa remains suspicious, however, of the motivations of Ennahda members and expresses fear about indoctrination of average

Tunisians into radical forms of Islam.[33] Amira Yahyaoui denies such allegations and insists that the Ennahda party is not radical: "They couldn't have won now with a fundamentalist Islamist agenda, but maybe in 10 years. . . . For now they have to be reassuring."[34]

Thus, the power of social media to connect women around their collective call for sociopolitical change has been unprecedented. Nevertheless, what we have seen is just the tip of the iceberg in terms of the potential that the Internet offers these women. From my analysis of the "Moroccan Women's Rights" Facebook site, it becomes obvious that both men and women rally around the same issues pertaining to women and social change. Women and men alike debate and argue in the social network site. Their debates are an example of the potential political use of the Internet to effect change. My analysis of Tunisian women's blogs shows that while Tunisian women lack a concrete feminist strategy of resistance to effect change, they are nevertheless using the Internet as a means to raise feminist consciousness and further their feminist goals. The Internet is also a space where they can keep each other up to date about the latest legislation and projects. It is a space wherein they can help to organize actions via online petitions and e-mail campaigns to politicians. Through interaction with such technologies, they have employed alternative forms of self-representation. In doing so, they dispute prevailing constructions of gender in their societies. The Internet, appropriated by these women as a tool of representation, has also become their tool of resistance.

Nevertheless, these women bloggers and Facebook users, however well connected, are not the whole story. As Duncan J. Watts notes in his book *Everything Is Obvious Once You Know the Answer*, the spread of an idea or taste also depends on "a critical mass of easily influenced people who influence other easy-to-influence people. When this critical mass existed, even an average individual was capable of triggering a large cascade."[35] In Andrew Delbanco's review of a book about Harriet Beecher Stowe's influential *Uncle Tom's Cabin*, the author reveals that the first print run was five thousand copies. Within a year, three hundred thousand copies of the book had been sold in America and over a million were sold in Britain. Yet more than ten times the number who bought the book may have been influenced by it because it came out during a pre-electronic social networking era when reading aloud to family and friends was common practice and the principal means of disseminating information.[36] And the response changed American history—just as the response to women's electronic social media is changing history now.

NOTES

1. Dave Eickelman and Jon Anderson, *New Media in the Muslim World: The Emerging Public Sphere*, 2nd Edition (Bloomington: Indiana University Press, 2003), 1.

2. Ibid., 14.

3. Dave Eickelman, "Inside the Islamic Revolution," in *Revolutionaries and Reformers: Contemporary Islamist Movements in the Middle* East, ed. Rubin Barry (Albany: State University of New York Press, 2003), 204.

4. Deborah Wheeler, "Curses and Blessings: Women and the Internet Revolution in the Arab World," in *Women and Media in the Middle East: Power through Self-Expression*, ed. Naomi Sakr (London: I. B. Tauris & Co. Ltd., 2004), 144.

5. Miriam Cooke and Bruce Lawrence, eds. *Muslim Networks from Hajj to Hip Hop* (Chapel Hill: University of North Carolina Press, 2005), 11.

6. For more information about Internet censorship in Morocco, refer to OpenNet Initiative, a Web site about Internet censorship in the mena region (the Middle East and North Africa). https://opennet.net/research/regions/mena (26 March 2013).

7. Steven Erlanger and Souad Mekhennet. "Family Code Gets Nudge but Women Seek a push," *New York Times* on the Web, 18 August 2009, http://www.nytimes.cazom/2009/08/19/world/africa/19tangiers.html?_r=1 (15 September 2009).

8. "The Moudawana: Five Years Later," August 20, 2009, http://bisahha.blogspot.com (July 7, 2011).

9. Nidal Chaouki, November 16, 2006, comment on Facebook post "Moroccan Women in the Past and Today (La femme marocaine dans le passé et aujourd'hui)," November 15, 2006, http://www.facebook.com/topic.php?uid=2217515955&topic=2076 (accessed November 2, 2009).

10. For the "Philosophie et spiritualité" Web site, visit http://sergecar.perso.neuf.fr.

11. Nadya Chamor, "La Feminite entre Nature et Culture," Facebook post, July 19 2009, http://www.facebook.com/topic.php?uid=24115319304&topic=11791 (accessed November 2, 2009).

12. Wiam, December 4, 2006, comment on Facebook post "F as Feminist!" December 2, 2006, http://www.facebook.com/topic.php?uid=2217515955&topic=2139 (accessed November 4, 2009).

13. Ibid.

14. Ibid.

15. Wiam, comment on Facebook post "F as Feminist!!"

16. Ibid.

17. Adnane, December 6, 2006, comment on Facebook post "F as Feminist!!" December 2, 2006, http://www.facebook.com/topic.php?uid=2217515955&topic=2139 (accessed November 4, 2009).

18. Myriam, December 6, 2006, comment on Facebook post "F as Feminist!!" December 2, 2006, http://www.facebook.com/topic.php?uid=2217515955&topic=2139 (accessed November 4, 2009).

19. Zineb, December 6, 2006, comment on Facebook post "F as Feminist!!" December 2, 2006, http://www.facebook.com/topic.php?uid=2217515955&topic=2139 (accessed November 4, 2009).

20. One example of such articles on Tunisian women bloggers is: Kristen Mctiche, "A Blogger at Arab Spring's Genesis," *The New York Times*, October 12, 2011, http://www.nytimes.com/2011/10/13/world/africa/a-blogger-at-arab-springs-genesis.html?_r=1 (accessed May 30, 2012).

21. Lina Ben Mhenni, "Tunisia: Unemployed Man's Suicide Attempt Sparks Riots," blog post, December 23, 2010, http://atunisiangirl.blogspot.com (accessed March 20, 2011).

22. Lina Ben Mhenni, "Sidi Bouzid is Burning," blog post, December 19, 2010, http://atunisiangirl.blogspot.com/2010/12/sidi-bouzid-is-burning.html (accessed March 20, 2011).

23. Lina Ben Mhenni, "You Cannot Stop Us from Writing!" blog post, January 3, 2011, http://atunisiangirl.blogspot.com/2011/01/you-cant-stop-us-from-writing.html (accessed May 28, 2012).

24. Emna Ben Jemaa, "Je suis une citoyenne Tunisienne qui a peur," blog post, January 2, 2011, http://emmabenji.canalblog.com/archives/2011/01/02/index.html (accessed May 30, 2012).

25. Emna Ben Jemaa, "En Deuil," blog post, January 10, 2011, http://emmabenji.canalblog.com/archives/2011/01/10/index.html (accessed May 29, 2012).

26. Amira Yahyaoui, "Women's Forum for the Economy and Society: Building the Future with Women's Vision," Global Meeting 2011, http://www.womens-forum.com/speaker/global-meeting-2011/amira-yahyaoui (accessed May 28, 2012).

27. Ibid.

28. Mehrezia Labidi, "Tunisia's Women are at the Heart of its Revolution," *Guardian*, March 23, 2012, http://www.guardian.co.uk/commentisfree/2012/mar/23/tunisia-women-revolution (accessed May 28, 2012).

29. Ibid.

30. "The Unfinished Revolution of Tunisia's Women," blog post, March 8 2012, http://eurobdnews.blogspot.com/2012/03/unfinished-revolution-of-tunisias-women.html#!/2012/03/unfinished-revolution-of-tunisias-women.html (accessed May 28, 2012).

31. Ibid.

32. Emna Ben Jemaa, "Ennahda et la Chariaa, la Comédie Continue," blog post, March 26, 2012, http://emmabenji.canalblog.com/archives/2012/03/26/23861947.html (accessed May 30, 2012).

33. Ibid.

34. Louise Loftus, "Mixed Messages for Tunisian Women," *The New York Times*, November 21, 2011, http://www.nytimes.com/2011/11/21/world/middleeast/mixed-messages-for-tunisian-women.html (accessed May 30, 2012).

35. Nicholas A. Christakis, "The Trouble with Common Sense," review of *Everything Is Obvious Once You Know the Answer*, by Duncan J. Watts, *The New York Times*, June 24, 2011, Sunday Book Review, http://www.nytimes.com/2011/06/26/books/review/book-review-everything-is-obvious-once-you-know-the-answer-by-duncan-j-watts.html (accessed July 14, 2011).

36. Andrew Delbanco, "The Impact of Uncle Tom's Cabin," review of *Uncle Tom's Cabin*, by Harriet Beecher Stowe, *The New York Times*, June 24, 2011, Sunday Book Review, http://www.nytimes.com/2011/06/26/books/review/book-review-mightier-than-the-sword-by-david-s-reynolds.html?pagewanted=all (accessed July 14, 2011).

Conclusion

This book has focused on women's authorship, feminisms, and politics in Africa. It traces the various authors' contribution to political and revolutionary debates, and their efforts to bring about social and political change. It also demonstrates how the authors articulate a uniquely African vision of political and social change. The literature and films produced by these women dwell on certain key moments and themes that are particular to Africa. These include law reform and family codes; linguistic tensions between French, Berber, and Arabic languages; as well as concern for an authentic identity vis-à-vis Islamic fundamentalism and Western imperialism.

Their engagement with the major social and political issues of their day generates reflection on modernity and provides a mode for entry into the public sphere. The public sphere in Africa, like the public sphere Habermas describes in his theories, is a stereotypically masculinist institution. Habermas' theories about the public sphere also refer to its potential for change.[1] Using the power of their literary and media discourses, female authors have used the public sphere's transformative mechanisms to demand change. Habermas theorizes the public sphere in two different ways. One is based on his view of nineteenth century society. The other emerges from his own political project of the pragmatics of language (his theory of communicative action). Adding the role of discourse and communicative action in Habermas' model sheds more light on women authors' interventions through the public sphere of cultural production. Habermas' concept of communicative action implies the potential negotiation of alternative identity conceptions. To give examples of alternative public spheres, he cites "popular science and literary publics, religious and artistic publics, feminist and 'alternative publics.'"[2] In his book *The Theory of Communicative Action*, Habermas argues that the state's exercise of power is challenged by citizens' communicative power in the political public sphere.[3] Such communicative power depends on whether agreement is reached on what has been communicated. Only then can communicative action be "oriented to reaching understanding."[4] Achieving understanding, according to him, is "the inherent telos of speech."[5]

The women authors included in this book have gone public through literature, film, and Internet discourse, thus constituting female authorship as dialogic. They speak through literature and media, but it is the readers' understanding of their speech that plays a role in effecting change. The public sphere of their cultural production becomes therefore an inclusive community of discourse. In order to show how female authors used their literature, film, and Internet discourse to achieve political ends, I approached their literary and media discourses historically as well as aesthetically. Aesthetically, the book links women authors' demand for change to their use of different genres to inscribe the gender notions of hierarchy that they contested. These are the notions that denied women free agency by defining them only in relation to their social location within the private sphere. Women authors employ different genres and enact various communicative acts and discursive strategies for the public dissemination of their message. They engage a network of discourses as they seek to link their gender concerns with wider social, political, and economic issues. Their use of aesthetic and political strategies to achieve political agency is not specific to their feminist discourse but part of a general discourse where both male and female writers participate, thus overcoming the gender divide. In her book *Revolution in Poetic Language*, Julia Kristeva argues that political revolution involves a revolution in artistic practice.[6] Being aware that language is a means of women's oppression as well as a means to fight against that oppression, women authors re-appropriate for their own feminist purposes established genres such as novels, plays, autobiography, testimonials, as well as film and social media, in this way subverting conventions and deemphasizing the binary opposition between the private and public spheres. Taken as a whole, their narratives constitute a vital engagement with women's struggle for autonomy and change.

Historically, I addressed how Habermas' optimistic vision of the transformative potential of the public sphere worked in specific instances, notably Bessie Head's ecofeminist vision, through her involvement in community development and its ultimate impact on the ecological, social, and political transformation of rural communities in Botswana; the writings and research of women writers like Assia Djebar, who fostered a feminism that began to name issues never discussed before such as sexuality, domestic and state violence, and political repression; the changes in oppressive family laws, initiated by women activists who campaigned for change in personal status codes regulating marriage, divorce, child custody, and male guardianship, among other issues; and women's actual contribution to change of government through involvement in Arab Spring and through literary texts that denounce human rights abuses. Malika Oufkir's *Stolen Lives* and Yvonne Vera's *The Stone Virgins* have become part of a more general testimony for a truth-and-reconciliation process that portends greater democratization in their countries. Oufkir and Vera's public persona, and their expatriation and disassociation from visions of postcolonial nations propagated by dictatorial regimes, positioned them to be spokeswomen for political reform. Women authors thus used their writing and media discourses to demand reforms that eventually led, though to a limited extent, to women's civil agency.

Habermas' theory of the public sphere as being, above all, a literary space for debating issues relating to civil society, seems to correspond to what these writers felt themselves to be doing. His model of communicative action also shows how women authors have used the communicative power of their literary and media discourses to challenge the power of their nation-states and influence decision making and laws. Women's literary and media action translates into freedom to critique their governments and thus contribute to public discourse regarding women who have largely been silenced by patriarchal and political structures. The literary and media works act in a way as "alternative publics," within which they experience the freedom to critique patriarchal and political structures. Women's activism has speeded the reform of such political structures, for instance, in recent movements, sweeping across North Africa. The book shows how women's online postings on Facebook, Twitter, and blogs have helped push for political and gender reform at the grassroots level, thus breaking the culture of silence and engaging in political action and group initiatives. These women see political revolution as the solution not only to their countries' crises but also to their personal plight as women. Critics have praised the bold, revolutionary spirit of these women's online activism for what they see as a new mode of women's writing. Women activists have, nonetheless, been affected by repressive politics in their countries. They have been subjected to torture, rape, and imprisonment, including leading political activists.

Nearly every woman writer, filmmaker, and Internet activist included in this book has been affected by repressive politics in her country. During the first decade following Ghana's independence, and under Kwame Nkrumah's repressive regime, Ama Ata Aidoo endured not only imprisonment but also torture by prison guards who threatened her with death. In an interview, she states that she refrained from writing between 1970 and 1977 because of the oppressive political regime in Ghana at the time, which was characterized by military brutality and the persecution of Ghana's intelligentsia.[7] Also subjected to censorship by oppressive regimes is Nigerian Tess Onwueme, who has to experiment with different techniques in her writings in order to evade persecution. Her political commitment is evident in her allusions to the local problem of unemployment as well as in the general political allegory that relates national problems to globalization. Through satire, she aims to raise political consciousness and issue a call for reform of Nigeria's politics. Censorship, bureaucracy, and bans of all sorts are also what compelled Assia Djebar to live and write in France, to publish abroad, and later choose to reside in the United States. Djebar wrote her novels *Le Blanc d'Algerie* (*The White of Algeria*) and *Vaste est La Prison* (*So Vast the Prison*) to denounce the civil war of the 1990s between Islamic fundamentalists and the state, and to lament the persecution of Algerian intellectuals, among whom were some of her former colleagues. She writes in *Vaste est La Prison*: "I thought that by dint of writing about those who died last century in my country in flames, the blood of men today (the blood of History and oppression of women) was rising again to splatter my writing and condemn me to silence."[8] Determining that life, even in today's Algeria, is dangerous, she has remained in exile and decided not to return to Algeria. Yvonne Vera opted for exile in Canada because of Zimbabwe's dictatorship. She was never persecuted as a writer, but had she published, before she died, her last and most political novel *Obedience*, set in 2002, in the week before the presidential election, she might have been persecuted by Robert Mugabe's repressive regime. Vera was posthumously recognized by the Zimbabwean government. The obituary makes no mention, however, of her novel *The Stone Virgins*.[9]

Emerging in Africa today is a whole new group of writers and filmmakers that has been educated in radical politics and possesses a progressive impulse. Leila Merrakshi, a self-exiled Moroccan filmmaker living in France, who shocked cinematic circles with her candid film *Marock*, was in hiding when her film came under critical scrutiny. The critical backlash against literature and films like Merrakshi's is a complex issue that is entangled with the hypermasculinity that continues to hold sway in Africa's cultural and literary discourses. Such criticism is also more familiarly attributed to masculinist political discourse, which dismisses women's concerns as irrelevant to politics. The sociopolitical space in much of Africa remains a masculine order. Women fall lower than men in terms of educational opportunities, and female illiteracy rates are high in all African countries. Women's political participation is also low. The majority of African women did not gain suffrage till the postindependence period. In countries such as Algeria, Ghana, and Nigeria, women gained the right to vote only after the overthrow of colonial rule, while in South Africa Black women did not gain the right to vote until 1994.

Despite hurdles to women's full participation in politics, women writers, filmmakers, and feminist activists are negotiating new democratic structures and changing the contexts of how Africa is read and viewed in the twenty-first century. In the coming decades, it will be fascinating to see to what extent future generations of women will benefit socioculturally and politically from the writings and films these female producers of culture have left them. The question is how will the past influence new emerging writers of the twenty-first century in Africa? And how are sociocultural and political movements like the Arab Spring, as well as other recent events across Africa, going to impact women's literary and cultural production in the future? My book has integrated women's literature with nonliterary genres in a new study of African women's cultural production. I have developed new ways of examining unexplored issues through the different generations of women authors who provide diverse perspectives on contentious issues in contemporary Africa. I hope this book will be a useful baseline for scholars and students who want to understand how African women's writing has developed generationally as well as across genres.

NOTES

1. Jürgen Habermas, "Further Reflections on the Public Sphere," in *Habermas and the Public Sphere*, ed. Craig Calhoun (Cambridge, MA: MIT Press, 1992), 429.
2. Jürgen Habermas, "Excerpt from *Between Facts and Norms: Contributions to a Discourse Theory of Law and Democracy,*" in *The Idea of the Public Sphere*, ed. Jostein Gripsrud, Hallvard Moe, Anders Molander and Graham Murdock (Lanham, MD: Lexington Books, 2010), 194.
3. Jürgen Habermas, *Theory of Communicative Action: Reason and the Rationalization of Society, Volume 1*, trans. Thomas McCarthy (Boston: Beacon Press, 1984), 342.
4. Ibid., 295.
5. Ibid., 287.
6. Julia Kristeva, *Revolution in Poetic Language* (La Révolution du Language Poé tique, 1974). Translated by Margaret, Waller (New York: Columbia University Press, 1984).
7. Jeanette Toomer, "Barnard College Celebrates African Women Artists," in *New York Amsterdam News*, Vol. 88, issue 44, 1997, 23.
8. Assia Djebar, *So Vast the Prison* (*Vaste est La Prison*) translated by Betsy Wing (New York: Seven Stories Press, 1995), 347.
9. Refer to Dorobta Pucherova, *The Ethics of Dissident Desire in Southern African Writing* (WVT: Wissenschaftlicher Verlag Trier, 2011).

Bibliography

Abouzeid, Leila. *The Last Chapter*. Translated by John Liechety. Cairo: American University Press, 2003.

———. *Year of the Elephant: A Moroccan Woman's Journey toward Independence*. Translated by Barbara Parmenter. Austin: University of Texas Press, 1989.

Abrahams, Cecil. *The Tragic Life: Bessie Head and Literature in Southern Africa*. Trenton, NJ: Africa World Press, 1990.

Accad, Evelyn. *Sexuality and War: Literary Masks of the Middle East*. New York: New York University Press, 1990.

Achebe, Chinua. *Hopes and Impediments: Selected Essays 1965-1987*. London: Heinemann, 1988.

Adams, Melinda. "Regional Women's Activism: African Women's Networks and the African Union." In *Global Feminism: Transnational Women's Activism, Organizing and Human Rights*, edited by Mira Marx Ferree and Aili Mari Tripp, 187–218. New York: New York University Press, 2006.

Adler, Michelle. "Bessie Head." In *Between the Lines: Interviews with Bessie Head, Sheila Roberts, Ellen Kuzwayo, Miriam Tlatli*, edited by Craig Mackenzie and Cherry Clayton, 5–29. South Africa: National English Library Museum, 1989.

Afkhami, Mahnaz, ed. *Faith and Freedom: Women's Human Rights in the Muslim World*. Syracuse, NY: Syracuse University Press, 1995.

African National Congress. "Statement of the National Executive Committee of the African National Congress on the Emancipation of Women in South Africa." *Agenda (Durban)* 8 (May 2, 1990): 19–23.

Aguiar, Susan. *The Bitch is Back: Wicked Women in Literature*. Carbondale: Board of Trustees, Southern Illinois University, 2001.

Ahmed, Aijaz. *In Theory: Classes, Nations, Literatures*. London: Verso, 1992.

———. "Jameson's Rhetoric of Otherness and the 'National Allegory.'" *Social Text* 17 (1987): 3–25.

Ahmed, Leila. *Women and Gender in Islam: Historical Roots of a Modern Debate*. New Haven, CT: Yale University Press, 1992.

Aidoo, Ama Ata. "Conference Presentation to the Dia Center for the Arts." In *Critical Fictions: The Politics of Imaginative Writing*, edited by Philomena Mariani, 151–154. Seattle: Bay Press, 1991.

———. *Diplomatic Pounds and Other Stories* (Oxfordshire: Ayebia Clarke Publishing Limited, 2012).

———. *Our Sister Killjoy: Or, Reflections from a Black-eyed Squint.* Harlow, Essex: Longman Drumbeat, 1977.

———. "The African Woman Today." In *Sisterhood, Feminisms and Power: From Africa to the Diaspora*, edited by Obioma Nnaemeka, 47–50. Trenton, NJ: Africa World Press, 1998.

Alexander, M. Jacqui, and Chandra Mohanty, eds. *Feminist Genealogies, Colonial Legacies and Democratic Futures*. New York: Routledge, 1997.

Al-Hassan Golley, Nawar. *Arab Women's Lives Retold: Exploring Identity through Writing*. Syracuse, NY: Syracuse University Press, 2007.

Al Jabri, Abed Mohammed. *Democracy, Human Rights and Law in Islamic Thought*. New York: L. B. Tauris Publishers, 2008.

Alloula, Malek. *The Colonial Harem*. Translated by Myrna Godzich and Wlad Godzich. Introduced by Barbara Harlow. Minneapolis: University of Minnesota Press, 1986.

Amadiune, Ifi. *Male Daughters, Female Husbands*. London: Zed Books Ltd., 1987.

Amnesty International. "Amnesty International Report 2009: The State of the World's Human Rights." Accessed September 14, 2010. http://report2009.amnesty.org.

———. "Amnesty International Report 2010: The State of the World's Human Rights." Accessed January 4, 2011. http://report2010.amnesty.org.

Anderson, Benedict. *Imagined Communities: Reflections on the Origin and Spread of Nationalism*. New York: Verso, 1991.

Andrade, Susan. *The Nation Writ Small: African Fictions and Feminisms, 1958-1988*. Durham, NC: Duke University Press, 2011.

Appiah, Kwame Anthony. *In My Father's House: Africa in the Philosophy of Culture*. Oxford: Oxford University Press, 1992.

Arendt, Hannah, ed. *Illuminations: Essays and Reflections*. New York: Schocken Books, 1969[1968].

Arndt, Susan. *The Dynamics of African Feminism: Defining and Classifying African-Feminist Literatures*. Trenton, NJ: Africa World Press, 2002.

Awam, Amkpa. *Theater and Postcolonial Desires*. London: Routledge, 2004.

Azodo, Ada Uzoamaka, and Gay Alden Wilentz, eds. *Emerging Perspectives on Ama Ata Aidoo*. Trenton, NJ: Africa World Press, 1999.

Babana-Hampton, Safoi. "Bringing into Focus Narrative Text and Subtext in Moroccan Film: Marock's Hors-Champ." *The Journal of North African Studies* 15, no. 3 (September 2010): 289–303.

Badran, Margot. "Understanding Islam, Islamism and Islamic Feminism." *The Journal of Women's History* 13 (2001): 47–52.

Badran, Margot, and Miriam Cooke, eds. *Opening the Gates: A Century of Arab Feminist Writing*. London: Virago Press, 1990.

Balibar, Etienne, and Immanuel Maurice Wallerstein. *Race, Nation, Class: Ambiguous Identities*. London: Verso, 1991.

Banham, Martin, James Gibbs, and Femi Osofisan, eds. *African Theater: Playwrights & Politics*. Bloomington: Indiana University Press, 2001.

Banks, Kathryn, and Joseph Harris, eds. *Exposure: Revealing Bodies, Unveiling Representations*. Oxford: Peter Lang Publishing, Inc., 2004.

Baraka, Amiri. "Black Revolutionary Theater." 1969. In *The Norton Anthology of African-American Literature*, edited by Henry Louis Gates, Jr. and Nellie Y. McKay, 1899–1902. New York: W. W. Norton & Co., 1997.

Barakat, Halim, ed. *Contemporary North Africa: Issues of Development and Integration*. Washington, DC: Center for Contemporary Arab Studies, 1985.

Barthet, Stella B., ed. *Shared Waters: Soundings in Postcolonial Literatures*. Amsterdam: Rodopi, 2009.

Bauman, Richard. *Story, Performance and Event: Contextual Studies of Oral Narrative*. Cambridge: Cambridge University Press, 1986.

Bauman, Zygmunt. *Wasted Lives: Modernity and Its Outcasts*. Oxford: Blackwell Publishing Ltd., 2004.

Benjamin, Walter. *Arcade Project*. Translated by Howard Eiland and Kevin Mclaughlin. Cambridge, MA: Belknap Press of Harvard University, 1999.

———. "The Task of the Translator." In *Illuminations: Essays and Reflections*, edited by Hannah Arendt, translated by Harry John, 69–82. New York: Schocken Books, 1969.

———. "Theses on the Philosophy of History." In *Illuminations: Essays and Reflections*, edited by Hannah Arendt, 253–264. New York: Schocken Books, 1968.

Benlyazid, Farida. *Bab Sma Maftouh (A Door to the Sky)*. Film. Directed by Farida Benlyazid. Produced by France Media, Centre Cinématographique Marocain, SATPEC. Morocco: 1988.

Bensmaia, Réda. "*La Nouba des Femmes du Mont Chenoua*: Introduction to the Cinematic Fragment." *World Literature Today* 70, no.4 (1996): 877–884.

———. "The Vanished Mediators: On the Nature of Violence in Algeria." *Parallax* 4, no. 2.7 (1998): 3–16.

Berndt, Katrin. *Female Identity in Contemporary Zimbabwean Fiction*. Bayreuth, Germany: Eckhard Breitlinger, Bayreuth University, 2005.

Bhabha, Homi K. "On Subaltern Secularism." *Journal* 6 (1995): 5–7. Accessed October 20, 2008. http://waf.gn.apc.org/journal6p5.html.

———. *The Location of Culture*. New York: Routledge, 1994.

Blanchot, Maurice, Elizabeth Rottenberg, and Jacques Derrida. *The Instant of My Death*. Stanford, CA: Stanford University Press, 2000.

Boehmer, Elleke. "A Postcolonial Aesthetic: Repeating Upon the Present." In *Rerouting the Postcolonial: New Directions for the New Millennium*, edited by Janet Wilson (et al.), 170–181. Abingdon: Routledge, 2010.

Boukhari, Karim. "Marock: Le Film de Tous Les Tabous." *Telquel* 223 (2005). Accessed January 5, 2009. http://www.telquel-online.com/223/couverture_223_1.shtml.

Bourdieu, Pierre. "Fourth Lecture: The Universal Corporatism: The Role of Intellectuals in the Modern World." *Poetics Today* 12, no. 4 (1991): 655–669.

Borg Barthet, Stella. *Shared Waters: Soundings in Postcolonial Literatures*. New York: Rodopi, 2009.

Brecht, Bertolt. *Caucasian Chalk Circle*. New York: Grove Press, 1966.

Bull-Christiansen, Lene. *Tales of the Nation: Feminist Nationalism or Patriotic History: Defining National History and Identity in Zimbabwe*. Uppsala, Sweden: Nordiska Afrikainstitutet, 2004.

Butler, Judith. *Precarious Life: The Powers of Violence and Mourning*. New York: Verso, 2006.

Calhoun, Craig. *Habermas and the Public Sphere*. Cambridge, MA: MIT Press, 1992.

Calinescu, Matei. *Five Faces of Modernity: Modernism, Avant-garde, Decadence, Kitsch, Postmodernism*. Durham, NC: Duke University Press, 1987.

Carter, Sandra Gayle. "Farida Benlyazid's Moroccan Women." *Quarterly Review of Film and Video* 17, no. 4 (2000): 343–369.

Chakrabarty, Dipesh. *Provincializing Europe: Postcolonial Thought and Historical Difference*. Princeton, NJ: Princeton University Press, 2000.

Chatterjee, Partha. *Nationalist Thought in the Colonial World*. London: Zed Books, 1986.

———. *The Nation and Its Fragments*. Delhi: Oxford University Press, 1995.

Cherifati-Merabtine, Doria. "Algeria at a Crossroads: National Liberation, Islamization and Women." In *Gender and National Identity: Women and Politics in Muslim Societies*, edited by Valentine M. Moghadam, 40–61. London: Oxford University Press, 1994.

Chow, Rey. "'It's You, and Not Me': Domination and 'Othering' in Theorizing the 'Third World.'" In *Coming to Terms: Feminism, Theory, Politics*, edited by Elizabeth Weed, 152–161. New York: Routledge, 1989.

Christakis, Nicholas. "The Trouble with Common Sense." Review of *Everything Is Obvious Once You Know the Answer*, by Duncan J. Watts. *The New York Times*, June 24, 2011. Accessed July 14, 2011. http://www.nytimes.com/2011/06/26/books/review/book-review-everything-is-obvious-once-you-know-the-answer-by-duncan-j-watts.html.

"Chronology (Assia Djebar)." *World Literature Today* 70, no. 4 (Autumn 1996): 800.

Cixous, Hélène. "Castration or Decapitation?" Translated by Annette Kuhn. *Signs* 7, no.1 (1981): 41–55.

———. *"Coming to Writing" and Other Essays* . Edited by Deborah Jenson. Cambridge, MA: Harvard University Press, 1991.

———. "The Laugh of the Medusa." Translated by Keith Cohen and Paula Cohen. *Signs* 1 (1976): 875–893.

Cohen, Roger. "King's Wrath: Morocco Family Tale of 2 Decades." *The New York Times*, January 25, 1994. Accessed January 2, 2011. http://www.nytimes.com/1994/01/25/world/king-s-wrath-morocco-family-tale-of-2decades.html.

Cole, Catherine M., Takyiwaa Manuh, and Stephan Miescher, eds. *Africa After Gender?* Bloomington: Indiana University Press, 2007.

Cooke, Miriam. *Women Claim Islam: Creating Islamic Feminism through Literature*. New York: Routledge, 2001.

Cooke, Miriam, and Lawrence Bruce, eds. *Muslim Networks from Hajj to Hip Hop*. Chapel Hill: University of North Carolina Press, 2005.

Cooper, Brenda. "*Chaiba the Algerian* versus *Our Sister Killjoy*: The Case for a Materialist Black Aesthetic." *English in Africa* 12, no. 2 (1985): 21–51.

Cornwall, Andrea, ed. *Readings in Gender in Africa*. Bloomington: Indiana University Press, 2005.

Coundouriotis, Eleni. "Authority and Invention in the Fiction of Bessie Head." *Research in African Literature* 21, no. 2 (1996): 17–32.

———. *Claiming History: Colonialism, Ethnography and the Novel*. New York: Columbia University Press, 1999.

Davidson, Basil. *Black Star: A View of the Life and Times of Kwame Nkrumah*. London: Allen Lane, 1973.

———. *The Black Man's Burden: Africa and the Curse of the Nation-State*. New York: Times Books, 1992.

Davies, Lizzy. "France Accused 44 Years on Over Moroccan's Vanishing." *Guardian*, October 29, 2009. Accessed January 2, 2011. http://www.guardian.co.uk/world/2009/oct/29/france-accused-over-moroccans-vanishing.

Davies, Miranda, ed. *Third World Second Sex 2*. London: Zed Books, 1987.

De Lauretis, Teresa. *Technologies of Gender: Essays on Theory, Film and Fiction*. Bloomington: Indiana University Press, 1987.

Delbanco, Andrew. "The Impact of Uncle Tom's Cabin." Review of *Uncle Tom's Cabin*, by Harriet Beecher Stowe. *The New York Times*, June 24, 2011, Sunday Book Review. Accessed July 14, 2011. http://www.nytimes.com/2011/06/26/books/review/book-review-mightier-than-the-sword-by-david-s-reynolds.html?pagewanted=all.

Derrida, Jacques. *On Cosmopolitanism and Forgiveness*. New York: Routledge, 2001.

Derrida, Jacques, and Elizabeth Roudinesco. *For What Tomorrow: A Dialogue*. Translated by Jeff Fort. San Francisco: Stanford University Press, 2004.

Diamond, Irene, and Gloria Feman Orenstein, eds. *Reweaving the World: The Emergence of Ecofeminism*. San Francisco: Sierra Club Books, 1990.

Djebar, Assia. *Fantasia: An Algerian Cavalcade*. Translated by Dorothy Blair. London: Quartet Books, 1993.

———. "Interview by Oussila Tamzali." *Cinéma Arabe* 10/11 (1978): 64–70.

———. *La femme sans Sépulture*. Paris: Albin Michel, 2002.

———. *La Nouba des femmes du Mont Chenoua*. Directed by Assia Djebar. Algeria, 1978. Distributed in the United States by Women Make Movies, New York.

———. "Untitled Speech for 1997 Prix Fonlon-Nichols." *The African Literature Association Bulletin* 23, no. 2 (September 1997): 21–22.

———. *Vaste est le prison*. Paris: Albin Michel, 1995.

———. *Women of Algiers in Their Apartment*. Translated by Marjolijn de Jager. Charlottesville: University Press of Virginia, 1992.

———. *Zerda ou les Chants de l'Oubli*. Directed by Assia Djebar. Algeria, 1982.

Doane, Mary Anne. *Femmes Fatales: Feminism, Film Theory, Psychoanalysis*. New York: Routledge, 1991.

Donadey, Anne. "Rekindling the Vividness of the Past: Assia Djebar's Films and Fiction." *World Literature Today* 70, no. 4 (1996): 885–892.

Douglas, Susan J. *The Rise of Enlightened Sexism: How Pop Culture Took Us from Girl Power to Girls Gone Wild*. New York: St. Martin's Press, 2010.

Dubey, Madhu. "The 'True Lie' of the Nation: Fanon and Feminism." *Differences* 10, no. 2 (1998): 1–29.

Dunphy, Catherine. "Yvonne Vera, 40: A Powerful Voice Quelled." *Toronto Star* (May 30, 2005).

Dunton, Chris. *Make Man Talk True: Nigerian Drama in English Since 1970*. London: Hans Zell Publishers, 1992.

———. "'Wheyting Be Dat?': The Treatment of Homosexuality in African Literature." *Research in African Literature* 20, no. 3 (1989): 422–448.

Eagleton, Terry, ed. *Nationalism, Colonialism, and Literatures*. Minneapolis: University of Minnesota Press, 1990.

Edward, Brian. "*Marock* in Morocco: Reading Moroccan Films in the Age of Circulation." *Journal of North African Studies* 12 (2007): 287–307.

Eickelman, Dave. "Inside the Islamic Revolution." In *Revolutionaries and Reformers: Contemporary Islamist Movements in the Middle East*, edited by Barry Rubin, 203–217. Albany: State University of New York Press, 2003.

Eickelman, Dave, and Jon Anderson. *New Media in the Muslim World: The Emerging Public Sphere*. Bloomington: Indiana University Press, 2003.

Eilerson, Gillian Stead. *Bessie Head: Thunder Behind her Ears*. Portsmouth, NH: Heinemann, 1995.

Eke, Maureen. "Introduction: Who Shall Silence the Drums? Another Women's War." In *What Mama Said: An Epic Drama*, by Onsonye Tess Onwueme, 7–12. Detroit, MI: Wayne State University Press, 2003.

Ekpo, Denis. "The Aporia of Post-Colonial Anger: Dissidence and Difference in Africa's Contemporary Literary Discourse." *Social Semiotics* 9, no. 1 (Apr 1999): 5–22.

El Bouih, Fatna. *Talk of Darkness*. Translated by Mustapha Kamal and Susan Slyomovics. Austin: University of Texas Press, 2008.

———. "This Time I Choose When to Leave." Interview. *Middle East Report* (Spring 2001): 218. Accessed September 30, 2010. http://www.merip.org/mer/mer218/time-i-choose-when-leave.

Elder, Arlene. *Narrative Shape-Shifting: Myth, Humor, & History in the Fiction of Ben Okri, B. Kojo Laing and Yvonne Vera*. Rochester, NY: James Currey, 2009.

Emenyonu, Ernest N., ed. *War in African Literature Today*. New York: James Currey, 2008.

Ennaji, Mohammed. *Serving the Master: Slavery and Society in Nineteenth-Century Morocco*. Translated by Seth Graebner. New York: St. Martin's Press, 1999.

Eppel, Shari. *Developing a Transformation Agenda for Zimbabwe*. Cape Town, South Africa: Idasa Publishers, 2009.

———. "'Gukurahundi': The Need for Truth and Reparation." In *Zimbabwe: Injustice and Political Reconciliation*, eds. Brian Raftopoulos and Tyrone Savage, 43–62. Harare, Zimbabwe: Weaver Press, 2005.

Epprecht, Marc. "The 'Unsaying' of Indigenous Homosexualities in Zimbabwe: Mapping a Blindspot in an African Masculinity." *Journal of Southern African Studies* 24, no. 4 (1998): 631–651.

Erlanger, Steven, and Souad Mekhennet. "Family Code Gets Nudge but Women Seek a Push." *The New York Times*, August 18, 2009. Accessed September 15, 2009. http://www.nytimes.com/2009/08/19/world/africa/19tangiers.html.

Fanon, Frantz. *A Dying Colonialism*. Translated by Chevalier Haakon. New York: Grove Weidenfeld, 1965.

———. *Black Skin, White Masks*. New York: Grove Press, 1967.

———. *The Wretched of the Earth.* Translated by Constance Farrington. New York: Grove Press, 1968.

Fashina, Nelson. "Alienation and Revolutionary Vision in East African Postcolonial Dramatic Literature." *Ufahamu: A Journal of African Studies* 35, no. 2 (2009). Accessed December 1, 2009. http://escholarship.org/uc/item/63k8d46k.

Felman, Shoshana, and Dori Laub. *Testimony: Crises of Witnessing in Literature, Psychoanalysis, and History*. New York: Routledge, 1992.

Fletcher, Angus. *Allegory: The Theory of a Symbolic Mode*. Ithaca, NY: Cornell University Press, 1964.
Foucault, Michel. *Power and Knowledge* . New York: Pantheon Books, 1980.
———. *Power/Knowledge: Selected Interviews and Other Writings, 1972-1977*. New York: Pantheon Books, 1980.
Francke, Lizzie. "Revolution on the Quiet." *The Guardian* (March 1995): 213.
Frazer, Nancy. "Rethinking the Public Sphere: A Contribution to the Critique of Actually Existing Democracy." In *Habermas and the Public Sphere*, edited by Craig Calhoun, 109-42. Cambridge, MA: MIT Press, 1992.
Freud, Sigmund. *Medusa's Head.* London: Hogarth Press, 1955.
Gabriel, Teshome. "Third Cinema as Guardian of Popular Memory: Towards a Third Aesthetics." In *Questions of Third Cinema*, edited by Jim Pines and Paul Willemen, 53-64. London: BFI Pub., 1989.
———. "Towards a Critical Theory of Third World Films." In *Questions of Third Cinema*, edited by Jim Pines and Paul Willemen, 30-52. London: BFI Pub., 1989.
Gates, Jr., Henry Louis, and Nellie Y. McKay, eds. *The Norton Anthology of African-American Literature*. New York: W. W. Norton & Co., 1996.
Gellner, Ernest, and Charles Micaud, eds. *Arabs and Berbers: From Tribe to Nation in North Africa*. Lexington, MA: Lexington Books, 1972.
Gilroy, Paul. *The Black Atlantic: Modernity and Double Consciousness*. Cambridge, MA: Harvard University Press, 1993.
Girard, Rene. *Mensonge Romantique Et Verite Romanesque*. Paris: Grasset, 1961.
Ghambou, Mokhtar. "Malika Oufkir and the American Making of a Moroccan Star." Accessed February 25, 2010. http://www.wafin.com/oufkir.phtml.
Ghosh, Bishnupriya, and Brinda Bose, eds. *Interventions: Feminist Dialogues on Third World Women's Literature and Film*. New York: Garland Publishing, Inc., 1997.
Goodman, Robin Truth. *World, Class, Women: Global Literature, Education and Feminism.* New York: Routledge, 2004.
Gourdine, Angeletta K. M. *Difference Place Makes: Gender, Sexuality, and Diaspora Identity*. Columbus: Ohio State University Press, 2002.
Green, Mary Jean. "Dismantling the Colonizing Text: Anne Hebert's *Kamouraska* and Assia Djebar's *L'Amour, la Fantasia*." *The French Review* 66, no. 6 (1993): 956–966.
Gripsrud, Jostein, Hallvard Moe, Anders Molander, and Graham Murdock, eds. *The Idea of the Public Sphere*. Lanham, MD: Lexington Books, 2010.
Guha, Ranajit. *A Subaltern Studies Reader*. Minneapolis: University of Minnesota Press, 1997.
Habermas, Jürgen. "Excerpt from *Between Facts and Norms: Contributions to a Discourse Theory of Law and Democracy*." In *The Idea of the Public Sphere*, edited by Jostein Gripsrud, Hallvard Moe, Anders Molander and Graham Murdock, 184–204. Lanham, MD: Lexington Books, 2010.
———. "Further Reflections on the Public Sphere." In *Habermas and the Public Sphere*, edited by Craig Calhoun, 421-61. Cambridge, MA: MIT Press, 1992.
———. "The Public Sphere." In *Media Studies: A Reader*, edited by Paul Marris and Sue Thornham, 92–98. Edinburgh, UK: Edinburgh University Press, 1996.
———. *The Theory of Communicative Action: Reason and the Rationalization of Society, Volume One*. Translated by Thomas McCarthy. Boston: Beacon Press, 1984.
Habila, Helon. "Obituary: Yvonne Vera." *The Guardian*, April 27, 2005. Accessed October 8, 2007. http://books.guardian.co.uk/news/articles/0,6109,1471087,00.html.
Hafez, Sabry. "Shifting Identities in Maghrebi Cinema: The Algerian Paradigm." *Alif: Journal of Comparative Poetics* 15 (1995): 39–80.
Hall, Michael. "Leila Abouzeid's *Year of the Elephant*: A Postcolonial Reading." *Women: A Cultural Review* 6, no. 1 (1995): 67–84.
Haraway, Donna. "Situated Knowledges: The Science Question in Feminism and the Privilege of Partial Perspective." *Feminist Studies* 14, no. 3 (Fall 1998): 575–599.
Harbi, Mohammed. *L'Algérie et Son Destin: Croyants ou Citoyens*. Paris: Arcantere, 1992.
Hartmann, Heidi. "Capitalism, Patriarchy and Job Segregation by Sex." *Signs* 1, no. 3 (1976): 137–168.

Hartsock, Nancy. "The Feminist Standpoint: Developing the Ground for a Specifically Feminist Historical Materialism." In *Discovering Reality: Feminist Perspectives on Epistemology, Metaphysics, Methodology, and Philosophy of Science*, edited by Sandra Harding and Merill B. Hintikka, 283–310. Dordrecht, Netherlands: Kluwer Academic Publishers, 2003.

Hawley, John C., ed. *Cross-Addressing: Resistance Literature and Cultural Border*. Albany, NY: SUNY Press, 1996.

Head, Bessie. *A Question of Power*. London: Heinemann, 1974.

———. "Autobiographical Essay." *Ms. Magazine*, November 1975, 72–75.

———. *The Collector of Treasures and Other Botswana Village Tales*. London: Heinemann Educational, 1977.

———. *Maru*. London: Heinemann, 1995[1972].

———. *Serowe: Village of the Rain Wind*. London: Heinemann, 1981.

———. *When Rain Clouds Gather*. London: Heinemann, 1995[1969].

Hélie Lucas, Marie Aimée. "Bound and Caged by the Family Code." In *Third World Second Sex 2*, edited by Miranda Davies, 3-15. London: Zed Books, 1987.

———. "Women, Nationalism and Religion in the Algerian liberation Struggle." In *Opening the Gates: A Century of Arab Feminist Writing*, edited by Margot Badran and Miriam Cooke, 105–114. London: Virago Press, 1990.

Herman, Judith. *Trauma and Recovery*. New York: Basic Books, 1992.

Hirschi, Mohammed. "The Ethics and Politics of Leila Marrakshi's *Marock*." *South Central Review* 28, no. 1 (Spring 2008): 93.

Houdaifa, Hicham, and Fedoua Tounassi. "*Marock*: Le Vrai Debat." *Le Journal L'Hebdomadaire* (May 27-June 2, 2006): 24.

hooks, bell. *Ain't I a Woman*. Boston: South End Press, 1981.

———. *Talking Back: Thinking Feminist, Thinking Black*. Boston: South End Press, 1989.

Hountondji, Paulin. *African Philosophy: Myth and Reality*. Bloomington: Indiana University Press, 1983[1976].

Hughes, Stephen. *Morocco Under Hassan II*. New York: Ithaca Press, 2006.

Hunter, Eva. "Feminism, Islam and the Modern Moroccan Woman in the Works of Leila Abouzeid." *African Studies* 65, no. 2 (2006): 139–155.

Hurley, Anthony, Renée Larrier, and Joseph Mclaren, eds. *Migrating Words and Worlds: Pan-Africanism Updated*. Trenton, NJ: Africa World Press, 1999.

Hutcheon, Linda. *A Poetics of Postmodernism: History, Theory, Fiction*. New York: Routledge, 1988.

Ibrahim, Huma. *Subversive Identities in Exile*. Charlottesville: University Press of Virginia, 1996.

Inegbe, Stephen. "Drama and Theater in Nigeria after Soyinka: Trend, Focus and Development." *Africa e Mediterrano* 4/03 (2007): 46. Accessed December 15, 2009. http://www.africaemediterraneo.it/articoli/art_enegbe_4_03.doc.

"Interview with Mehdi Ben Barka's Son Bachir," November 1999. Accessed December 15, 2010. http://www.marxist.com/appeals-old/ben_barka/interview.html.

Irele, Abiola. *The African Imagination: Literature in Africa and the Black Diaspora*. Oxford: Oxford University Press, 2001.

Irigaray, Luce. "Women on the Market." In *This Sex Which Is Not One*, translated by Catherine Porter, 170–191. Ithaca, NY: Cornell University Press, 1985.

Jameson, Fredric. "Modernism and Imperialism." In *Nationalism, Colonialism, and Literatures*, edited by Terry Eagleton, 43–68. Minneapolis: University of Minnesota Press, 1990.

———. *Postmodernism, or the Cultural Logic of Late Capitalism*. Durham, NC: Duke University Press, 1991.

———. "Third World Literature in the Era of Multinational Capitalism." *Social Text* 15 (1986): 65–88.

Jaywardena, Kumari. *Feminism and Nationalism in the Third World*. London: Zed Books, 1986.

Jeancolas, Pierre. *Le Cinéma des Français; La Véme République, 1958-1978*. Paris: Stock, 1979.

Jolly, Rosemary. "'Intersecting Marginalities': The Problem of Homophobia in South African Women's Writing." In *Cross-Addressing: Resistance Literature and Cultural Border*, edited by John C. Hawley, 107–120. Albany, NY: SUNY Press, 1996.

Jones, Eldred Durosimi, Eustace Palmer, and Marjorie Jones, eds. *Critical Theory & African Literature Today*. Trenton, NJ: Africa World Press, 1994.

Joseph, Suad, and Afsaneh Najmabadi. *Encyclopedia of Women and Islamic Cultures: Family, Law & Politics*. Leiden, Netherlands: Brill, 2005.

Kahf, Mohja. "Spare Me the Sermon on Muslim Women." *Washington Post*, October 5, 2008. Accessed November 4, 2009. http://www.washingtonpost.com/wpdyn/content/article/2008/10/03/AR2008100301968.html.

Kandiyoti, Deniz. "Bargaining with Patriarchy." *Gender and Society* 2, no. 3 (September 1988): 274–290.

———. "Identity and Its Discontents." In *Colonial Discourse and Postcolonial Theory*, edited by Patrick Williams and Laura Chrisman, 376–391. New York: Columbia University Press, 1994.

Kaplan, Ann E. *Psychoanalysis & Cinema*. London: Routledge, 1990.

Kasambala, Tiseke, and Georgette Gagnon. *Zimbabwe: "Bullets for Each One of You": State-Sponsored Violence Since March 29 Elections*. New York: Human Rights Watch, 2008.

Khatibi, Abdelkébir. "Double Criticism: The Decolonization of Arab Sociology." In *Contemporary North Africa: Issues of Development and Integration*, edited by Halim Barakat, 9–19. Washington, DC: Center for Contemporary Arab Studies, 1985.

Kishwar, Madhu. "Why I Am Not a Feminist?" *Manushi: A Journal of Women and Society* 61 (November/December 1990): 2–8.

Kolawole, Mary Ebun Modupe. *Womanism and African Consciousness*. Trenton, NJ: Africa World Press, 1997.

Kristeva, Julia. *Black Sun: Depression and Melancolia*. New York: Columbia University Press, 1989.

———. *Revolution in Poetic Language* (La Révolution du Language Poé tique, 1974). Translated by Margaret Waller. New York: Columbia University Press, 1984.

Kusunose, Keiko. "Bessie Head and Pan-Africanism." In *Migrating Words and Worlds: Pan-Africanism Updated*, edited by Anthony Hurley, Renée Larrier and Joseph Mclaren, 233–246. Trenton, NJ: Africa World Press, 1999.

Kwame, Arhin. *The Life and Work of Kwame Nkrumah: Papers of a Symposium Organized by the Institute of African Studies*. Trenton, NJ: Africa World Press, 1993.

Labidi, Mehrezia. "Tunisia's Women are at the Heart of its Revolution." *The Guardian*, March 23, 2012. Accessed May 28, 2012. http://www.guardian.co.uk/commentisfree/2012/mar/23/tunisia-women-revolution.

Laroui, Abdellah. *L'Ideologie Arabe Contemporaine: Essai Critique*. Paris: Maspero, 1973.

———. *The Crisis of the Arab Intellectual: Traditionalism or Historicism?* Berkeley: University of California Press, 1976.

Lazarus, Neil. "Doubting the New World Order: Marxism, Realism, and the Claims of Postmodernist Cultural Theory." *Differences: A Journal of Feminist Cultural Studies* 3, no. 3 (1991): 94–138.

———. *Nationalism and Cultural Practice in the Postcolonial World*. Cambridge: Cambridge University Press, 1999.

———. *Resistance in Postcolonial African Fiction*. New Haven, CT: Yale University Press, 1993.

———. *The Postcolonial Unconscious*. Cambridge: Cambridge University Press, 2011.

Lazreg, Marnia. *The Eloquence of Silence: Algerian Women in Question*. New York: Routledge, 1994.

Le Jeune, Philippe. *Le Pacte Autobiographique*. Paris: Seuil, 1975.

Lewis, Desiree. *Living on a Horizon: Bessie Head and the Politics of Imagining*. Trenton, NJ: Africa World Press, 2007.

Loftus, Louise. "Mixed Messages for Tunisian Women." *The New York Times*, November 21, 2011. Accessed May 30, 2012. http://www.nytimes.com/2011/11/21/world/middleeast/mixed-messages-for-tunisian-women.html.

Lyons, Tanya. *Guns and Guerilla Girls: Women in the Zimbabwean National Liberation Struggle*. Trenton, NJ: World Africa Press, 2004.
Lyotard, Jean Francois. *Differend: Phrases in Dispute*. Translated by George Van Den Abeele. Minneapolis: University of Minnesota Press, 1988.
———. *The Postmodern Condition: A Report on Knowledge*. Minneapolis: University of Minnesota Press, 1984.
Mackenzie, Craig. *Bessie Head*. New York: Twayne Publishers, 1999.
Mackenzie, Craig, and Cherry Clayton, eds. *Between the Lines: Interviews with Bessie Head, Sheila Roberts, Ellen Kuzwayo, Miriam Tlatli*. South Africa: National English Library Museum, 1989.
Mahmoud, Saba. *The Politics of Piety: The Islamic Revival and the Feminist Subject*. Princeton, NJ: Princeton University Press, 2005.
Mama, Amina. "Sheroes and Villains: Conceptualizing Colonial and Contemporary Violence Against Women in Africa." In *Feminist Genealogies, Colonial Legacies and Democratic Futures*, eds. M. Jacqui Alexander and Chandra Mohanty, 46–52. New York: Routledge, 1997.
Mamdani, Mamdouh. *Citizen and Subject: Contemporary Africa and the Legacy of Late Colonialism*. Princeton, NJ: Princeton University Press, 1996.
Manuh, Takyiwah. "Women and Their Organizations During the Convention Peoples' Party Period." In *The Life and Work of Kwame Nkrumah: Papers of a Symposium Organized by the Institute of African Studie*s, edited by Arhin Kwame, 101–127. Trenton, NJ: Africa World Press, 1993.
Mariani, Philomena, ed. *Critical Fictions: The Politics of Imaginative Writing*. Seattle: Bay Press, 1991.
Marris, Paul, and Sue Thornham, eds. *Media Studies: A Reader*. Edinburgh, UK: Edinburgh University Press, 1996.
Martin, Florence. *Screens and Veils: Maghrebi Women's Cinema*. Bloomington: Indiana University Press, 2011.
Marx Ferree, Mira, and Aili Mari Tripp, eds. *Global Feminism: Transnational Women's Activism, Organizing and Human Rights*. New York: New York University Press, 2006.
Marx-Scouras, Danielle. "Muffled Screams / Stifled Voices." *Yale French Studie*s 82 (1993): 172–182.
McClintock, Anne. *Imperial Leather: Race, Gender, and Sexuality in Colonial Contest*. New York: Routledge, 1995.
———. "'No Longer in a Future Heaven': Women and Nationalism in South Africa." *Transition* 51 (1991): 104–123.
———. "The Angel of Progress: Pitfalls of the Term 'Postcolonialism.'" *Social Text* 31/32 (1992): 84–98.
Mclintock, Anne, Aamir Mufti, and Ella Shohat. *Dangerous Liaisons: Gender, Nation and Postcolonial Perspectives*. Minneapolis: University of Minnesota Press, 2004[1997].
Mctiche, Kristen. "A Blogger at Arab Spring's Genesis." *New York Times*, October 12, 2011. Accessed May 30, 2012. http://www.nytimes.com/2011/10/13/world/africa/a-blogger-at-arab-springs-genesis.html?_r=1.
Mediene, Benamar. "Algeria: Social Crisis or Crisis of Meanings." Translated by Abdel Gaffeur. Conference paper originally entitled "Aujourd'hui l'Algérie: Crise Sociale ou Crise du Sens." Presented at "Algeria: In and Out of French: A Conference on Politics and Culture in Postcolonial Algeria," Cornell University, Ithaca, NY, October 3, 1996.
Mémmi, Albert. *The Colonizer and the Colonized*. Boston: Beacon Press, 1991[1965].
Mernissi, Fatima. "Arab Women's Rights and the Muslim State in the Twenty-First Century: Reflections on Islam as Religion and State." In *Faith and Freedom: Women's Human Rights in the Muslim World*, edited by Mahnaz Afkhami, 33–50. Syracuse, NY: Syracuse University Press, 1995.
———. *Dreams of Trespass: Tales of a Harem Girlhood*. Reading, MA: Addison-Wesley, 1994.
———. *The Veil and the Male Elite: A Feminist Interpretation of Women's Rights in Islam*. Translated by Mary Jo Lakeland. Reading, MA: Addison-Wesley, 1991.

Merrakshi, Leila. *Marock.* Film. Directed by Leila Merrakshi. Distributed by Pan Européenne Distribution, France and Morocco: 2005.

Miles, Rosalind. *Women and Power*. London: Macdonald, 1985.

Mmembe, Achille. "The Banality of Power and the Aesthetics of Vulgarity in the Postcolony." *Public Culture* 4, no. 2 (1992): 1–30.

Moghadam, Valentine M., ed. *Gender and National Identity: Women and Politics in Muslim Societies*. London: Oxford University Press, 1994.

———. *Modernizing Women: Gender and Social Change in the Middle East*. Boulder, CO: Lynne Rienner Publishers, 2003.

Mohanty, Chandra, Ann Russo, and Lourde Torres, eds. *Third World Women and the Politics of Feminism*. Bloomington: Indiana University Press, 1991.

Moore, David Chioni. "The Bessie Head–Langston Hughes Correspondence, 1960–1961." *Research in African Literatures* 41, no. 3 (2010): 1–20.

Mortimer, Mildred, ed. *Maghrebian Mosaic: A Literature in Transition*. Boulder, CO: Lynne Rienner Publishers, 2001.

———. *Writing from the Hearth: Public, Domestic, and Imaginative Space in Francophone Women's Fiction of Africa and the Caribbean*. Landham, MD: Lexington Books, 2007.

Muchemwa, Kizito, and Robert Muponde, eds. *Manning the Nation: Father Figures in Zimbabwean Literature and Society*. Harare, Zimbabwe: Weaver Press, 2007.

Mudimbe, Valentin Y. *The Idea of Africa*. Bloomington: Indiana University Press, 1994.

———. *The Invention of Africa: Gnosis, Philosophy, and the Order of Knowledge*. Bloomington: Indiana University Press, 1988.

Mulvey, Laura. "Moving bodies." Interview with Moufida Tlatli. *Sight and Sound* 5, no. 3 (1995): 18–20.

———. *Visual and Other Pleasures*. Bloomington: Indiana University Press, 1989.

Munro, Ian. "Cultural Production in the Maghreb: The Example of Leila Abouzeid." Conference paper presented at the African Literature Association Convention. Madison, WI, 2004.

———. "Interview with Leila Abouzeid, Moroccan Writer." *Journal of Commonwealth and Postcolonial Studies* 10, no. 2 (2004): 1–15.

Muponde, Robert, and Mandivavarira Maodzwa-Taruvinga, eds. *Sign and Taboo: Perspectives on the Poetic Fiction of Yvonne Vera*. Harare, Zimbabwe: Weaver Press, 2002.

Musila, Grace. "'A Man Can Try': Negotiating Manhoods in Colonial Urban Spaces in Dambudzo Marechera's *The House of Hunger* and Yvonne Vera's *Butterfly Burning*." In *Manning the Nation: Father Figures in Zimbabwean Literature and Society*, edited by Kizito Muchemwa and Robert Muponde, 142–155. Harare, Zimbabwe: Weaver Press, 2007.

Mwangi, Evan. *Africa Writes Back to the Self: Metafiction, Gender, Sexuality*. Albany: State University of New York Press, 2009.

Naaman, Dorit. "Woman/Nation: A Postcolonial Look at Female Subjectivity." *Quarterly Review of Film and Video* 17, no. 4 (2000): 333–342.

Naficy, Hamid. *An Accented Cinema: Exilic and Diasporic Filmmaking*. Princeton, NJ: Princeton University Press, 2001.

Nasta, Susheila, ed. *Motherlands: Black Women's Writing from Africa, the Caribbean, and South Asia*. New Brunswick, NJ: Rutgers University Press, 1992.

Nederveen Pieterse, Jan, and Bhikhu Parekh, eds. *The Decolonization of Imagination: Culture, Knowledge and Power*. London: Zed Press Ltd., 1995.

Needham, Anuradha Dingwaney. "An Interview with Ama Ata Aidoo." *The Massachusetts Review* 36, no. 1 (1995): 123–133.

———. *Using the Master's Tools: Resistance and the Literature of the African and South-Asian Diasporas*. London: Macmillan Press Ltd., 2000.

Nelson, Cary, and Lawrence Grossberg, eds. *Marxism and the Interpretation of Culture*. Urbana: University of Illinois Press, 1988.

Newcomb, Rachel. *Women of Fes: Ambiguities of Urban Life in Morocco*. Philadelphia: University of Pennsylvania Press, 2009.

Nfah-Abbenyi, Juliana Makuchi. *Gender in African Women's Writing: Identity, Sexuality and Difference*. Bloomington: Indiana University Press, 1997.

Nhongo-Simbanegavi, Josephine. *For Better or Worse? Women and ZANLA in Zimbabwe's Liberation Struggle*. Harare, Zimbabwe: Weaver Press, 2000.
Nisan, Mordechai. *Minorities in the Middle East: A History of Struggle and Self-Expression*. London: McFarland & Company, Inc. Publishers, 2002.
Nkrumah, Kwame. *Africa Must Unite*. New York: Frederick A. Praeger Inc., 1963.
———. *Consciencism*. New York: Monthly Review Press, 1970.
Nnaemeka, Obioma. "Mapping African Feminisms." In *Readings in Gender in Africa*, ed. Andrea Cornwall, 31–40. Bloomington: Indiana University Press, 2005.
———. " Nego-Feminism: Theorizing, Practicing, and Pruning Africa's Way." *Signs* 29, no. 2 (2004): 357–386.
———, ed. *Sisterhood, Feminism, and Power: From Africa to the Diaspora*. Trenton, NJ: Africa World Press, 1998.
Obafemi, Olu. "Towards Feminist Aesthetics in Nigerian Drama: The Plays of Tess Onwueme." In *Critical Theory & African Literature Today*, edited by Eldred Durosimi Jones, Eustace Palmer, and Marjorie Jones, 84–100. Trenton, NJ: Africa World Press, 1994.
O'Brien, Anthony. *Against Normalization: Writing Radical Democracy in South Africa*. Durham, NC: Duke University Press, 2001.
Ogundipe-Leslie, Molara. "Stiwanism: Feminism in an African Context." In *African Literature: An Anthology of Criticism and Theory*, edited by Tejumola Olaniyan and Ato Quayson, 542–550. Oxford: Blackwell Publishing Ltd., 2007.
———. "The Female Writer and Her Commitment." *African Literature Today* 15 (1987): 5–13.
Ojo-Ade, Femi. "Bessie Head's Alienated Heroine: Victim or Villain?" *Ba Shiru: A Journal of African Languages and Literature* 8, no. 2 (1977): 13–21.
Okri, Ben. *The Famished Road*. London: Vintage, 2009[1991].
Olaniyan, Tejumola and Ato Quayson, eds. *African Literature: An Anthology of Criticism and Theory*. Oxford: Blackwell Publishing Ltd., 2007.
Onwueme, Osonye Tess. *No Vacancy*. Trenton, NJ: Africa World Press, 2005.
———. *What Mama Said: An Epic Drama*. Detroit, MI: Wayne State University Press, 2003.
Orlando, Valérie. *Francophone Voices of the "New" Morocco in Film and Print: (Re)presenting a Society in Transition*. New York: Palgrave Macmillan, 2009.
———. *Screening Morocco: Contemporary Depictions in Film of a Changing Society*. Athens, OH: Ohio University Press, 2011.
Orwell, George. *1984*. New York: Penguin Books Ltd., 1949 [1977].
Oufkir, Malika, and Michele Fitoussi. *Stolen Lives: Twenty Years in a Desert Jail*. Translated by Ros Schwartz. New York: Hyperion, 2001.
Oussedik, Fatma. "Masculin/Féminin: Les Algériens Et Le Mouvement des Femmes." *Pouvoirs* 86 (1998): 117–128.
Oyewumi, Oyeronke. *The Invention of Women: Making an African Sense of Western Gender Discourses*. Minneapolis: University of Minnesota Press, 1997.
Park, Thomas, and Aomar Boum. *Historical Dictionary of Morocco*. Oxford: The Scarecrow Press, 2005.
Parpart, Jane. "Maculinities, Race and Violence in the Making of Zimbabwe." In *Manning the Nation: Father Figures in Zimbabwean Literature and Society*, edited by Kizito Z. Muchemwa and Robert Muponde, 102–114. Harare, Zimbabwe: Weaver Press, 2007.
Pennell, C.R. *Morocco since 1830*. New York: New York University Press, 2000.
Pines, Jim, and Paul Willemen, eds. *Questions of Third Cinema*. London: BFI Publishing, 1989.
Pollack, Kenneth M., Daniel L. Byman, Akram Al-Turk, et al., *The Arab Awakening: America and the Transformation of the Middle East*. Washington, DC: Brookings Institution Press, 2011.
Pontecorvo, Gillo, and Franco Solinas. *The Battle of Algiers*. Film. Directed by Gillo Pontecorvo. Co-Produced by Igor Film and Casbah Film. Algeria: 1966.
Porter, Catherine, trans. *This Sex Which Is Not One*. Ithaca, NY: Cornell University Press, 1985.

Pratt, Mary Louise. *Imperial Eyes: Travel Writing and Transculturation.* New York: Routledge, 2008[1992].
Primorac, Ranka. "Obituary: Yvonne Vera (1964-2005)." *The Journal of Commonwealth Literature* (Sage Publications) 40 , no. 3 (2005): 149–152. doi: 10.1177/0021989405056981.
Pucherova, Dobrota. "A Romance that Failed: Bessie Head and Black Nationalism in 1960's South Africa." *Research in African Literatures* 42, no. 2 (Summer 2011): 105–124.
———. *The Ethics of Dissident Desire in Southern African Writing*. Trier, Germany: Wissenschaftlicher Verlag Trier, 2011.
Radner, Hilary. *Neo-Feminist Cinema: Girly Films, Chick Flicks and Consumer Culture*. New York: Routledge, 2011.
Raftopoulos, Brian, and Tyrone Savage. *Zimbabwe: Injustice and Political Reconciliation.* Harare, Zimbabwe: Weaver Press, 2005.
Ranger, Terrence. "History has its Ceiling: The Pressures of the Past in the *Stone Virgins*." In *Sign and Taboo: Perspectives on the Poetic Fiction of Yvonne Vera,* edited by Robert Muponde and Mandivavarira Maodzwa-Taruvinga, 203–216. Harare, Zimbabwe: Weaver Press, 2002.
———. "Missionaries, Migrants and the Manyika: The Invention of Ethnicity in Zimbabwe." In *The Creation of Tribalism in Southern Africa*, edited by Leroy Vail, 118–150. Berkeley: University of California Press, 1991.
Reiter, Rayna. *Toward an Anthropology of Women*. New York: Monthly Review Press, 1975.
Rice, Alison. *Time Signatures: Contextualizing Contemporary Francophone Autobiographical Writing from the Maghreb*. Lanham, MD: Lexington Books, 2006.
Rich, Adrienne. *Blood, Bread, and Poetry: Selected Prose, 1979-85*. New York: W. W. Norton & Co., Ltd., 1986.
Rooney, Caroline. "Dangerous Knowledge and the Poetics of Survival: A Reading of *Our Sister Killjoy* and *A Question of Power*." In *Motherlands: Black Women's Writing from Africa, the Caribbean, and South Asia*, edited and introduced by Susheila Nasta, 99–128. New Brunswick, NJ: Rutgers University Press, 1992.
Rose, Jacqueline. "On the 'Universality' of Madness: Bessie Head's *A Question of Power*." *Critical Inquiry* 20 (Spring 1994): 404–405.
Rosenstone, Robert. "History in Images/History in Words: Reflections on the Possibility of Really Putting History onto Film." *American Historical Review* 93, no. 5 (December 1988): 1173–1185.
Rotimi, Ola. *Hopes of the Living Dead: A Drama of Struggle*. Ibadan, Nigeria: Spectrum Books, 1988.
Sadiqi, Fatima. "Feminization of Public Space: Women's Activism, the Family Law and Social Change in Morocco." *Journal of Middle East Women's Studies* 2, no. 2 (2006): 1–37.
Said, Edward. *Culture and Imperialism*. New York: Knopt, 1993.
———. *Orientalism*. New York: Vintage Books, 1978.
Sakr, Naomi, ed. *Women and Media in the Middle East: Power through Self-Expression.* London: I. B.Tauris & Co. Ltd., 2004.
Samantrai, Ranu. "Caught at the Confluence of History: Ama Ata Aidoo's Necessary Nationalism." *Research in African Literature* 26, no. 2 (1995): 140–157.
Sandoval, Chela. *Methodology of the Oppressed*. Minneapolis: University of Minnesota Press, 2000.
Sarte, Jean-Paul. *No Exit and Three Other Plays*. Translated by Abel Lionel. New York: Vintage International, 1989.
Scarry, Elaine. *The Body in Pain: The Making and the Unmaking of the World*. New York: Oxford University Press, 1985.
Scott, Joan W. *Gender and the Politics of History*. New York: Columbia University Press, 1999.
Segal, Ronald. *Islam's Black Slaves: The Other Black Diaspora*. New York: Farrar Straus and Giroux, 2001.
Sherzer, Dina, ed. *Cinema, Colonialism, Postcolonialism: Perspectives from the French and Francophone Worlds*. Austin: University of Texas Press, 1996.

Shirazi, Faeghi, ed. *Muslim Women in War and Crisis: Representation and Reality*. Austin: University of Texas Press, 2010.

Shohat, Ella. "Notes on the 'Post-colonial.'" *Social Text* 31/32 (1992): 99–113.

———. "Post-Third-Worldist Culture: Gender, Nation, and the Cinema." In *Feminist Genealogies, Colonial Legacies, Democratic Futures*, edited by M. Jacqui Alexander and Chandra Mohanty, 183–209. New York: Routledge, 1997.

Shohat, Ella, and Robert Stam. *Unthinking Eurocentrism: Multiculturalism and the Media*. New York: Routledge, 1994.

Showalter, Elaine. *The Female Malady: Women, Madness and English Culture 1830-1980*. London: Virago, 1987.

Silverman, Kaja. "Historical Trauma and Male Subjectivity." In *Psychoanalysis & Cinema*, edited by Ann E. Kaplan, 110–127. London: Routledge, 1990.

———. *The Threshold of the Visible World*. New York: Routledge, 1996.

Simarski, Lynn Teo. "North African Cinema: Through North African Eyes." *Saudi Aramco World*, February 1992, 30–35. Accessed January 20, 2000. http://www.saudiaramcoworld.com/issue/199201/through.north.african.eyes.htm.

Singh, Jaspal K., and Rajemdra Chetty. *Trauma, Resistance, Reconstruction in Post-1994 South African Writing*. New York: Peter Lang, 2010.

Skalli, Loubna H. Through a Local Prism: Gender, Globalization, and Identity in Moroccan Women's Magazines. Lanham, MD: Lexington Books, 2006.

Slaughter, Joseph. "Narration in International Human Rights Law." *Comparative Literature and Culture* 9, no. 1 (March 2007): 2–15. http://docs.lib.purdue.edu/clcweb/vol9/iss1/19.

———. *The Human Rights, Inc.: The World Novel, Narrative Form and International Law*. New York: Fordham University Press, 2007.

Slyomovics, Susan. "Reparations in Morocco: The Symbolic Dirham." In *Waging War, Making Peace: Reparations and Human Rights*, edited by Susan Slyomovics and Barbara Rose Johnston. Vancouver, BC: University of British Columbia Press, 2008.

———. Review of *Stolen Lives: Twenty Years in a Desert Jail*, by Malika Oufkir and Michele Fitoussi. *Boston Review* 26, no. 6, January, 2002. http://bostonreview.net/BR26.6/slyomovics.html.

———. *The Performance of Human Rights in Morocco*. Philadelphia: University of Pennsylvania Press, 2005.

Slyomovics, Susan, and Barbara Rose Johnston, eds. *Waging War, Making Peace: Reparations and Human Rights*. Vancouver, BC: University of British Columbia Press, 2008.

Smaoui, Barrada. "Assia Djebar: Comment Travaillent les Écrivains." *Jeune Afrique* 19, no. 2 (1988): 197–205.

Smith, Sidonie, and Julia Watson, eds. *Women, Autobiography, Theory: A Reader*. Madison: University of Wisconsin Press, 1998.

Soyinka, Wole. *Myth, Literature, and the African World.* Cambridge: Cambridge University Press, 1976.

Spivak, Gayatri. "Can the Subaltern Speak?" In *Marxism and the Interpretation of Culture*, edited by Cary Nelson and Lawrence Grossberg, 271–313. Urbana: University of Illinois Press, 1988.

———. "Diasporas Old and New: Women in the Transnational World." In *Revolutionary Pedagogies: Cultural Politics, Instituting Education, and the Discourse of Theory*, edited by Peter Pericles Trifonas, 3–29. New York: Routledge, 2000.

———. *Outside in the Teaching Machine*. New York: Routledge, 1993.

———. "Teaching for the Times." *The Decolonization of Imagination: Culture, Knowledge and Power*, edited by Jan Nederveen Pieterse and Bhikhu Parekh, 177–202. London: Zed Press Ltd., 1995.

Spurr, David. *The Rhetoric of Empire: Colonial Discourse in Journalism, Travel Writing, and Imperial Administration*. Durham, NC: Duke University Press, 1993.

Stam, Robert, Robert Burgoyne, and Sandy Flitterman-Lewis, eds. *New Vocabularies in Film Semiotics*. New York: Routledge, 1992.

Starhawk (Miriam Simos). "Power, Authority and Mystery: Earth-Based Spirituality and Ecofeminism." In *Reweaving the World: The Emergence of Ecofeminism*, edited by Irene Diamond and Gloria Feman Orenstein, 73–86. San Francisco: Sierra Club Books, 1990.

Stolberg, Sheryl Gay, and Robert Pear. "Wary Centrists Posing Challenge in Health Care Vote." *New York Times*, February 27, 2010. Accessed February 28, 2010. http://www.nytimes.com/2010/02/28/us/politics/28health.html.

Stone, Judy. "'Silences of the Palace' Has Everybody Talking: Director Moufida Tlatli Honored at S.F. Festival," *San Francisco Chronicle*, April 23, 1995. Accessed February 20, 2000. http://www.sfgate.com/cgi-bin/article.cgi?f=/c/a/1995/04/23/PK45698.DTL&ao=2.

Stora, Benjamin. *Histoire de L'Algérie Coloniale: 1830-1954*. Paris: La Découverte, 1994.

———. *Histoire de La Guerre d'Algérie: 1954-1962*. Paris: La Découverte & Syros, 1993.

Stratton, Florence. *Contemporary African Literature and the Politics of Gende*r. New York: Routledge, 1994.

Tamale, Sylvia. "African Feminism: How Should we Change?" *Development* 49, no. 1 (2006): 38–41.

———. ed. *African Sexualities: A Reader*. Oxford: Pambazuka Press, 2011.

Taubin, Amy. "The Silences of the Palace." *The Village Voice*, April 16, 1996. http://www.villagevoice.com.

Tlatli, Moufida. *Samt Al Kusur (Silences of the Palace)*. Film. Directed by Moufida Tlatli. Co-Produced by Cinétéléfilms, Mat Films and Canal Horizons. Tunisia: 1994.

Trifonas, Peter Pericles, ed. *Revolutionary Pedagogies: Cultural Politics, Instituting Education, and the Discourse of Theory*. New York: Routledge, 2000.

Tucker, Margaret. "A Nice-Time Girl Strikes Back: An Essay on Bessie Head's *A Question of Power*." *Research in African Literatures* 19, no. 2 (1988): 170–181.

Uko, Iniobong. *Gender and Identity in the Work of Osonye Tess Onwueme*. Trenton, NJ: African World Press, 2004.

Vail, Leroy, ed. *The Creation of Tribalism in Southern Africa*. Berkeley: University of California Press, 1991.

Vambe, Maurice T. "Problems of Representing the Zimbabwean War of Liberation in Mutasa's *The Contact*, Samupindi's *Pawns* & Vera's *The Stone Virgins*." In *War in African Literature Today*, edited by Ernest N. Emenyonu, 87–102. New York: James Currey, 2008.

Vera, Yvonne. *Nehanda*. Harare, Zimbabwe: Baobab Books, 1993.

———. *The Stone Virgins*. New York: Farrar, Sraus and Giroux, 2002.

Vigne, Randolph, ed. *A Gesture of Belonging: Letters from Bessie Head, 1965-1979*. Portsmouth, NH: Heinemann, 1991.

Vincendeau, Ginette. "Melodramatic Realism: On Some French Women's Film in the 1930s." *Screen* 3 (Summer 1989): 51.

Vogl, Mary. *Picturing the Maghreb: Literature, Photography, (Re)presentation*. Boston: Rowman & Littlefield Publishers, 2003.

Wadud, Amina. *Qur'an and Woman: Rereading the Sacred Text from a Woman's Perspective*. Oxford: Oxford University Press, 1999[1992].

Ware, Cellestine. *Woman Power: The Movement for Women's Liberation*. New York: Tower Publications, 1970.

Wa Thiong'o, Ngugi. *Moving the Centre: The Struggle for Cultural Freedom*. Portsmouth, NH: Heinemann, 1993.

Weed, Elizabeth, ed. *Coming to Terms*: *Feminism, Theory, Politics*. New York: Routledge, 1989.

Wheeler, Deborah. "Curses and Blessings: Women and the Internet Revolution in the Arab World." In *Women and Media in the Middle East: Power through Self-Expression*, edited by Naomi Sakr, 138–161. London: I. B.Tauris & Co. Ltd., 2004.

Whiting, Denean. *Frantz Fanon: Conflicts and Feminisms*. Boston: Rowman & Littlefield Publishers, Inc., 1998.

Wilentz, Gay Alden. "The Politics of Exile: Reflections of a Black-Eyed Squint in *Our Sister Killjoy*." In *Emerging Perspectives on Ama Ata Aidoo*, edited by Ada Uzoamaka Azodo and Gay Alden Wilentz, 79–92. Trenton, NJ: Africa World Press, 1999.

Wilford, Rick, and Robert Miller, eds. *Women, Ethnicity and Nationalism: The Politics of Transition.* London: Routledge, 1998.

Willey, Elizabeth. "National Identities, Tradition and Feminism." In *Interventions: Feminist Dialogues on Third World Women's Literature and Film*, edited by Bishnupriya Ghosh and Brinda Bose, 4–25. New York: Garland Publishing, Inc., 1997.

Williams, Daniel. "2 Activists (and 2 Views) of Women's Rights in Morocco." *New York Times*, June 10, 2008. Accessed November 1, 2009. http://www.nytimes.com/2008/06/10/world/africa/10iht-letter.1.13598220.html.

Williams, Patrick, and Laura Chrisman, eds. *Colonial Discourse and Postcolonial Theory.* New York: Columbia University Press, 1994.

Williams, Raymond. "Realism and the Contemporary Novel." In *The Long Revolution*. Westport, CT: Greenwood Press, 1975.

Wilson-Tagoe, Nana. "Representing Culture and Identity: African Women Writers and National Cultures." In *Africa After Gender?*, edited by Catherine M. Cole, Takyiwaa Manuh and Stephan Miescher, 233–238. Bloomington: Indiana University Press, 2007.

Winant, Howard. "Gayatri Spivak on the Politics of the Postcolonial Subject." Interview with Gayatri Spivak. *Socialist Review* 90, no. 3 (1990): 85–97.

Woodhull, Winifred. "Feminism and Islamic Tradition." *Studies in Twentieth Century* 17, no. 1 (Winter 1993): 26–44.

Yahyaoui, Amira. "Women's Forum for the Economy and Society: Building the Future with Women's Vision." Global Meeting 2011. Accessed May 28, 2012. http://www.womens-forum.com/speaker/global-meeting-2011/amira-yahyaoui.

Young, Robert. *Colonial Desire, Hybridity in Theory, Culture and Race*. London: Routledge, 1995.

Zekri, Khalid. *Fictions du Réel. Modernité Romanesque et Écriture du Réel au Maroc: 1990-2006.* Paris: L'Harmattan, 2006.

Zenenga, Praise. "'Boys': Performing Manhood in Zimbabwean Drama." In *Manning the Nation: Father Figures in Zimbabwean Literature and Society*, edited by Kizito Muchemwa and Robert Muponde, 127-41. Harare, Zimbabwe: Weaver Press, 2007.

Index

About the Author

Touria Khannous is assistant professor in the Department of Foreign Languages and the International Studies Program at Louisiana State University. She has published articles on women's writing from Africa and the African diaspora, African cinema, black diaspora studies, and cultural studies.

www.ingramcontent.com/pod-product-compliance
Lightning Source LLC
Chambersburg PA
CBHW051252200926
51612CB00001B/20
* 9 7 8 0 7 3 9 1 7 0 4 1 0 *